MILITARY AIRCRAFT
VISUAL GUIDE

MILITARY AIRCRAFT
VISUAL GUIDE
MORE THAN 90 OF THE WORLD'S GREATEST FIGHTING AIRPLANES

GENERAL EDITOR: DAVID DONALD

amber
BOOKS

This edition first published in 2008 by
Amber Books Ltd
74–77 White Lion Street
London
N1 9PF
United Kingdom
www.amberbooks.co.uk

ISBN 978-1-905704-89-7

Project Editor: James Bennett
Additional material: Robert Jackson

Previously published in a different format as part of the reference set *Airplane*

All images courtesy Aerospace/Art-Tech except 190–191 © Pixelpushers Inc.

Printed in Thailand

Contents

Fokker Dr.I

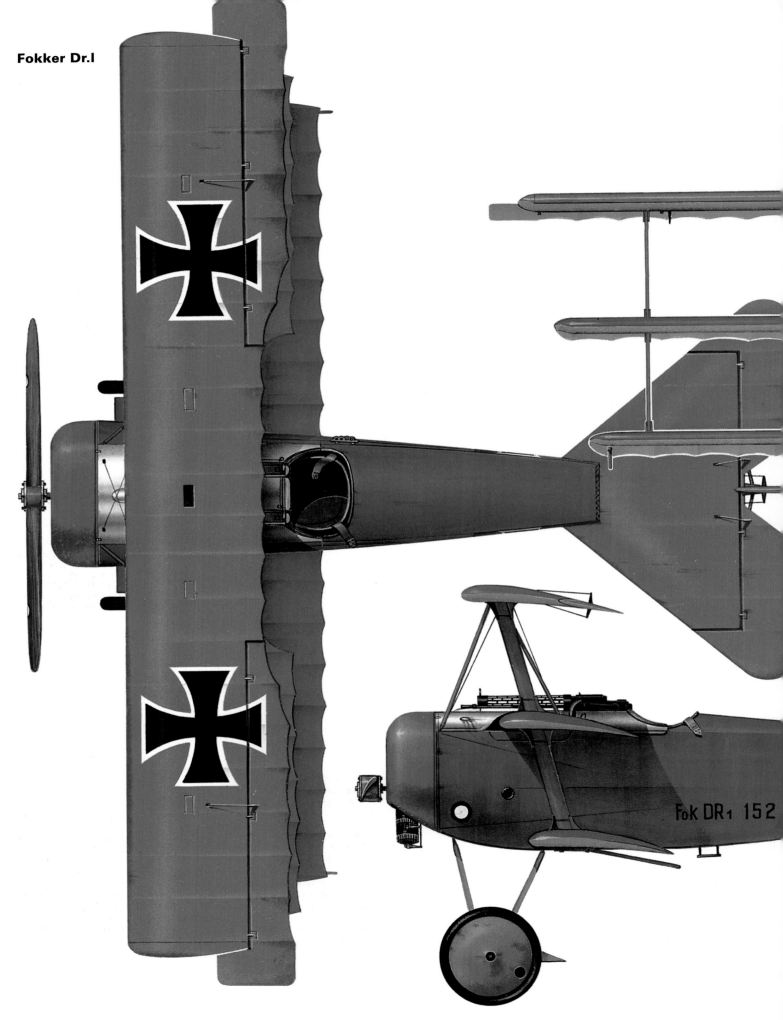

Fok DR₁ 152

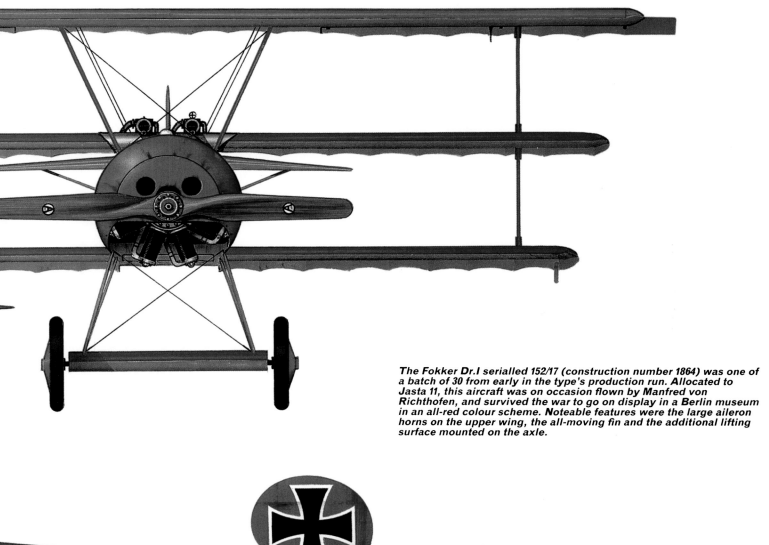

The Fokker Dr.I serialled 152/17 (construction number 1864) was one of a batch of 30 from early in the type's production run. Allocated to Jasta 11, this aircraft was on occasion flown by Manfred von Richthofen, and survived the war to go on display in a Berlin museum in an all-red colour scheme. Noteable features were the large aileron horns on the upper wing, the all-moving fin and the additional lifting surface mounted on the axle.

Specification
Fokker Dr.I
Type: single-seat fighting scout

Powerplant: one 82-kW (110-hp) Oberursel Ur.II nine-cylinder rotary piston engine

Performance: maximum speed 185 km/h (115 mph) at sea level; 165 km/h (103 mph) at 4000 m (13,125 ft); climb to 1000 m (3,280 ft) 2 minutes 55 seconds; service ceiling 6100 m (20,015 ft); range 300 km (186 miles); endurance 1 hour 20 minutes

Weights: empty 406 kg (894 lb); maximum take-off 586 kg (1,291 lb)

Dimensions: span upper 7.12 m (23 ft 7 in), centre 6.23 m (20 ft 5¼ in), lower 5.7 m (18 ft 8½ in); length 5.77 m (18 ft 11 in); height 2.95 m (9 ft 8 in); wing area, including axle fairing 18.66 m^2 (200.85 sq ft)

Armament: two 7.92 mm (0.31 in) LMG 08/15 machine-guns, each with 500 rounds

Few aircraft were more colourful than the Albatros D.Vs, and this example is no exception. Later aircraft were delivered with pre-dyed 'lozenge' fabric on the wing fabric. Jasta 5 was the best-known of the Albatros operators, its ranks including many important aces. This particular aircraft was a D.V, and is believed to have been flown by Klein. If so, this is the aircraft in which he was shot down by McCudden.

Iain Wyllie

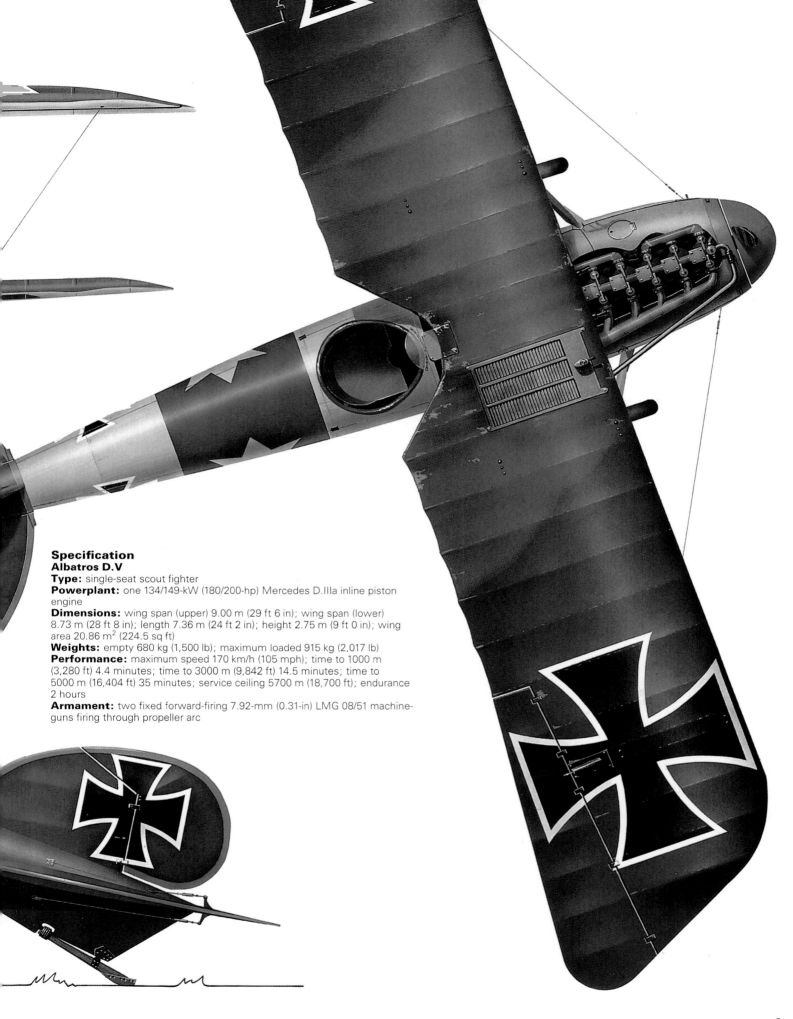

Specification
Albatros D.V
Type: single-seat scout fighter
Powerplant: one 134/149-kW (180/200-hp) Mercedes D.IIIa inline piston
engine
Dimensions: wing span (upper) 9.00 m (29 ft 6 in); wing span (lower)
8.73 m (28 ft 8 in); length 7.36 m (24 ft 2 in); height 2.75 m (9 ft 0 in); wing
area 20.86 m^2 (224.5 sq ft)
Weights: empty 680 kg (1,500 lb); maximum loaded 915 kg (2,017 lb)
Performance: maximum speed 170 km/h (105 mph); time to 1000 m
(3,280 ft) 4.4 minutes; time to 3000 m (9,842 ft) 14.5 minutes; time to
5000 m (16,404 ft) 35 minutes; service ceiling 5700 m (18,700 ft); endurance
2 hours
Armament: two fixed forward-firing 7.92-mm (0.31-in) LMG 08/51 machine-
guns firing through propeller arc

A Camel of 'B' Flight, No. 210 Sqn, RAF, on the Western Front. After the old No. 10 (Naval) Sqn, RNAS, was re-numbered No. 210 in the Royal Air Force on 1 April 1918 the horizontal bars (black for 'A' Flight, red for 'B' and blue for 'C', all separated by white bars) were omitted from the nose, and the flight was simply denoted by a letter just aft of the cockpit. The squadron was heavily involved in fighting at the time of the German offensive in mid-1918, before returning to routine coastal patrol work in July.

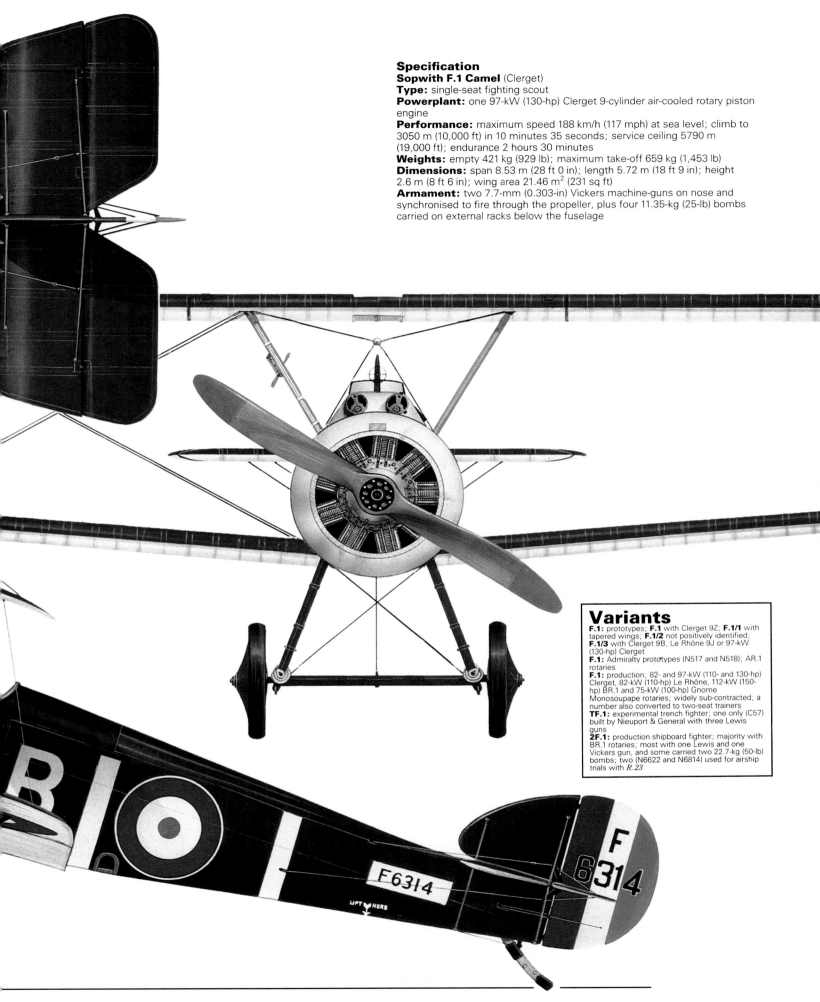

Specification

Sopwith F.1 Camel (Clerget)

Type: single-seat fighting scout

Powerplant: one 97-kW (130-hp) Clerget 9-cylinder air-cooled rotary piston engine

Performance: maximum speed 188 km/h (117 mph) at sea level; climb to 3050 m (10,000 ft) in 10 minutes 35 seconds; service ceiling 5790 m (19,000 ft); endurance 2 hours 30 minutes

Weights: empty 421 kg (929 lb); maximum take-off 659 kg (1,453 lb)

Dimensions: span 8.53 m (28 ft 0 in); length 5.72 m (18 ft 9 in); height 2.6 m (8 ft 6 in); wing area 21.46 m² (231 sq ft)

Armament: two 7.7-mm (0.303-in) Vickers machine-guns on nose and synchronised to fire through the propeller, plus four 11.35-kg (25-lb) bombs carried on external racks below the fuselage

Variants

F.1: prototypes; **F.1** with Clerget 9Z; **F.1/1** with tapered wings; **F.1/2** not positively identified; **F.1/3** with Clerget 9B, Le Rhône 9J or 97-kW (130-hp) Clerget

F.1: Admiralty prototypes (N517 and N518); AR.1 rotaries

F.1: production; 82- and 97-kW (110- and 130-hp) Clerget, 82-kW (110-hp) Le Rhône, 112-kW (150-hp) BR.1 and 75-kW (100-hp) Gnome Monosoupape rotaries; widely sub-contracted; a number also converted to two-seat trainers

TF.1: experimental trench fighter; one only (C57) built by Nieuport & General with three Lewis guns

2F.1: production shipboard fighter; majority with BR.1 rotaries; most with one Lewis and one Vickers gun, and some carried two 22.7-kg (50-lb) bombs; two (N6622 and N6814) used for airship trials with *R.23*

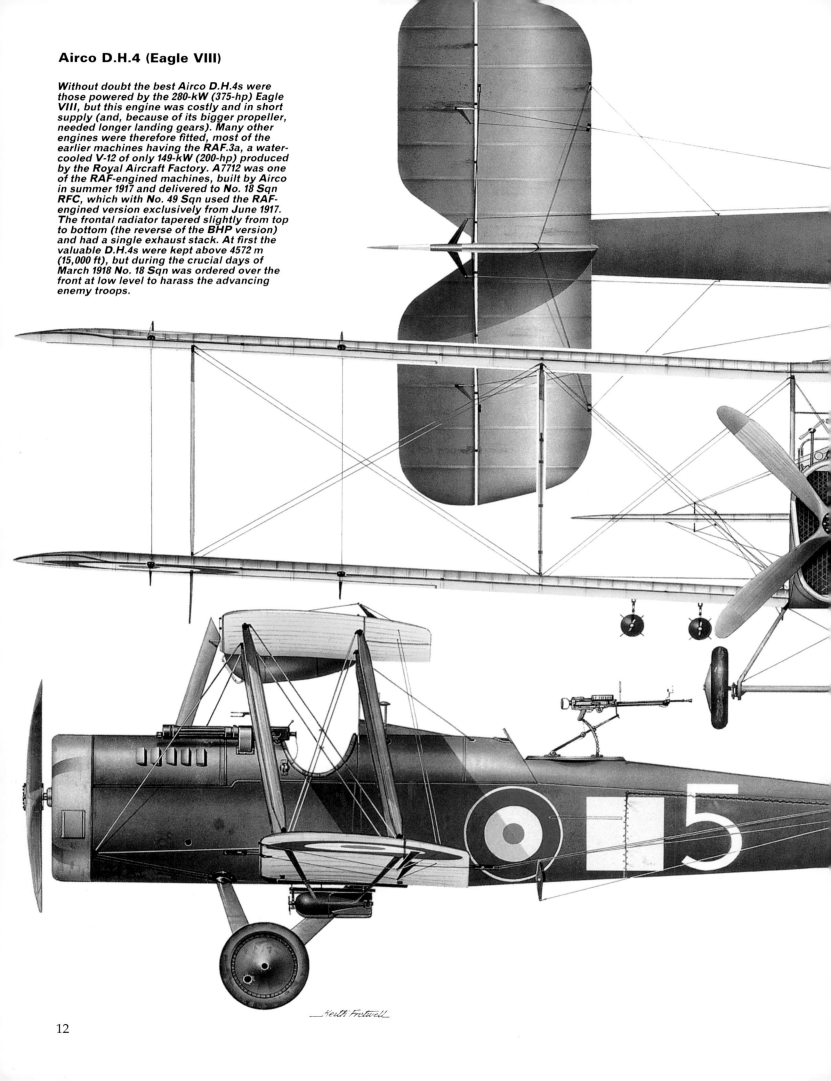

Airco D.H.4 (Eagle VIII)

Without doubt the best Airco D.H.4s were those powered by the 280-kW (375-hp) Eagle VIII, but this engine was costly and in short supply (and, because of its bigger propeller, needed longer landing gears). Many other engines were therefore fitted, most of the earlier machines having the RAF.3a, a water-cooled V-12 of only 149-kW (200-hp) produced by the Royal Aircraft Factory. A7712 was one of the RAF-engined machines, built by Airco in summer 1917 and delivered to No. 18 Sqn RFC, which with No. 49 Sqn used the RAF-engined version exclusively from June 1917. The frontal radiator tapered slightly from top to bottom (the reverse of the BHP version) and had a single exhaust stack. At first the valuable D.H.4s were kept above 4572 m (15,000 ft), but during the crucial days of March 1918 No. 18 Sqn was ordered over the front at low level to harass the advancing enemy troops.

Keith Fretwell

Specification
Airco D.H.4 (Eagle VIII)
Type: two-seat bomber
Powerplant: one 280-kW (375-hp) Rolls-Royce Eagle VIII water-cooled V-12 piston engine
Performance: maximum speed 230 km/h (143 mph) at sea level; cruising speed about 174 km/h (108 mph); time to reach 4572 m (15,000 ft) 16.5 minutes; service ceiling 6700 m (22,000 ft); endurance (maximum) 6 hours 45 minutes
Weights: empty 1083 kg (2,387 lb); loaded (clean) 1575 kg (3,472 lb), (two 104-kg/230-lb bombs) 1784 kg (3,932 lb)
Dimensions: span 12.92 m (42 ft 4.625 in); length (Eagle) 9.347 m (30 ft 8 in); height (Eagle VIII) 3.353 m (11 ft 0 in); wing area 40.32 m² (434 sq ft)
Armament: one 7.7-mm (0.303-in) Vickers machine-gun firing ahead; single or twin Lewis of same calibre mounted on observer's Scarff ring; racks under lower wing for two bombs of 104 kg (230 lb), four of 50.8 kg (112 lb), depth charges or other stores

Specification
Breguet Bre.19 A.2

Type: two-seat day bomber

Powerplant: one 383-kW (513-hp) Renault 12Kd water-cooled 12-cylinder Vee engine

Performance: maximum speed 235 km/h (146 mph) at sea level; climb to 5000 m (16,405 ft) in 29 minutes 50 seconds; absolute ceiling 6900 m (22,640 ft); maximum range 1200 km (746 miles)

Weights: empty 1722 kg (3,796 lb); normal loaded 2347 kg (5,174 lb); maximum take-off 3110 kg (6,856 lb)

Dimensions: span 14.83 m (48 ft 7¾ in); length 9.51 m (31 ft 2½ in); height 3.69 m (12 ft 1¼ in); wing area 50.00 m² (538.2 sq ft)

Armament: one forward-firing synchronised Vickers 7.7-mm (0.303-in) machine-gun with 500 rounds, two Lewis 7.7-mm (0.303-in) guns on Scarff TO-7 ring mounting on rear cockpit and one ventral 7.7-mm (0.303-in) gun with 1,522 rounds, plus a maximum internal bombload of 400 kg (882 lb) and 400 kg (882 lb) on external racks

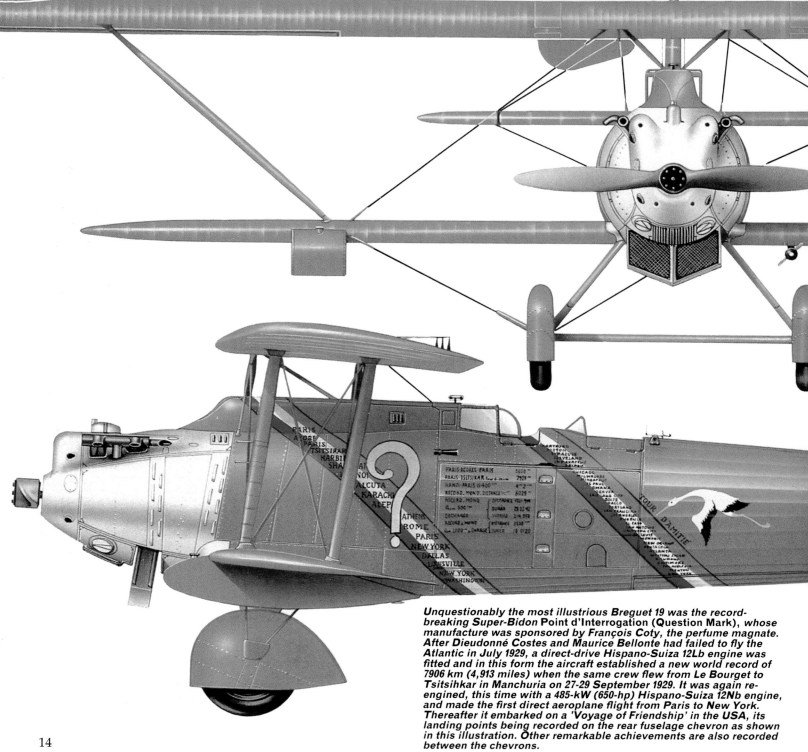

Unquestionably the most illustrious Breguet 19 was the record-breaking Super-Bidon Point d'Interrogation (Question Mark), whose manufacture was sponsored by François Coty, the perfume magnate. After Dieudonné Costes and Maurice Bellonte had failed to fly the Atlantic in July 1929, a direct-drive Hispano-Suiza 12Lb engine was fitted and in this form the aircraft established a new world record of 7906 km (4,913 miles) when the same crew flew from Le Bourget to Tsitsihkar in Manchuria on 27-29 September 1929. It was again re-engined, this time with a 485-kW (650-hp) Hispano-Suiza 12Nb engine, and made the first direct aeroplane flight from Paris to New York. Thereafter it embarked on a 'Voyage of Friendship' in the USA, its landing points being recorded on the rear fuselage chevron as shown in this illustration. Other remarkable achievements are also recorded between the chevrons.

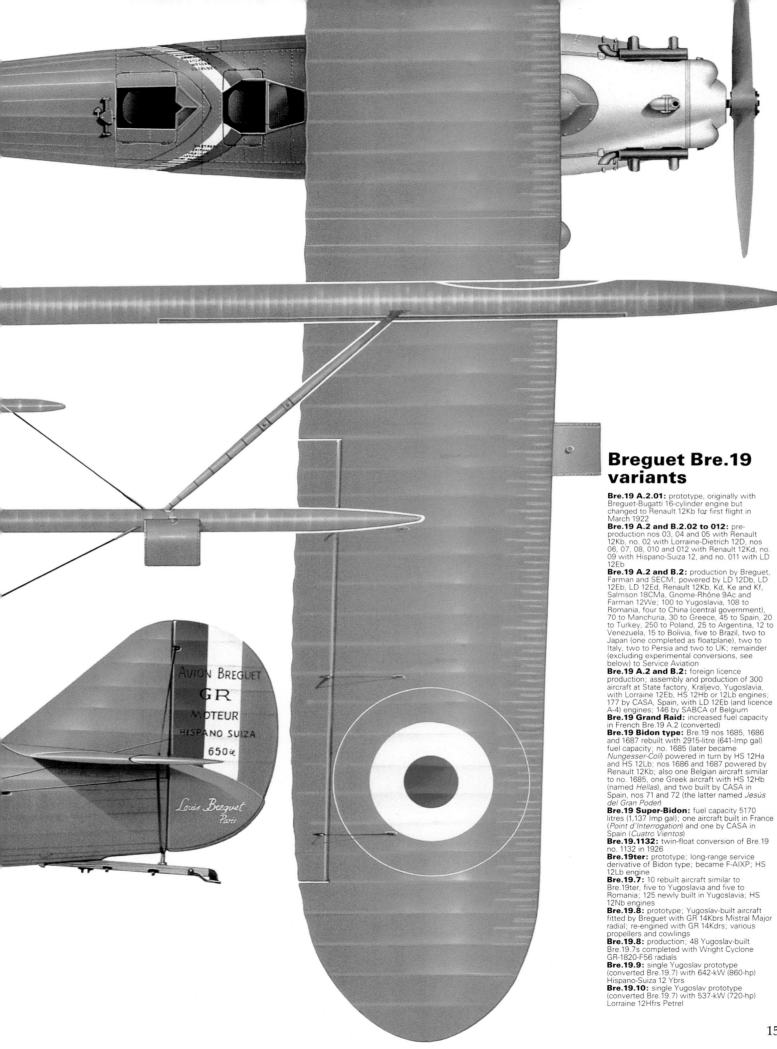

Breguet Bre.19 variants

Bre.19 A.2.01: prototype, originally with Breguet-Bugatti 16-cylinder engine but changed to Renault 12Kb for first flight in March 1922

Bre.19 A.2 and B.2.02 to 012: pre-production nos 03, 04 and 05 with Renault 12Kb, no. 02 with Lorraine-Dietrich 12D, nos 06, 07, 08, 010 and 012 with Renault 12Kd, no. 09 with Hispano-Suiza 12, and no. 011 with LD 12Eb

Bre.19 A.2 and B.2: production by Breguet, Farman and SECM; powered by LD 12Db, LD 12Eb, LD 12Ed, Renault 12Kb, Kd, Ke and Kf, Salmson 18CMa, Gnome-Rhône 9Ac and Farman 12We; 100 to Yugoslavia, 108 to Romania, four to China (central government), 70 to Manchuria, 30 to Greece, 45 to Spain, 20 to Turkey, 250 to Poland, 25 to Argentina, 12 to Venezuela, 15 to Bolivia, five to Brazil, two to Japan (one completed as floatplane), two to Italy, two to Persia and two to UK; remainder (excluding experimental conversions, see below) to Service Aviation

Bre.19 A.2 and B.2: foreign licence production; assembly and production of 300 aircraft at State factory, Kraljevo, Yugoslavia, with Lorraine 12Eb, HS 12Hb or 12Lb engines; 177 by CASA, Spain, with LD 12Eb (and licence A-4) engines; 146 by SABCA of Belgium

Bre.19 Grand Raid: increased fuel capacity in French Bre.19 A.2 (converted)

Bre.19 Bidon type: Bre.19 nos 1685, 1686 and 1687 rebuilt with 2915-litre (641-Imp gal) fuel capacity; no. 1685 (later became *Nungesser-Coli*) powered in turn by HS 12Ha and HS 12Lb; nos 1686 and 1687 powered by Renault 12Kb; also one Belgian aircraft similar to no. 1685, one Greek aircraft with HS 12Hb (named *Hellas*), and two built by CASA in Spain, nos 71 and 72 (the latter named *Jesús del Gran Poder*)

Bre.19 Super-Bidon: fuel capacity 5170 litres (1,137 Imp gal); one aircraft built in France (*Point d'Interrogation*) and one by CASA in Spain (*Cuatro Vientos*)

Bre.19.1132: twin-float conversion of Bre.19 no. 1132 in 1926

Bre.19ter: prototype; long-range service derivative of Bidon type; became F-AIXP; HS 12Lb engine

Bre.19.7: 10 rebuilt aircraft similar to Bre.19ter, five to Yugoslavia and five to Romania; 125 newly built in Yugoslavia; HS 12Nb engines

Bre.19.8: prototype; Yugoslav-built aircraft fitted by Breguet with GR 14Kbrs Mistral Major radial; re-engined with GR 14Kdrs; various propellers and cowlings

Bre.19.8: production; 48 Yugoslav-built Bre.19.7s completed with Wright Cyclone GR-1820-F56 radials

Bre.19.9: single Yugoslav prototype (converted Bre.19.7) with 642-kW (860-hp) Hispano-Suiza 12 Ybrs

Bre.19.10: single Yugoslav prototype (converted Bre.19.7) with 537-kW (720-hp) Lorraine 12Hfrs Petrel

Bulldog Mk IIA

Specification
Bulldog Mk IIA

Type: single-seat interceptor
Powerplant: one 328-kW (440-hp) Bristol Jupiter VIIF air-cooled radial piston engine
Performance: maximum speed 286 km/h (178 mph) at 34050 m (10,000 ft); climb to 6095 m (20,000 ft) in 14 minutes 30 seconds; service ceiling 8230 m (27,000 ft); normal range 499 km (310 miles)
Weights: empty 1008 kg (2,222 lb); maximum take-off 1660 kg (3,660 lb)
Dimensions: span 10.34 m (33 ft 11 in); length 7.67 m (25 ft 2 in); height 3.00 m (9 ft 10 in); wing area 28.47 m^2 (206.5 sq ft)
Armament: two forward-firing synchronised 7.7-mm (0.303-in) Vickers machine-guns on the sides of the nose, plus occasional provision for four 9-kg (20-lb) bombs

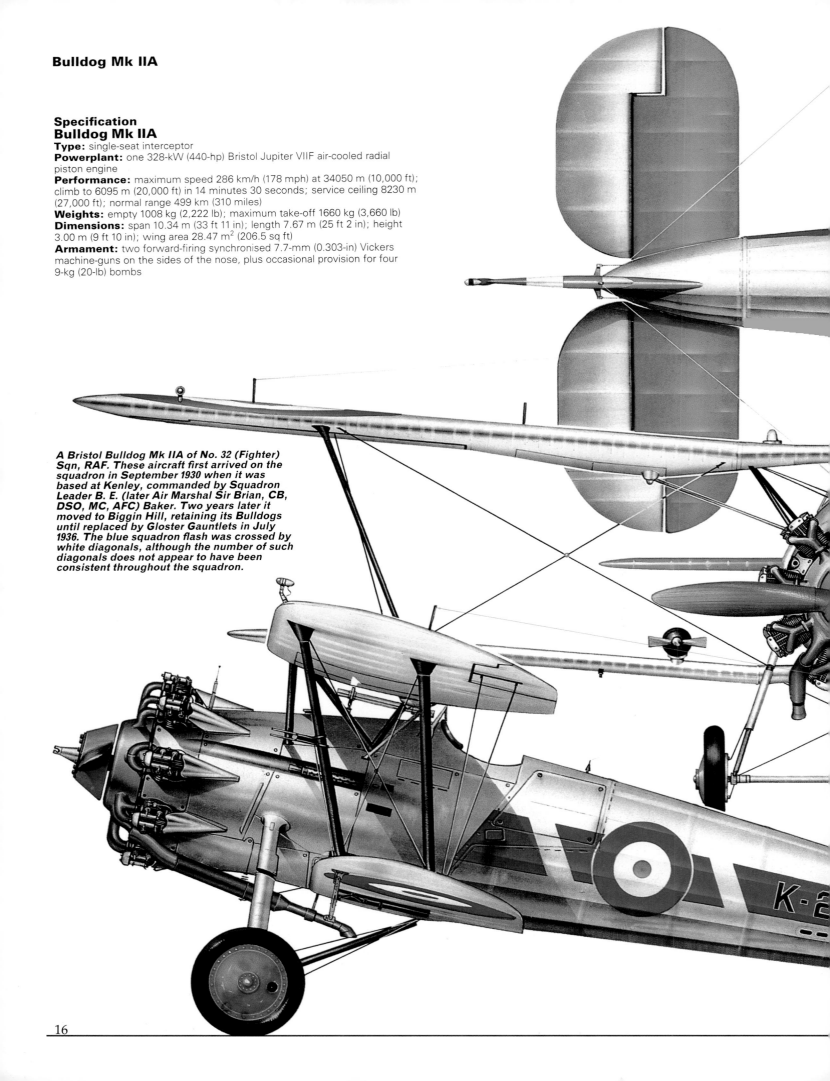

A Bristol Bulldog Mk IIA of No. 32 (Fighter) Sqn, RAF. These aircraft first arrived on the squadron in September 1930 when it was based at Kenley, commanded by Squadron Leader B. E. (later Air Marshal Sir Brian, CB, DSO, MC, AFC) Baker. Two years later it moved to Biggin Hill, retaining its Bulldogs until replaced by Gloster Gauntlets in July 1936. The blue squadron flash was crossed by white diagonals, although the number of such diagonals does not appear to have been consistent throughout the squadron.

Keith Fretwell.

Gloster Gladiator Mk I

A Gladiator Mk I of the second production batch shown in the markings of No. 73 (Fighter) Sqn. When deliveries of this fighter were first made in June that year the squadron was commanded by Squadron Leader Eric Stanley Finch at Debden, but moved to Digby in November where it gave up the biplanes in favour of the Hurricane the following July. As was fairly common in Fighter Command at the time, the yellow wheel discs and propeller boss denoted a 'B' Flight aircraft.

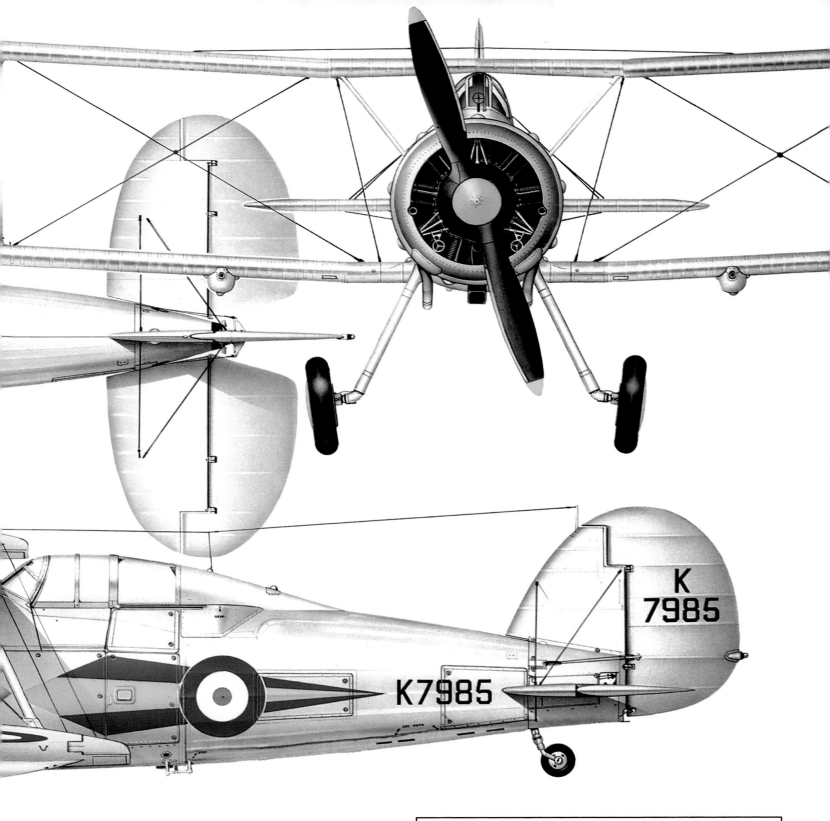

Specification
Gloster Gladiator Mk I

Type: single-seat interceptor biplane

Powerplant: one 627-kW (840-hp) Bristol Mercury IX air-cooled radial piston engine

Performance: maximum speed 407 km/h (253 mph) at 4420 m (14,500 ft); climb to 6095 m (20,000 ft) in 9 minutes 30 seconds; service ceiling 10060 m (33,000 ft); range 547 km (340 miles)

Weights: empty 1565 kg (3,450 lb); maximum take-off 2155 kg (4,750 lb)

Dimensions: span 9.83 m (32 ft 3 in); length 8.36 m (27 ft 5 in); height 3.15 m (10 ft 4 in); wing area 30.01 m² (323.0 sq ft)

Armament: two nose-mounted Vickers Mk V 7.7-mm (0.303-in) machine-guns each with 600 rounds, and two wing-mounted 7.7-mm (0.303-in) Lewis machine-guns each with one 97-round drum; later aircraft had all guns changed to Brownings, each fuselage gun with 600 rounds and each wing gun with 400 rounds

Gloster Gladiator variants

SS.37: one prototype (K5200) to Specification F7/30; first flown September 1934

Gladiator Mk I: 23 aircraft (K6129-K6151) completed with Vickers and Lewis guns; production for RAF in 1936-37

Gladiator Mk I: 208 aircraft (K7892-K8055, L7608-L7623 and L8005-L8032); production in 1937-38 for RAF; most completed with Browning guns, and some later converted to Mk II; some later passed to Egypt, Iraq and Greece

Gladiator Mk I: 147 aircraft built for export (Belgium 22, China 36, Eire 4, Greece 2, Latvia 26, Lithuania 14, Norway 6 and Sweden 37 (J8)

Gladiator Mk I: two aircraft (K6129 and K8039) converted to Sea Gladiator standard for trials

Sea Gladiator (Interim): 38 aircraft (N2265-N2302) modified on Mk II production line for Royal Navy

Gladiator Mk II: 252 aircraft (N2303-N2314, N5575-N5594, N5620-N5649, N5680-N5729, N5750-N5789, N5810-N5859 and N5875-N5924) for RAF; Mercury VIII or VIIIAS driving Fairey Reed 3-bladed propeller; 15 aircraft (N5835-N5849) sold to Portugal, and 6 (N5919-N5924) to Norway before delivery to RAF; others later passed to Finland (33), Greece (about 6), Egypt (27), South Africa (11) and Iraq (5)

Gladiator Mk II (J8A): 18 export aircraft for Sweden

Sea Gladiator: 60 full-standard aircraft for Royal Navy (N5500-N5549, N5565-N5574) with arrester hook, dinghy stowage and provision for two additional Browning guns in top wing

Hawker Hart

Specification
Hawker Hart

Type: two-seat light day bomber

Powerplant: one 392-kW (525-hp) Rolls-Royce Kestrel IB 12-cylinder Vee liquid-cooled engine

Performance: maximum speed 296 km/h (184 mph) at 1525 m (5,000 ft); climb to 3050 m (10,000 ft) in 8 minutes 20 seconds; service ceiling 6506 m (21,350 ft); range 692 km (430 miles)

Weights: empty 1148 kg (2,530 lb); maximum take-off 2066 kg (4,554 lb)

Dimensions: span 11.35 m (37 ft 3 in); length 8.94 m (29 ft 4 in); height 3.17 m (10 ft 5 in); wing area 32.33 m² (384.0 sq ft)

Armament: one fixed forward-firing 7.7-mm (0.303-in) Vickers Mk II or III machine-gun in port side of nose and one 7.7-mm (0.303-in) Lewis gun on rear cockpit mounting, plus a bombload of up to 236 kg (520 lb)

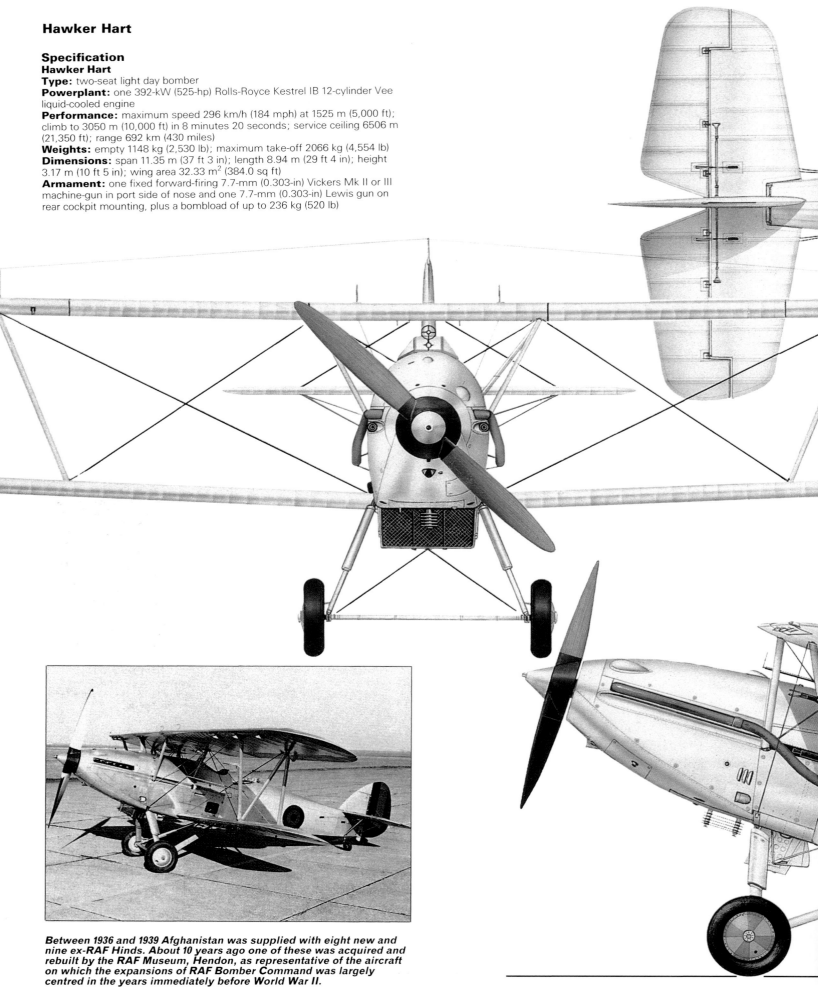

Between 1936 and 1939 Afghanistan was supplied with eight new and nine ex-RAF Hinds. About 10 years ago one of these was acquired and rebuilt by the RAF Museum, Hendon, as representative of the aircraft on which the expansions of RAF Bomber Command was largely centred in the years immediately before World War II.

Displaying the distinctive flashes of No. 604 (County of Middlesex) Sqn, Auxiliary Air Force, this Hawker Demon also bears the county badge (three seaxes) on the fin, and the commanding officer's pennant below the front cockpit sill. Based at Hendon from the date of its formation in 1930 until the outbreak of war in September 1939, No. 604 Sqn started life as a light bomber auxiliary squadron but changed to Demon fighters in 1935, retaining them until becoming a night fighter squadron with Blenheims. Among the squadron's famous pilots who flew Demons was Flight Lieutenant (later Group Captain) John Cunningham.

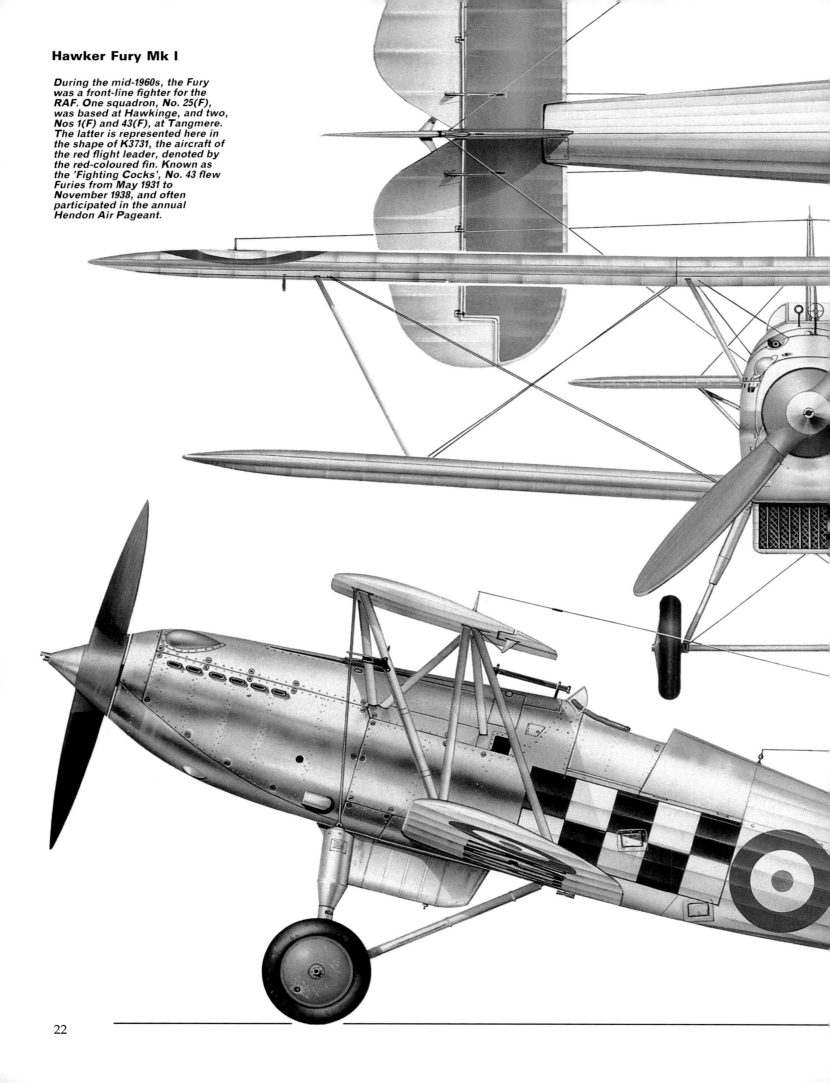

Hawker Fury Mk I

During the mid-1960s, the Fury was a front-line fighter for the RAF. One squadron, No. 25(F), was based at Hawkinge, and two, Nos 1(F) and 43(F), at Tangmere. The latter is represented here in the shape of K3731, the aircraft of the red flight leader, denoted by the red-coloured fin. Known as the 'Fighting Cocks', No. 43 flew Furies from May 1931 to November 1938, and often participated in the annual Hendon Air Pageant.

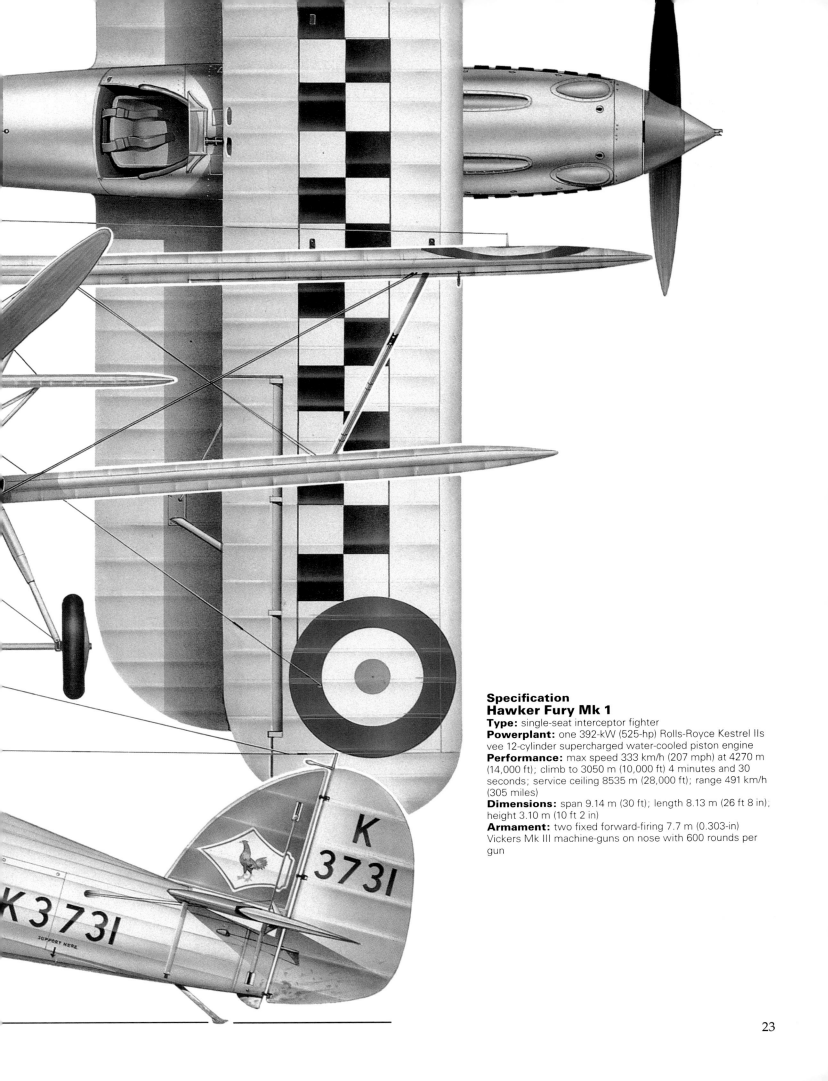

Specification
Hawker Fury Mk 1
Type: single-seat interceptor fighter
Powerplant: one 392-kW (525-hp) Rolls-Royce Kestrel IIs vee 12-cylinder supercharged water-cooled piston engine
Performance: max speed 333 km/h (207 mph) at 4270 m (14,000 ft); climb to 3050 m (10,000 ft) 4 minutes and 30 seconds; service ceiling 8535 m (28,000 ft); range 491 km/h (305 miles)
Dimensions: span 9.14 m (30 ft); length 8.13 m (26 ft 8 in), height 3.10 m (10 ft 2 in)
Armament: two fixed forward-firing 7.7 m (0.303-in) Vickers Mk III machine-guns on nose with 600 rounds per gun

The P-36A was the subject of a large **USAAC** order for fighters to augment the Seversky P-35s in service. Rapidly establishing itself as the service's main equipment, examples were on station in Hawaii during the attack on Pearl Harbor and rose to meet the Japanese, claiming a few victories. This aircraft is depicted in the colours of the 35th Pursuit Squadron at Langley Field, Virginia, in 1939-40. The unit moved to Mitchell Field, New York, during the latter years.

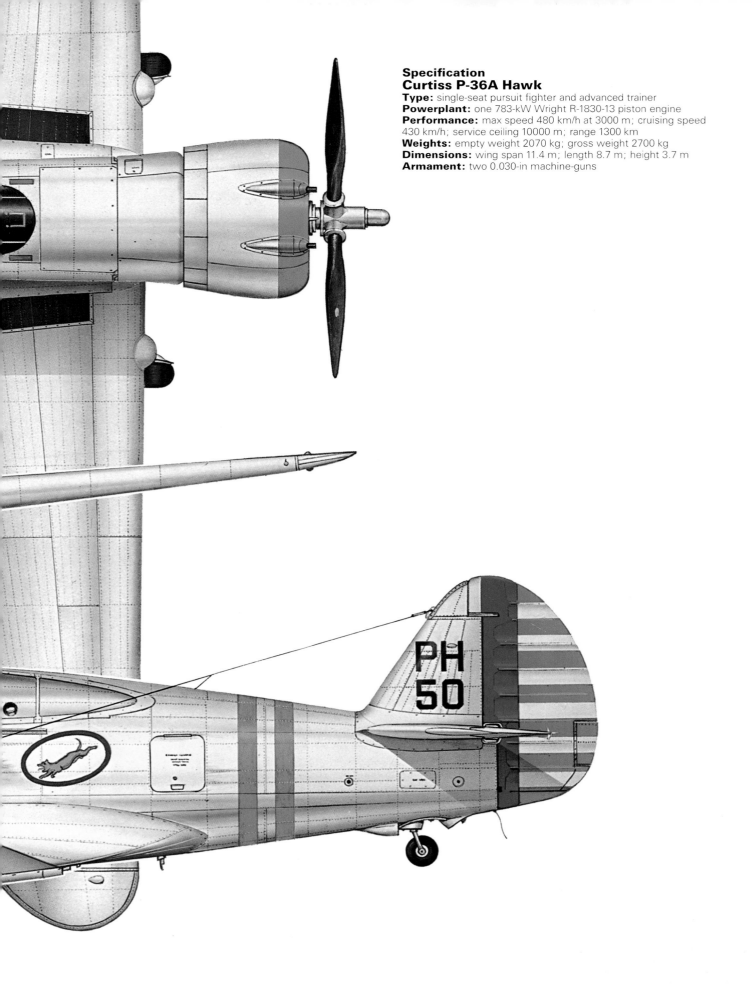

Specification
Curtiss P-36A Hawk
Type: single-seat pursuit fighter and advanced trainer
Powerplant: one 783-kW Wright R-1830-13 piston engine
Performance: max speed 480 km/h at 3000 m; cruising speed 430 km/h; service ceiling 10000 m; range 1300 km
Weights: empty weight 2070 kg; gross weight 2700 kg
Dimensions: wing span 11.4 m; length 8.7 m; height 3.7 m
Armament: two 0.030-in machine-guns

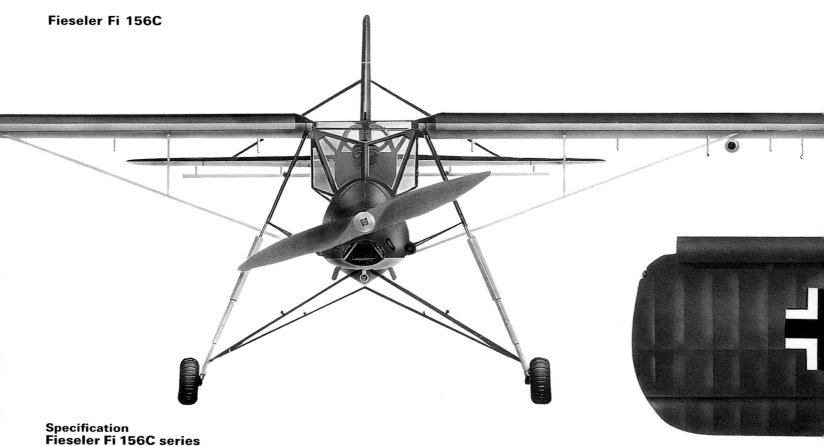

Specification
Fieseler Fi 156C series

Type: STOL liaison, observation and rescue aircraft
Powerplant: one 179-kW (240-hp) Argus As 10C-3 inverted V-8 air-cooled piston engine
Performance: maximum speed 175 km/h (109 mph); cruising speed 130 km/h (81 mph); range (standard wing fuel) 467 km (290 miles)
Weights: empty 930 kg (2,050 lb); normal loaded 1325 kg (2,920 lb)
Dimensions: span 14.25 m (46 ft 9 in); length 9.9 m (32 ft 5.76 in); height 3.0 m (10 ft 0 in); wing area 26.0 m² (279.86 sq ft)
Armament: provision for one 7.92-mm (0.312-in) MG15 machine-gun with four spare 75-round magazines.

Fieseler Storch variants

Fi 156 B: projected variants with movable leading-edge slats; not built
Fi 156C-0: pre-production version of an improved Fi 156A-1 with raised rear-cabin glazing to allow installation of a rear-firing 7.92-mm (0.31-in) machine-gun
Fi 156B-1: liaison and staff transport version
Fi 156C-2: reconnaissance version with one camera and two-man crew; some late examples equipped to carry one stretcher for casualty evacuation
Fi 156C-3: general-purpose version, some with improved Argus As 10P engine
Fi 156C-3/Trop: tropicalised version of the Fi 156C-3 with engine dust/sand filters
Fi 156C-5: similar to 156C-3 but with Argus As 10P engine as standard and provision to carry an underfuselage drop tank or camera installation
Fi 156C-5/Trop: tropicalised version of the above
Fi 156D-0: pre-production ambulance version with improved accommodation for one stretcher and an enlarged loading/unloading hatch; powered by Argus As 10C engine
Fi 156D-1: production version of the above with Argus As 10P engine as standard
Fi 156E-0: designation of 10 pre-production aircraft with a form of tracked landing gear, the main units each with two wheels in tandem linked by pneumatic rubber track; no further production
Fi 256: two examples only of larger capacity (5-seat) civil version, built at Morane-Saulnier factory at Puteaux, France, during 1943-44

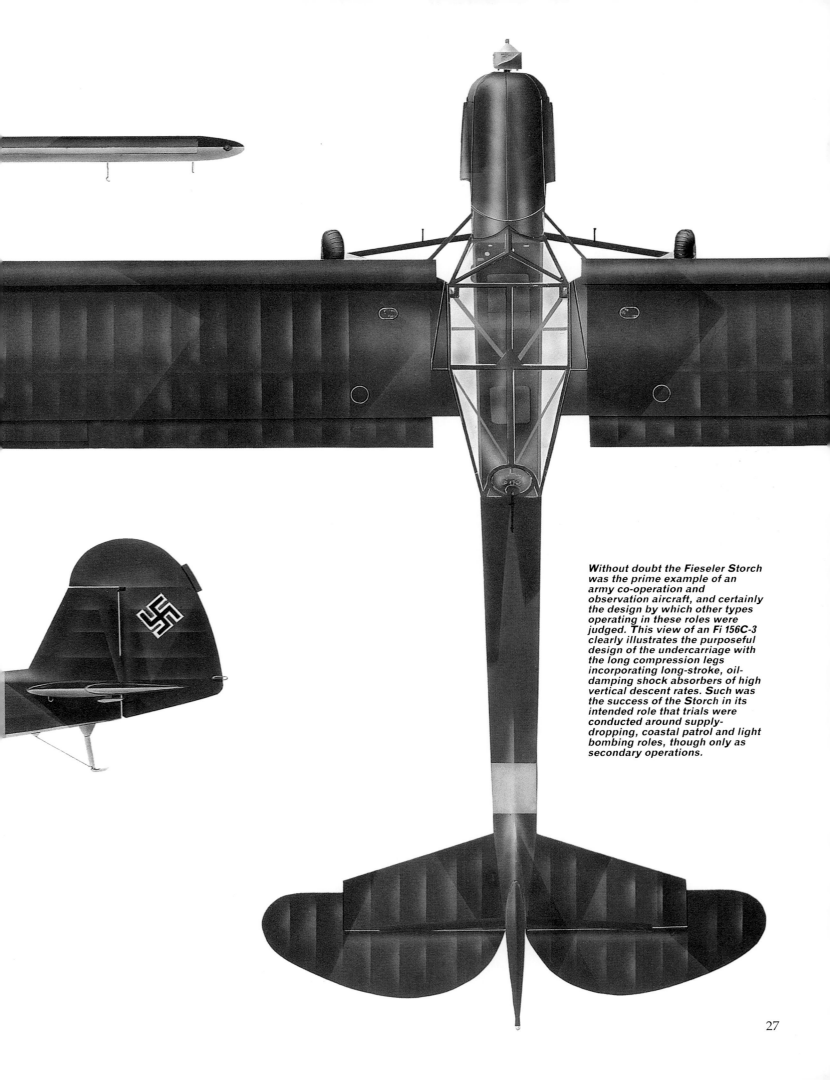

Without doubt the Fieseler Storch was the prime example of an army co-operation and observation aircraft, and certainly the design by which other types operating in these roles were judged. This view of an Fi 156C-3 clearly illustrates the purposeful design of the undercarriage with the long compression legs incorporating long-stroke, oil-damping shock absorbers of high vertical descent rates. Such was the success of the Storch in its intended role that trials were conducted around supply-dropping, coastal patrol and light bombing roles, though only as secondary operations.

Heinkel He 111H-16

Specification
Heinkel He 111H-16

Type: five-seat medium night bomber/pathfinder and glider tug
Powerplant: two 1006-kW (1,350-hp) Junkers Jumo 211F-2 inline piston engines
Performance: maximum speed 435 km/h (270 mph) at 600 m (19,685 ft); service ceiling 8500 m (27,890 ft); normal range 1950 km (1,212 miles)
Weights: empty 8680 kg (19,136 lb); maximum take-off 14000 kg (30,864 lb)
Dimensions: span 22.60 m (74 ft 1¾ in); length 16.40 m (53 ft 9½ in); height 4.00 m (13 ft 1¼ in); wing area 86.50 m² (931.1 sq ft)
Armament: one 20-mm MG FF cannon, one 13-mm (0.51-in) MG 131 and up to seven 7.92-mm (0.31-in) MG 15 and MG 81 machine-guns, plus one 2000-kg (4,409-lb) bomb carried externally and one 500-kg (1,102-lb) bomb internally, or eight 250-kg (551-kg) bombs all internally

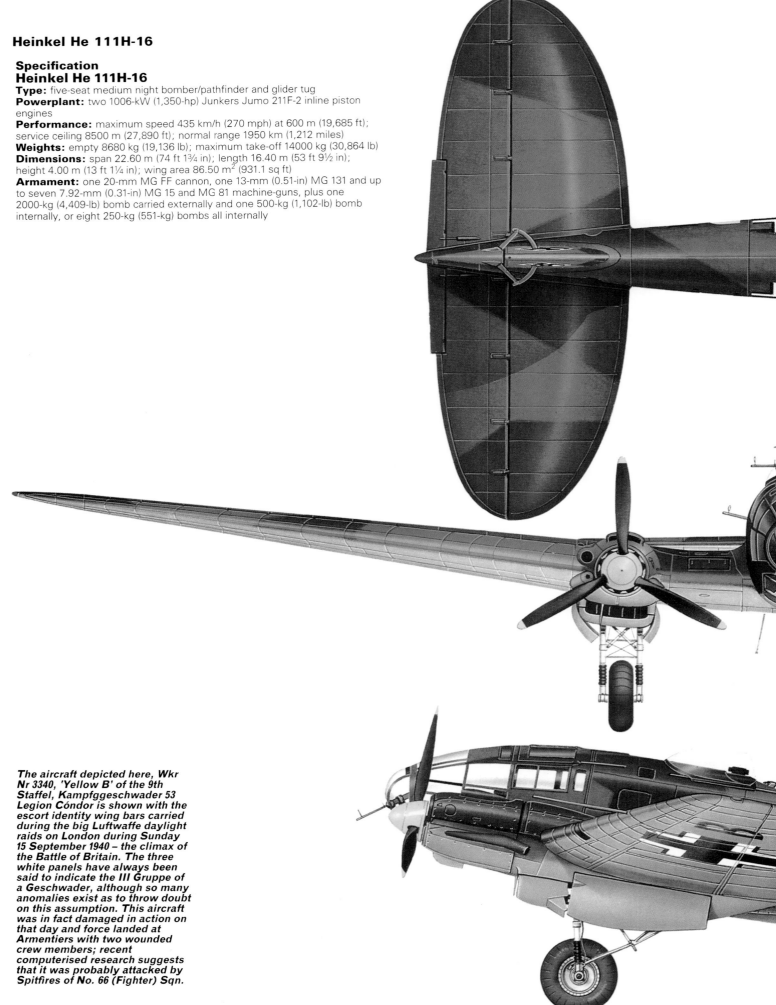

The aircraft depicted here, Wkr Nr 3340, 'Yellow B' of the 9th Staffel, Kampfggeschwader 53 Legion Cóndor is shown with the escort identity wing bars carried during the big Luftwaffe daylight raids on London during Sunday 15 September 1940 – the climax of the Battle of Britain. The three white panels have always been said to indicate the III Gruppe of a Geschwader, although so many anomalies exist as to throw doubt on this assumption. This aircraft was in fact damaged in action on that day and force landed at Armentiers with two wounded crew members; recent computerised research suggests that it was probably attacked by Spitfires of No. 66 (Fighter) Sqn.

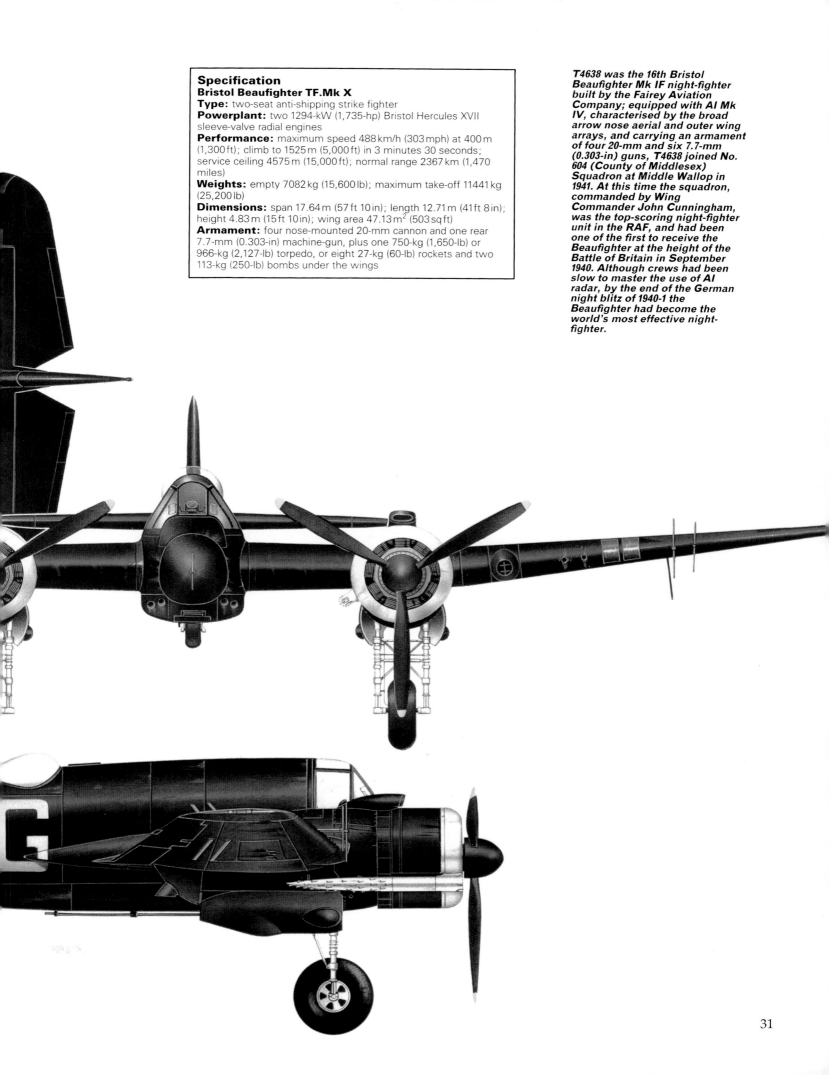

Specification
Bristol Beaufighter TF.Mk X
Type: two-seat anti-shipping strike fighter
Powerplant: two 1294-kW (1,735-hp) Bristol Hercules XVII sleeve-valve radial engines
Performance: maximum speed 488 km/h (303 mph) at 400 m (1,300 ft); climb to 1525 m (5,000 ft) in 3 minutes 30 seconds; service ceiling 4575 m (15,000 ft); normal range 2367 km (1,470 miles)
Weights: empty 7082 kg (15,600 lb); maximum take-off 11441 kg (25,200 lb)
Dimensions: span 17.64 m (57 ft 10 in); length 12.71 m (41 ft 8 in); height 4.83 m (15 ft 10 in); wing area 47.13 m² (503 sq ft)
Armament: four nose-mounted 20-mm cannon and one rear 7.7-mm (0.303-in) machine-gun, plus one 750-kg (1,650-lb) or 966-kg (2,127-lb) torpedo, or eight 27-kg (60-lb) rockets and two 113-kg (250-lb) bombs under the wings

T4638 was the 16th Bristol Beaufighter Mk IF night-fighter built by the Fairey Aviation Company; equipped with AI Mk IV, characterised by the broad arrow nose aerial and outer wing arrays, and carrying an armament of four 20-mm and six 7.7-mm (0.303-in) guns, T4638 joined No. 604 (County of Middlesex) Squadron at Middle Wallop in 1941. At this time the squadron, commanded by Wing Commander John Cunningham, was the top-scoring night-fighter unit in the RAF, and had been one of the first to receive the Beaufighter at the height of the Battle of Britain in September 1940. Although crews had been slow to master the use of AI radar, by the end of the German night blitz of 1940-1 the Beaufighter had become the world's most effective night-fighter.

Messerschmitt Bf 109E-7

Introduced into Luftwaffe service midway through the Battle of Britain in August 1940, the Messerschmitt Bf 109E-7 featured a modified fuel system and attachments for a ventral drop tank. Being equipped to carry the extra fuel, the new aircraft were able to provide effective escort for the big daylight raids over London in September 1940. 'Red 2' (no. 2058), depicted here, was being flown by Unteroffizier Klick of 3./LG 2 when it was shot down by RAF fighters in the famous raids on London of 15 September.

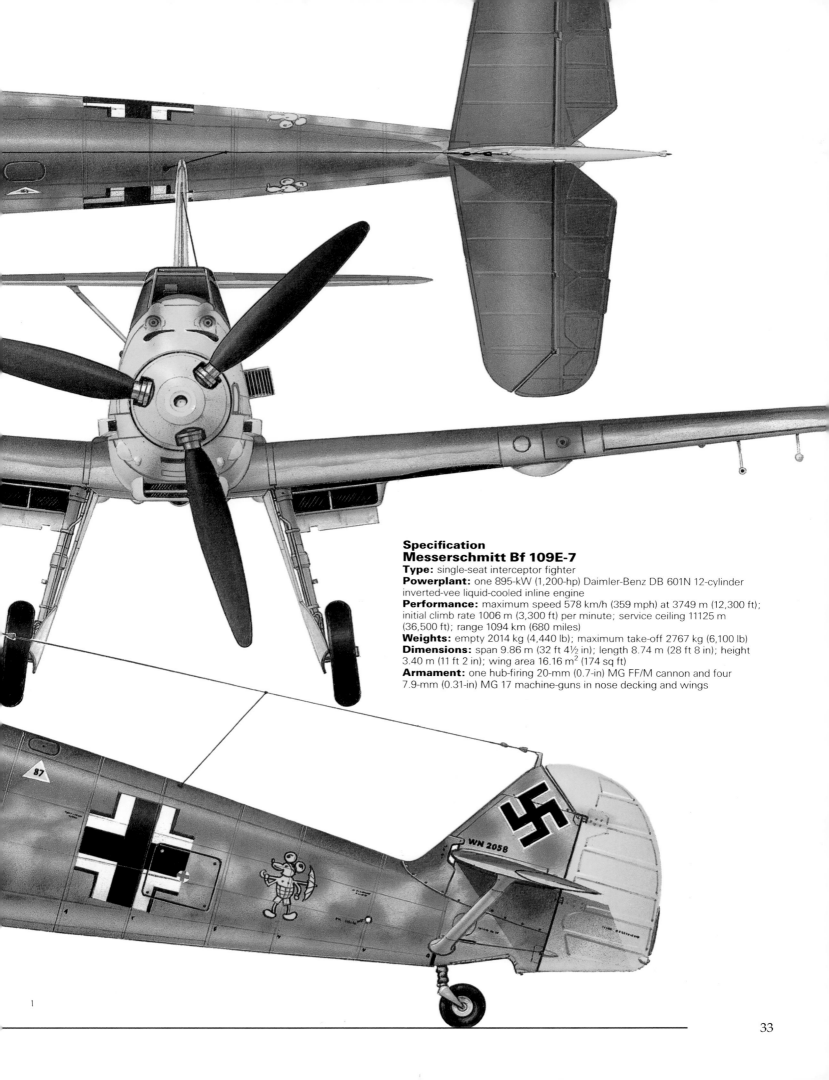

Specification
Messerschmitt Bf 109E-7
Type: single-seat interceptor fighter
Powerplant: one 895-kW (1,200-hp) Daimler-Benz DB 601N 12-cylinder inverted-vee liquid-cooled inline engine
Performance: maximum speed 578 km/h (359 mph) at 3749 m (12,300 ft); initial climb rate 1006 m (3,300 ft) per minute; service ceiling 11125 m (36,500 ft); range 1094 km (680 miles)
Weights: empty 2014 kg (4,440 lb); maximum take-off 2767 kg (6,100 lb)
Dimensions: span 9.86 m (32 ft 4½ in); length 8.74 m (28 ft 8 in); height 3.40 m (11 ft 2 in); wing area 16.16 m² (174 sq ft)
Armament: one hub-firing 20-mm (0.7-in) MG FF/M cannon and four 7.9-mm (0.31-in) MG 17 machine-guns in nose decking and wings

Short S.25 Sunderland III

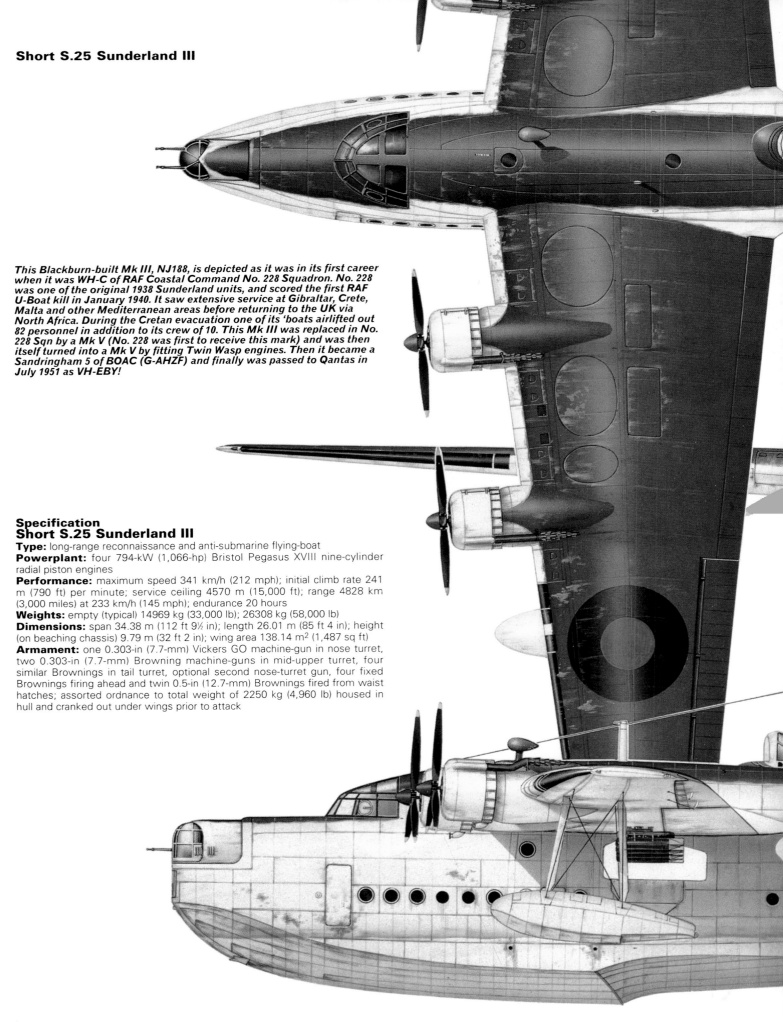

This Blackburn-built Mk III, NJ188, is depicted as it was in its first career when it was WH-C of RAF Coastal Command No. 228 Squadron. No. 228 was one of the original 1938 Sunderland units, and scored the first RAF U-Boat kill in January 1940. It saw extensive service at Gibraltar, Crete, Malta and other Mediterranean areas before returning to the UK via North Africa. During the Cretan evacuation one of its 'boats airlifted out 82 personnel in addition to its crew of 10. This Mk III was replaced in No. 228 Sqn by a Mk V (No. 228 was first to receive this mark) and was then itself turned into a Mk V by fitting Twin Wasp engines. Then it became a Sandringham 5 of BOAC (G-AHZF) and finally was passed to Qantas in July 1951 as VH-EBY!

Specification
Short S.25 Sunderland III
Type: long-range reconnaissance and anti-submarine flying-boat
Powerplant: four 794-kW (1,066-hp) Bristol Pegasus XVIII nine-cylinder radial piston engines
Performance: maximum speed 341 km/h (212 mph); initial climb rate 241 m (790 ft) per minute; service ceiling 4570 m (15,000 ft); range 4828 km (3,000 miles) at 233 km/h (145 mph); endurance 20 hours
Weights: empty (typical) 14969 kg (33,000 lb); 26308 kg (58,000 lb)
Dimensions: span 34.38 m (112 ft 9½ in); length 26.01 m (85 ft 4 in); height (on beaching chassis) 9.79 m (32 ft 2 in); wing area 138.14 m² (1,487 sq ft)
Armament: one 0.303-in (7.7-mm) Vickers GO machine-gun in nose turret, two 0.303-in (7.7-mm) Browning machine-guns in mid-upper turret, four similar Brownings in tail turret, optional second nose-turret gun, four fixed Brownings firing ahead and twin 0.5-in (12.7-mm) Brownings fired from waist hatches; assorted ordnance to total weight of 2250 kg (4,960 lb) housed in hull and cranked out under wings prior to attack

Hawker Hurricane Mk I

Specification
Hawker Hurricane Mk I

Type: single-seat interceptor fighter

Powerplant: one 768-kW (1,030-hp) Rolls-Royce Merlin III inline piston engine

Performance: maximum speed 511 km/h (318 mph) at 5500 m (18,000 ft); initial climb rate 770 m (2,520 ft) per minute; service ceiling 10970 m (36,000 ft); maximum range 740 km (460 miles)

Weights: empty 2118 kg (4,670 lb); maximum take-off 2994 kg (6,600 lb)

Dimensions: span 12.20 m (40 ft 0 in); length 9.59 m (31 ft 4 in); height 3.96 m (12 ft 11½ in); wing area 23.93 m² (257.6 sq ft)

Armament: eight 7.7-mm (0.303-in) Browning machine-guns with 2,660 rounds of ammunition

Representative of the classic RAF Battle of Britain Hurricane I, P3059 served with No. 501 (County of Gloucester) Squadron during August 1940. Aircraft of this Gloster Aircraft-produced batch, equipped from the outset with Rotol constant-speed propellers, started delivery to RAF fighter squadrons in May and continued throughout the Battle of Britain; it has been said that the Rotol propeller transformed the Hurricane's performance from 'disappointing' to one of 'acceptable mediocrity', and modified aircraft were certainly much sought after among squadrons equipped with aircraft having the older de Havilland two-position propeller.

Messerschmitt Bf 110C-4

Messerschmitt Bf 110C-4/B of 9. Staffel, Zerstörergeschwader 26 'Horst Wessel', shown carrying two 250-kg (551-lb) and four 100-kg (220-lb) bombs. This unit was among the first German units to be sent to the Mediterranean, being based at Palermo at the end of 1940.

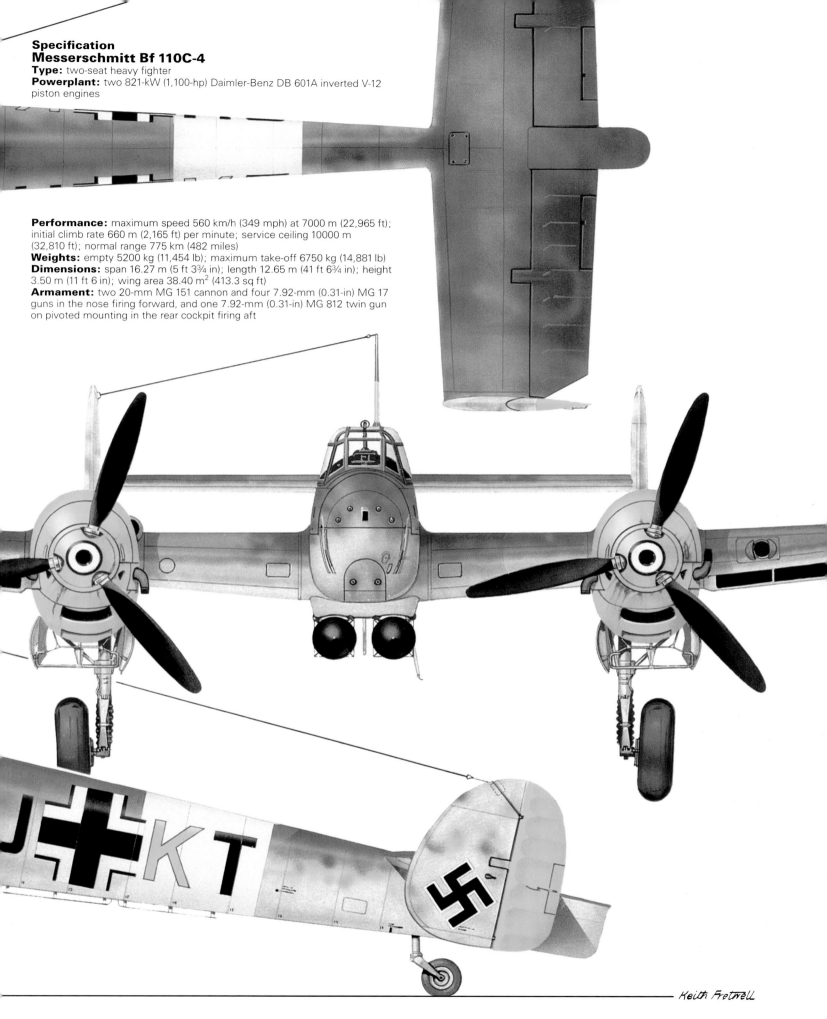

Specification
Messerschmitt Bf 110C-4
Type: two-seat heavy fighter
Powerplant: two 821-kW (1,100-hp) Daimler-Benz DB 601A inverted V-12 piston engines

Performance: maximum speed 560 km/h (349 mph) at 7000 m (22,965 ft); initial climb rate 660 m (2,165 ft) per minute; service ceiling 10000 m (32,810 ft); normal range 775 km (482 miles)
Weights: empty 5200 kg (11,454 lb); maximum take-off 6750 kg (14,881 lb)
Dimensions: span 16.27 m (5 ft 3¾ in); length 12.65 m (41 ft 6¾ in); height 3.50 m (11 ft 6 in); wing area 38.40 m² (413.3 sq ft)
Armament: two 20-mm MG 151 cannon and four 7.92-mm (0.31-in) MG 17 guns in the nose firing forward, and one 7.92-mm (0.31-in) MG 812 twin gun on pivoted mounting in the rear cockpit firing aft

Keith Fretwell

Halifax B.Mk I Series I

Specification
Halifax B.Mk I Series 1

Type: seven-seat heavy bomber
Powerplant: four 954-kW (1,280-hp) Rolls-Royce Merlin X V-12 engines
Performance: maximum speed 426 km/h (265 mph); service ceiling 6950 m (22,800 ft); initial climb 229 m (750 ft) per minute; range with 2631 kg (5,800 lb) bombload 3000 km (1,860 miles)
Weights: empty 15359 kg (33,860 lb); loaded 26308 kg (58,000 lb)
Dimensions: span 30.12 m (98 ft 10 in); length 21. 36 m (70 ft 1 in); height 6.32 m (20 ft 9 in); wing area 116 m^2 (1,250 sq ft)
Armament: normal bombload 5897 kg (13,000 lb) including mines or two torpedoes; (defensive) two 7.7-mm (0.303-in) Browning machine-guns in Boulton Paul nose turret, four in tail turret of same make, plus two Vickers 'K' machine-guns of same calibre aimed by hand through beam hatches

L9530 was one of the very first batch (L9485-9534) of production Halifaxes, delivered in the winter of 1940-41. Styled B.Mk I Series 1, it is shown after delivery to RAF No. 76 Sqn in Bomber Command's No. 4 Group at Middleton St George (today Tees-side Airport). The crest was applied by the pilot, Christopher Cheshire, brother of the more famous Leonard Cheshire who served with the first Halifax squadron, No. 35, and later went on to command No. 76. All bomb doors are shown open, and the projections aft of the trailing edge just outboard of the centre-section are fuel-jettison pipes. The 'acorn' carried above the fuselage, downstream of the navigator's astrodome, housed the rotatable direction-finding radio loop aerial.

Keith Fretwell

Junkers Ju 52/3mg7e

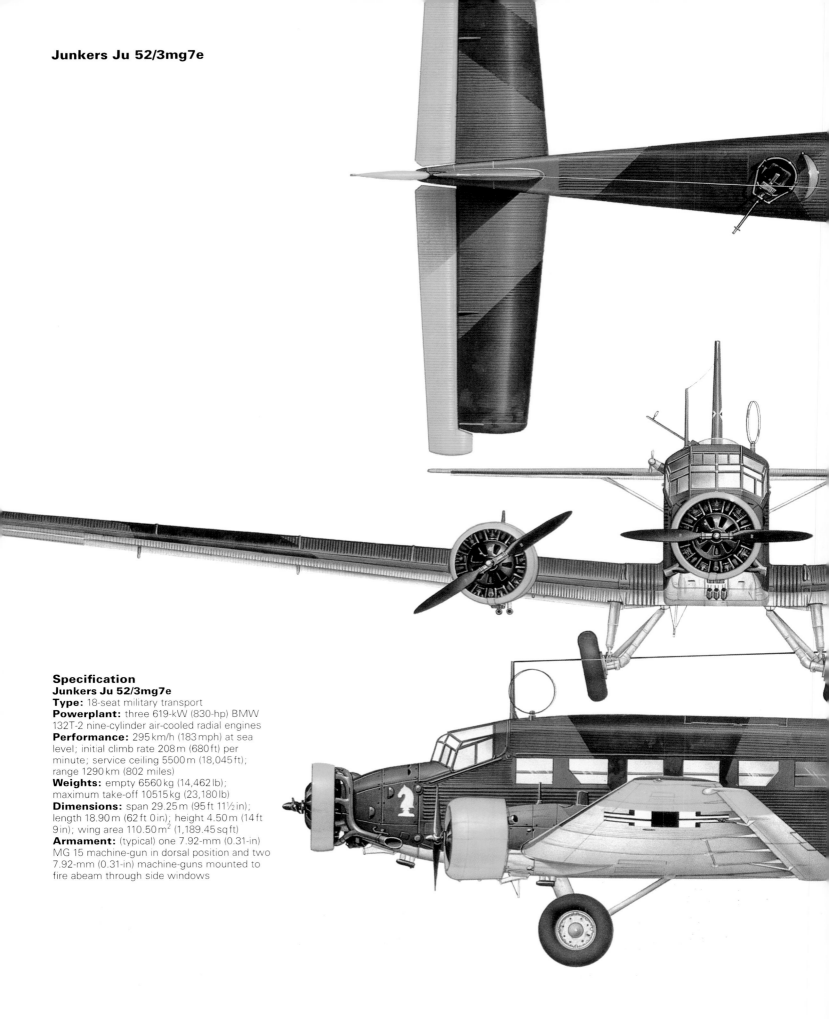

Specification
Junkers Ju 52/3mg7e
Type: 18-seat military transport
Powerplant: three 619-kW (830-hp) BMW 132T-2 nine-cylinder air-cooled radial engines
Performance: 295 km/h (183 mph) at sea level; initial climb rate 208 m (680 ft) per minute; service ceiling 5500 m (18,045 ft); range 1290 km (802 miles)
Weights: empty 6560 kg (14,462 lb); maximum take-off 10515 kg (23,180 lb)
Dimensions: span 29.25 m (95 ft 11½ in); length 18.90 m (62 ft 0 in); height 4.50 m (14 ft 9 in); wing area 110.50 m² (1,189.45 sq ft)
Armament: (typical) one 7.92-mm (0.31-in) MG 15 machine-gun in dorsal position and two 7.92-mm (0.31-in) machine-guns mounted to fire abeam through side windows

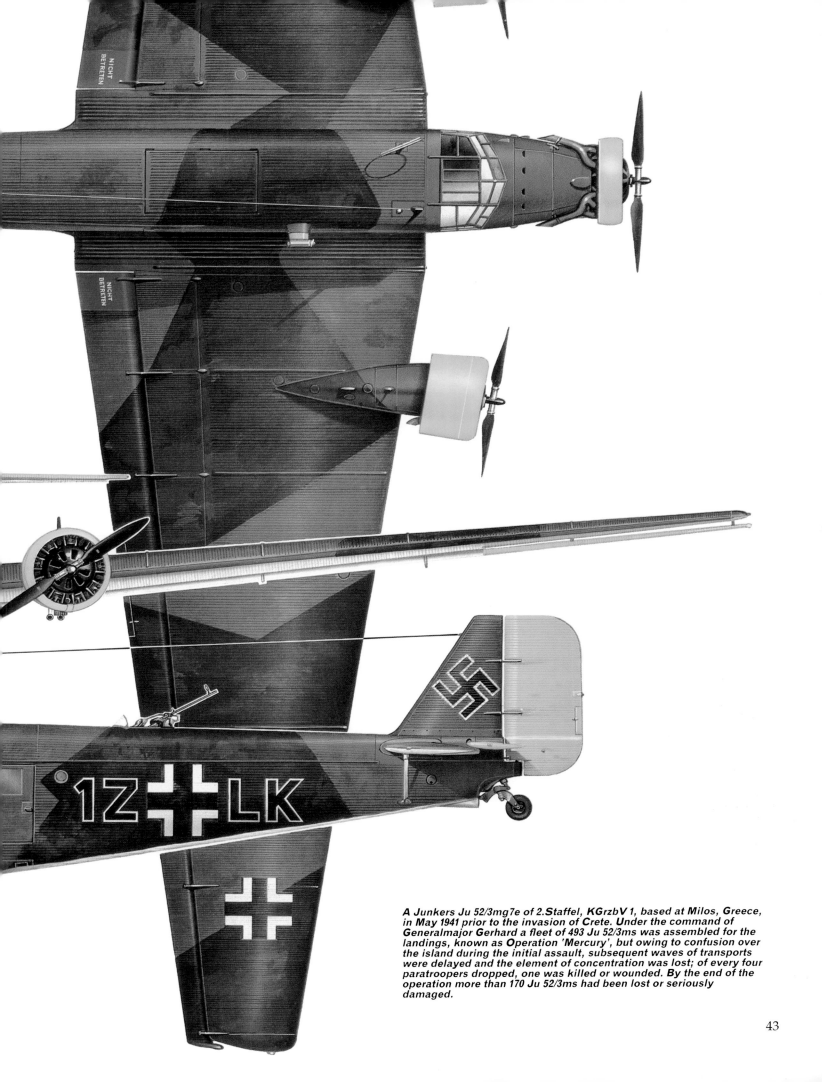

A Junkers Ju 52/3mg7e of 2.Staffel, KGrzbV 1, based at Milos, Greece, in May 1941 prior to the invasion of Crete. Under the command of Generalmajor Gerhard a fleet of 493 Ju 52/3ms was assembled for the landings, known as Operation 'Mercury', but owing to confusion over the island during the initial assault, subsequent waves of transports were delayed and the element of concentration was lost; of every four paratroopers dropped, one was killed or wounded. By the end of the operation more than 170 Ju 52/3ms had been lost or seriously damaged.

Vickers Wellington B.Mk III

Specification
Vickers Wellington B.Mk III

Type: six-crew medium bomber
Powerplant: two 1119-kW (1,500-hp) Bristol Hercules XI air-cooled 14-cylinder radial piston engines
Performance: maximum speed 410 km/h (255 mph) at 3810 m (12,500 ft); initial climb rate 283 m (930 ft) per minute; service ceiling 5790 m (19,000 ft); range 3540 km (2,200 miles) with 680 kg (1,500 lb) of bombs, or 2478 km (1,540 miles) with 2041 kg (4,500 lb) of bombs
Weights: empty 8417 kg (18,556 lb); maximum take-off 13381 kg (29,500 lb)
Dimensions: span 26.26 m (86 ft 2 in); length 18.54 m (60 ft 10 in); height 5.31 m (17 ft 5 in); wing area 78.04 m² (840.0 sq ft)
Armament: two 7.7-mm (0.303-in) machine-guns in nose turret, four similar weapons in tail turret, and one similar weapon in each rear fuselage beam position, plus a maximum bombload of 2041 kg (4,500 lb), or one 1814-kg (4,000-lb) bomb

Vickers Wellington variants

Type 271: B.9/32 first prototype (K4049) with Pegasus X; first flown 15 June 1936
Type 285 Wellington Mk I: prototype (L4212) with Pegasus X; flown 23 December 1937
Type 290 Wellington Mk I: production, 183 built at Weybridge (180) and Chester (3) with Pegasus XVIII; Vickers turrets and 'dustbin'
Type 408 Wellington Mk IA: production, 187 built at Weybridge and Chester with Pegasus XVIII; Nash and Thompson turrets and 'dustbin'
Type 416 Wellington Mk IC: production, 2,685 built at Weybridge (1,052), Chester (1,583) and Blackpool (50); **Type 423** covered conversion of all bombers to carry 4,000-lb (1814-kg) bomb; beam guns (no 'dustbin')
Type 298 Wellington Mk II: prototype (L4250) with Merlin X; first flown 3 March 1939
Type 406 Wellington B.Mk II: production, 400 built at Weybridge with Merlin X
Type 299 Wellington Mk III: prototypes, L4251 with Hercules HEISM, and P9238 with Hercules III
Type 417 Wellington B.Mk III: production, 1,517 built at Chester (737) and Blackpool (780) in 1941-43; fighter-towing experiments by Flight Refuelling
Type 410 Wellington Mk IV: prototype (R1220) with Pratt & Whitney Twin Wasp radials
Type 424 Wellington B.Mk IV: production, 220 built at Chester with Twin Wasps
Type 421 Wellington Mk V: first prototype (R3298) with Hercules III
Type 407 Wellington Mk V: second prototype (R3299) with Hercules VIII
Type 432 Wellington Mk VI: prototype (W5795) with Rolls-Royce Merlin (various)
Type 442 Wellington B.Mk VI: production, 63 built at Weybridge; Sperry bomb sight
Type 449 covered **Wellington Mk VIG** production; two aircraft to No. 109 Sqn
Type 430 Wellington Mk VII: prototype (T2545) cancelled; Merlin XX; production of 150 aircraft also cancelled
Type 429 Wellington GR.Mk VIII: production, with Pegasus XVIII; 397 built at Weybridge; 58 fitted with Leigh Light; provision to carry AS weapons (some aircraft with provision for torpedoes)
Type 437 Wellington IX: one transport prototype (P2522) converted from Wellington Mk IA; Hercules XVI
Type 440 Wellington B.Mk X: production, 3,803 built at Chester (2,434) and Blackpool (1,369); Hercules XI/XVI; **Type 619** covered post-war conversion to **Wellington T.Mk 10;** RP468 fitted with tail boom radar as G-ALUH; some sold to France in 1946; six to Royal Hellenic air force in April 1946
Type 454 Wellington Mk XI: prototype (MP502) with ASV Mk II; Hercules VI/XVI; **Type 459** covered MP545 with ASV Mk III

Type 458 Wellington GR.Mk XI: production, 180 built at Weybridge (105) and Blackpool (75); ASV Mk III and Hercules VIU/XVI
Type 455 Wellington GR.Mk XII: production, 58 built at Weybridge (50) and Chester (8); Leigh Light, ASV Mk III and Hercules VI/XVI; some to France in 1946
Type 466 Wellington GR.Mk XIII: production, 844 built at Weybridge (42) and Blackpool (802); Hercules XVI
Type 467 Wellington GR.Mk XIV: production, 841 built at Weybridge (53), Chester (538) and Blackpool (250); Hercules XVI; many supplied to France between April 1944 and July 1945; some sold to France in 1946
Wellington C.Mk XV: service conversion of Wellington Mk IAs to troop transport (originally designated **Wellington C.Mk IA**); accommodation for 18 troops
Wellington C.Mk XVI: service conversion of Wellington Mk ICs to troop transport (originally designated **Wellington C.Mk IC**); modification as for Wellington C.Mk XV
Type 487 Wellington T.Mk XVII: kits for service conversion to trainer with Mosquito-type AI radar; Hercules XVII
Type 490 Wellington T.Mk XVIII: production, 80 built at Blackpool plus conversion of some Wellington Mk XIs; Hercules XVI; Mosquito-type radar-equipped 'flying classroom'
Wellington T.Mk XIX: service conversion from Wellington Mk X to trainer
Type 416 Wellington (II): L4250 with experimental installation of 40-mm Vickers gun in dorsal position; Merlin X; also modified with twin fins
Type 418 Wellington DWI.Mk I: conversion of P2516 for mine detonation; Ford auxiliary power unit
Type 419 Wellington DWI.Mk II: conversion of L4356 for mine detonation; Gipsy Six auxiliary power unit
Type 435 Wellington Mk IC: conversion of T2977 to mount Turbinlite for comparison with Leigh Light
Type 439 Wellington Mk II: Z8416 with experimental installation of 40-mm Vickers gun in nose; Merlin X
Type 443 Wellington Mk V: W5816 with conversion to Hercules VIII testbed
Type 445 Wellington (II): Z8570/G as testbed for Whittle W2B/23 jet in tail; **Type 470** covered Wellington II W5389/G with Whittle W2B jet, and **Type 486** covered Wellington II W5518 with W2/700 jet
Type 478 Wellington Mk X: LN718 with trial installation of Hercules 100
Type 602 Wellington X: LN715 as engine testbed with two Rolls-Royce Dart turboprops
Type 638 Wellington X: NA 857 as engine testbed with Napier Naiads; not completed
Wellington III: X3268 with glider-towing clearance for Hadrian, Hotspur and Horsa

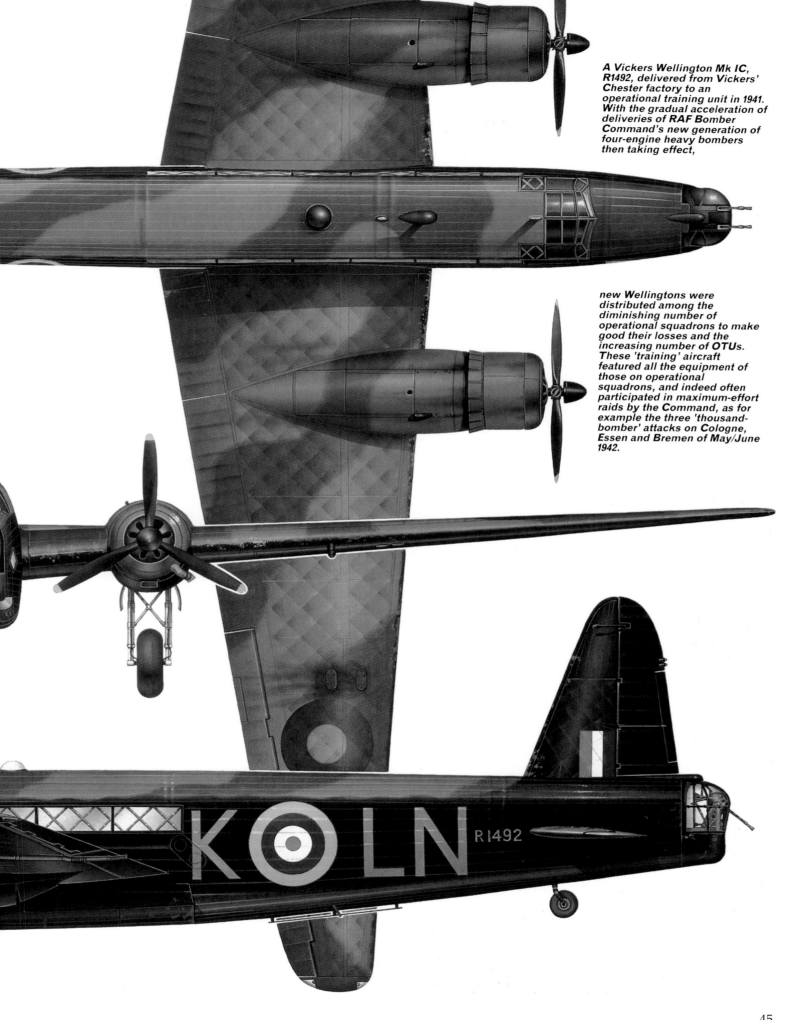

A Vickers Wellington Mk IC, R1492, delivered from Vickers' Chester factory to an operational training unit in 1941. With the gradual acceleration of deliveries of RAF Bomber Command's new generation of four-engine heavy bombers then taking effect,

new Wellingtons were distributed among the diminishing number of operational squadrons to make good their losses and the increasing number of OTUs. These 'training' aircraft featured all the equipment of those on operational squadrons, and indeed often participated in maximum-effort raids by the Command, as for example the three 'thousand-bomber' attacks on Cologne, Essen and Bremen of May/June 1942.

Grumman TBF-1 Avenger

This drawing depicts one of the first TBF-1s to come off the line at Bethpage in early 1942. Only about 200 were delivered with the national insignia as shown, a red border with white rectangles being added in June 1943. The colour scheme of sea blue fading through grey to a white underside was introduced in 1943, all earlier TBFs having the original scheme of sea green above and light grey below. Other points of interest include the kinked steel main legs, fixed slots ahead of the fabric-covered ailerons, and crew door in the side of the rear fuselage.

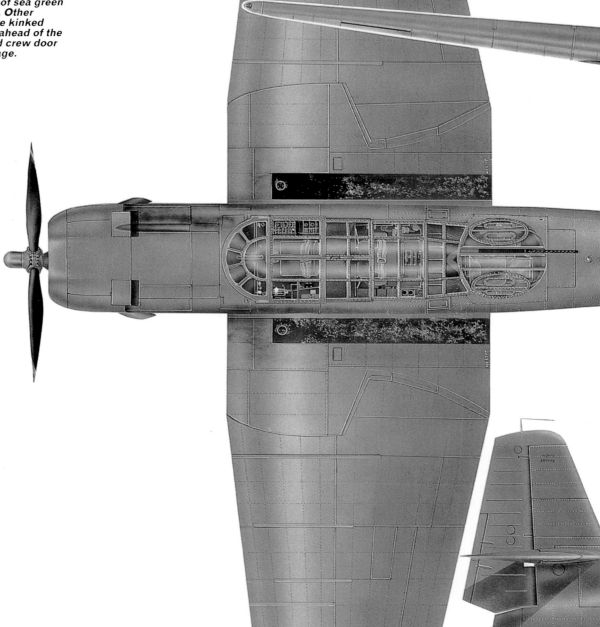

Specification
Grumman TBF-1 Avenger

Type: three-seat carrier-based torpedo-bomber

Powerplant: one 1268-kW (1,700-hp) Wright R-2600-8 Cyclone 14-cylinder two-row radial piston engine

Performance: maximum speed 436 km/h (271 mph); typical long-range cruise 233 km/h (145 mph); range on internal fuel 1778 km (1,105 miles)

Weights: empty (TBF-1C) 4788 kg (10,555 lb); maximum loaded 7876 kg (17,364 lb)

Dimensions: span 16.51 m (54 ft 2 in); length 12.2 m (40 ft 0.2 in); height 4.19 m (13 ft 9 in); wing area 45.52 m² (490 sq ft)

Armament: one 7.62-mm (0.3-in) gun firing ahead (in TBF-1C, two 12.7-mm/0.5-in), one 12.7-mm (0.5-in) in turret and one 7.62-mm (0.3-in) in lower rear position; internal bay for one 577-mm (22.7-in) torpedo or up to 907 kg (2,000 lb) of other stores.

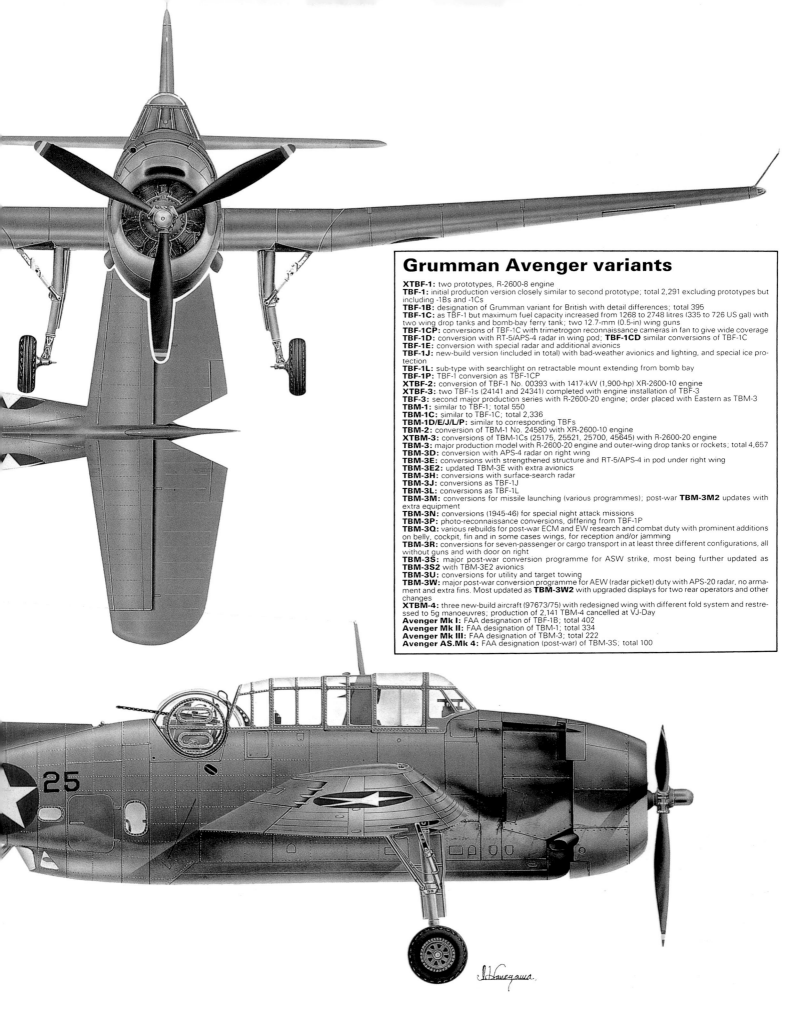

Grumman Avenger variants

XTBF-1: two prototypes, R-2600-8 engine
TBF-1: initial production version closely similar to second prototype; total 2,291 excluding prototypes but including -1Bs and -1Cs
TBF-1B: designation of Grumman variant for British with detail differences; total 395
TBF-1C: as TBF-1 but maximum fuel capacity increased from 1268 to 2748 litres (335 to 726 US gal) with two wing drop tanks and bomb-bay ferry tank; two 12.7-mm (0.5-in) wing guns
TBF-1CP: conversions of TBF-1C with trimetrogon reconnaissance cameras in fan to give wide coverage
TBF-1D: conversion with RT-5/APS-4 radar in wing pod; **TBF-1CD** similar conversions of TBF-1C
TBF-1E: conversion with special radar and additional avionics
TBF-1J: new-build version (included in total) with bad-weather avionics and lighting, and special ice protection
TBF-1L: sub-type with searchlight on retractable mount extending from bomb bay
TBF-1P: TBF-1 conversion as TBF-1CP
XTBF-2: conversion of TBF-1 No. 00393 with 1417-kW (1,900-hp) XR-2600-10 engine
XTBF-3: two TBF-1s (24141 and 24341) completed with engine installation of TBF-3
TBF-3: second major production series with R-2600-20 engine; order placed with Eastern as TBM-3
TBM-1: similar to TBF-1; total 550
TBM-1C: similar to TBF-1C; total 2,336
TBM-1D/E/J/L/P: similar to corresponding TBFs
TBM-2: conversion of TBM-1 No. 24580 with XR-2600-10 engine
XTBM-3: conversions of TBM-1Cs (25175, 25521, 25700, 45645) with R-2600-20 engine
TBM-3: major production model with R-2600-20 engine and outer-wing drop tanks or rockets; total 4,657
TBM-3D: conversion with APS-4 radar on right wing
TBM-3E: conversions with strengthened structure and RT-5/APS-4 in pod under right wing
TBM-3E2: updated TBM-3E with extra avionics
TBM-3H: conversions with surface-search radar
TBM-3J: conversions as TBF-1J
TBM-3L: conversions as TBF-1L
TBM-3M: conversions for missile launching (various programmes); post-war **TBM-3M2** updates with extra equipment
TBM-3N: conversions (1945-46) for special night attack missions
TBM-3P: photo-reconnaissance conversions, differing from TBF-1P
TBM-3Q: various rebuilds for post-war ECM and EW research and combat duty with prominent additions on belly, cockpit, fin and in some cases wings, for reception and/or jamming
TBM-3R: conversions for seven-passenger or cargo transport in at least three different configurations, all without guns and with door on right
TBM-3S: major post-war conversion programme for ASW strike, most being further updated as **TBM-3S2** with TBM-3E2 avionics
TBM-3U: conversions for utility and target towing
TBM-3W: major post-war conversion programme for AEW (radar picket) duty with APS-20 radar, no armament and extra fins. Most updated as **TBM-3W2** with upgraded displays for two rear operators and other changes
XTBM-4: three new-build aircraft (97673/75) with redesigned wing with different fold system and restressed to 5g manoeuvres; production of 2,141 TBM-4 cancelled at VJ-Day
Avenger Mk I: FAA designation of TBF-1B; total 402
Avenger Mk II: FAA designation of TBM-1; total 334
Avenger Mk III: FAA designation of TBM-3; total 222
Avenger AS.Mk 4: FAA designation (post-war) of TBM-3S; total 100

Mitsubishi A6M5c Reisen

Specification
Mitsubishi A6M5c Reisen

Type: carrier-based fighter-bomber

Powerplant: one 843-kW (1,130-hp) Nakajima NK1F Sakae 21 radial piston engine

Performance: maximum speed 565 km/h (351 mph); cruising speed 370 km/h (230 mph); climb to 6000 m (19,685 ft) in 7 minutes; service ceiling 11740 m (38,520 ft); maximum range 1922 km (1,194 miles)

Weights: empty 1876 kg (4,136 lb); maximum take-off 2733 kg (6,025 lb)

Dimensions: span 11.00 m (36 ft 1 in); length 9.12 m (29 ft 11.25 in); height 3.50 m (11 ft 6 in); wing area 21.3 m² (229.27 sq ft)

Armament: one 13.2-mm (0.52-in) Type 3 heavy machine-gun in the fuselage decking (breech in the cockpit), two 20-mm Type 99 cannon in the wings and two 13.2-mm (0.52-in) Type 3 guns in the wings outboard of the cannon, plus two 60-kg (132-lb) bombs under the wings (suicide mission, one 250-kg/551-lb bomb)

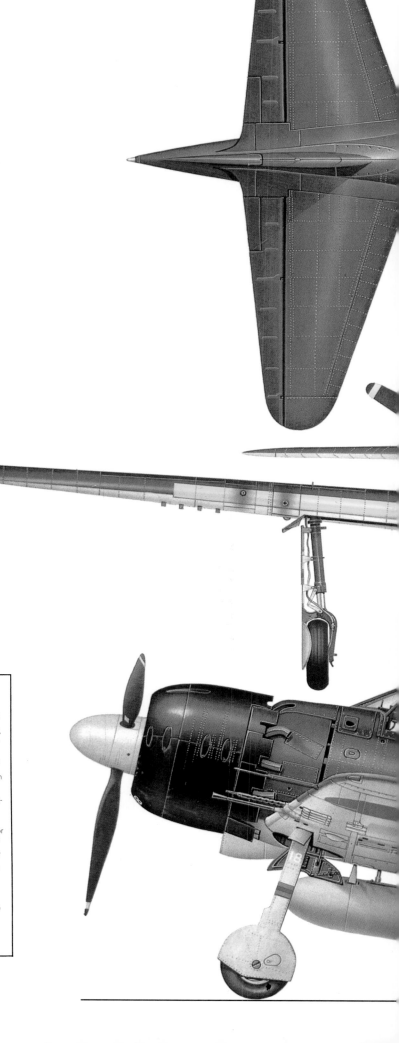

Mitsubishi A6M Reisen variants

Mitsubishi A6M1: first two prototypes, powered by the 582-kW (780-hp) Zuisei 13 engine

Mitsubishi A6M2: initial production version, powered by the 701-kW (940-hp) Sakae 12 engine, with an armament of two 20-mm and two 7.7-mm (0.303-in) guns, span 12.00 m (39 ft 4.5 in) and normal take-off weight 2410 kg (5,313 lb); initial aircraft of the batch, up to c/n 21, had an unreinforced rear spar, aircraft from c/n 22 onwards had the reinforced rear spar (both sub-types being designated **Model 11**), and from c/n 65 the wingtips were capable of manual folding (the sub-type being designated **Model 21**)

Mitsubishi A6M3 Model 32: improved production model powered by the 843-kW (1,130-hp) Sakae 21; from the fourth aircraft 20-mm cannon ammunition was increased, and later aircraft had square-tipped wings of 11.00 m (36 ft 1 in) span compared with the **A6M3 Model 22**'s rounded tips of 12.00 m (39 ft 4.5 in); normal take-off weight 2544 kg (5,609 lb)

Mitsubishi A6M4: unsuccessful experimental variant with turbocharged Sakae engine

Mitsubishi A6M5 Model 52: improved A6M3 with thicker wing skins, rounded wingtips and thrust-augmenting exhaust stacks; normal take-off weight 2733 kg (6,025 lb)

Mitsubishi A6M5a Model 52A: derivative of the A6M5 with thicker wing skins and improved Type 99 Model 2 Mark 3 cannon

Mitsubishi A6M5 Model 52B: improved A6M5a with extra protection, fire extinguishing system for the fuel tanks, and one 7.7-mm (0.303-in) machine-gun replaced by a 13.2-mm (0.52-in) Type 3 weapon

Mitsubishi A6M5c Model 52C: yet further improved model, with two 13.2-mm (0.52-in) Type 3 machine-guns added outboard of the cannon, armour behind the pilot, extra fuel capacity, and racks for eight 10-kg (22-lb) unguided air-to-air rockets

Mitsubishi A6M6c Model 53C: improved A6M5c with 903-kW (1,210-hp) Sakae 31 plus methanol/water boost, and self-sealing wing tanks

Mitsubishi A6M7 Model 63: dive-bomber version of the A6M6c intended for use from small carriers; centreline provision for one 250-kg (551-lb) bomb and underwing points for two 350-litre (77-Imp gal) drop tanks

Mitsubishi A6M8 Model 64: uprated model with 1164-kW (1,560-hp) Kinsei 62 engine, no fuselage guns, better protection, and normal take-off weight 3150 kg (6,945 lb)

Mitsubishi A6M2-K: dual-control trainer version of the A6M2

Mitsubishi A6M5-K: dual-control version of the A6M5

Nakajima A6M2-N: floatplane version of the A6M2 with single main float and two underwing stabilising floats; normal take-off weight 2460 kg (5,423 lb)

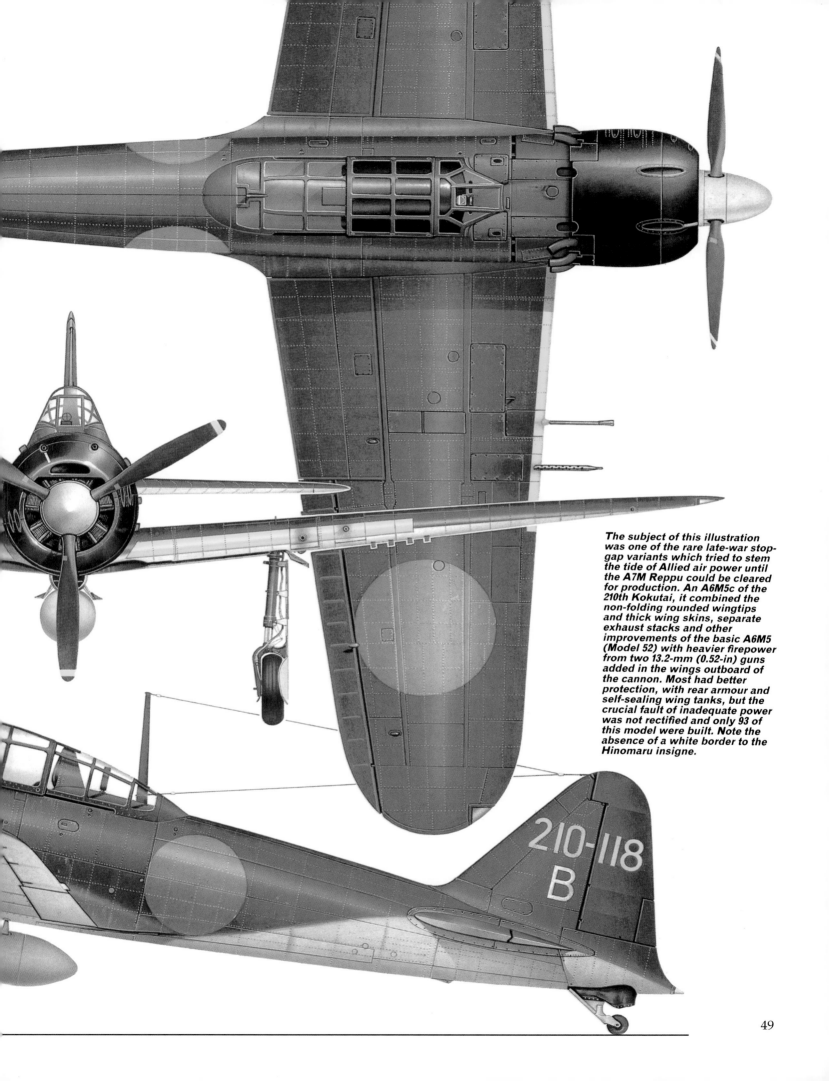

The subject of this illustration was one of the rare late-war stop-gap variants which tried to stem the tide of Allied air power until the A7M Reppu could be cleared for production. An A6M5c of the 210th Kokutai, it combined the non-folding rounded wingtips and thick wing skins, separate exhaust stacks and other improvements of the basic A6M5 (Model 52) with heavier firepower from two 13.2-mm (0.52-in) guns added in the wings outboard of the cannon. Most had better protection, with rear armour and self-sealing wing tanks, but the crucial fault of inadequate power was not rectified and only 93 of this model were built. Note the absence of a white border to the Hinomaru insigne.

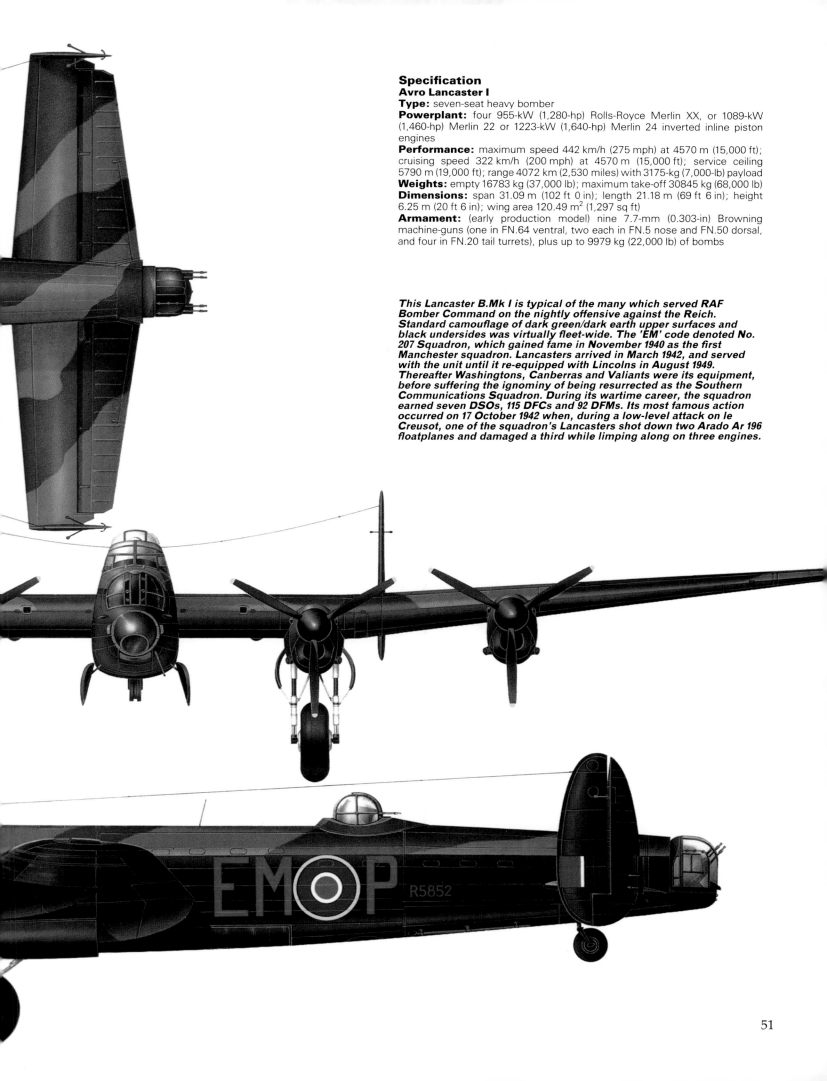

Specification
Avro Lancaster I
Type: seven-seat heavy bomber

Powerplant: four 955-kW (1,280-hp) Rolls-Royce Merlin XX, or 1089-kW (1,460-hp) Merlin 22 or 1223-kW (1,640-hp) Merlin 24 inverted inline piston engines

Performance: maximum speed 442 km/h (275 mph) at 4570 m (15,000 ft); cruising speed 322 km/h (200 mph) at 4570 m (15,000 ft); service ceiling 5790 m (19,000 ft); range 4072 km (2,530 miles) with 3175-kg (7,000-lb) payload

Weights: empty 16783 kg (37,000 lb); maximum take-off 30845 kg (68,000 lb)

Dimensions: span 31.09 m (102 ft 0 in); length 21.18 m (69 ft 6 in); height 6.25 m (20 ft 6 in); wing area 120.49 m² (1,297 sq ft)

Armament: (early production model) nine 7.7-mm (0.303-in) Browning machine-guns (one in FN.64 ventral, two each in FN.5 nose and FN.50 dorsal, and four in FN.20 tail turrets), plus up to 9979 kg (22,000 lb) of bombs

This Lancaster B.Mk I is typical of the many which served RAF Bomber Command on the nightly offensive against the Reich. Standard camouflage of dark green/dark earth upper surfaces and black undersides was virtually fleet-wide. The 'EM' code denoted No. 207 Squadron, which gained fame in November 1940 as the first Manchester squadron. Lancasters arrived in March 1942, and served with the unit until it re-equipped with Lincolns in August 1949. Thereafter Washingtons, Canberras and Valiants were its equipment, before suffering the ignominy of being resurrected as the Southern Communications Squadron. During its wartime career, the squadron earned seven DSOs, 115 DFCs and 92 DFMs. Its most famous action occurred on 17 October 1942 when, during a low-level attack on le Creusot, one of the squadron's Lancasters shot down two Arado Ar 196 floatplanes and damaged a third while limping along on three engines.

Hawker Typhoon F.Mk 1B

This aircraft represents the ultimate standard of build of the Typhoon IB, which accounted for all but approximately 105 of the entire production run. The four-bladed propeller was introduced in 1943 but did not completely supplant the original unit. The aircraft shown flew with No. 181 Sqn, 2nd Tactical Air Force, serving in France in June 1944, and is armed with rockets.

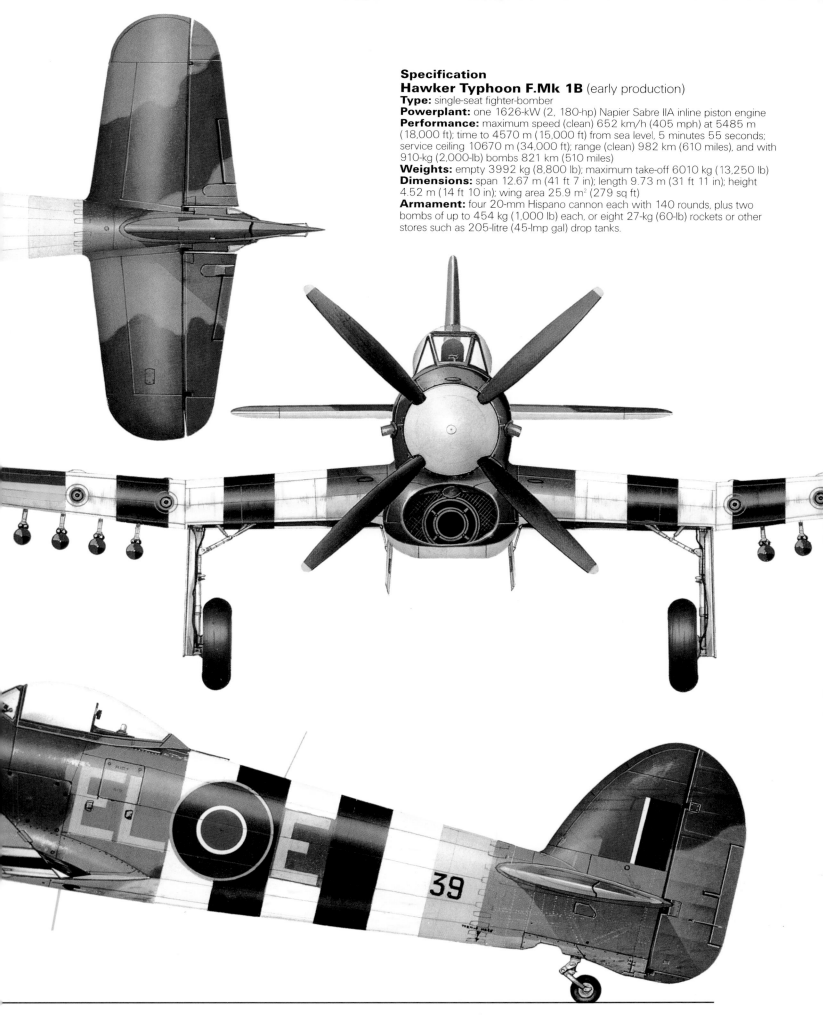

Specification
Hawker Typhoon F.Mk 1B (early production)
Type: single-seat fighter-bomber
Powerplant: one 1626-kW (2, 180-hp) Napier Sabre IIA inline piston engine
Performance: maximum speed (clean) 652 km/h (405 mph) at 5485 m (18,000 ft); time to 4570 m (15,000 ft) from sea level, 5 minutes 55 seconds; service ceiling 10670 m (34,000 ft); range (clean) 982 km (610 miles), and with 910-kg (2,000-lb) bombs 821 km (510 miles)
Weights: empty 3992 kg (8,800 lb); maximum take-off 6010 kg (13,250 lb)
Dimensions: span 12.67 m (41 ft 7 in); length 9.73 m (31 ft 11 in); height 4.52 m (14 ft 10 in); wing area 25.9 m² (279 sq ft)
Armament: four 20-mm Hispano cannon each with 140 rounds, plus two bombs of up to 454 kg (1,000 lb) each, or eight 27-kg (60-lb) rockets or other stores such as 205-litre (45-lmp gal) drop tanks.

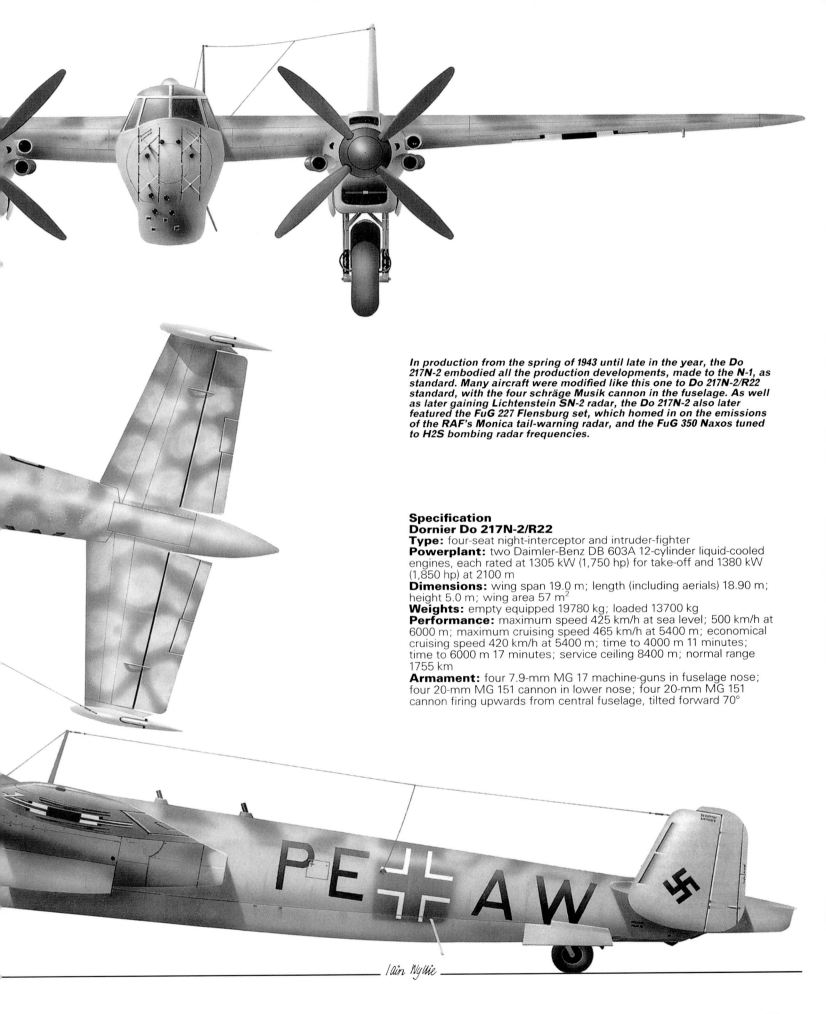

In production from the spring of 1943 until late in the year, the Do 217N-2 embodied all the production developments, made to the N-1, as standard. Many aircraft were modified like this one to Do 217N-2/R22 standard, with the four schräge Musik cannon in the fuselage. As well as later gaining Lichtenstein SN-2 radar, the Do 217N-2 also later featured the FuG 227 Flensburg set, which homed in on the emissions of the RAF's Monica tail-warning radar, and the FuG 350 Naxos tuned to H2S bombing radar frequencies.

Specification
Dornier Do 217N-2/R22
Type: four-seat night-interceptor and intruder-fighter
Powerplant: two Daimler-Benz DB 603A 12-cylinder liquid-cooled engines, each rated at 1305 kW (1,750 hp) for take-off and 1380 kW (1,850 hp) at 2100 m
Dimensions: wing span 19.0 m; length (including aerials) 18.90 m; height 5.0 m; wing area 57 m^2
Weights: empty equipped 19780 kg; loaded 13700 kg
Performance: maximum speed 425 km/h at sea level; 500 km/h at 6000 m; maximum cruising speed 465 km/h at 5400 m; economical cruising speed 420 km/h at 5400 m; time to 4000 m 11 minutes; time to 6000 m 17 minutes; service ceiling 8400 m; normal range 1755 km
Armament: four 7.9-mm MG 17 machine-guns in fuselage nose; four 20-mm MG 151 cannon in lower nose; four 20-mm MG 151 cannon firing upwards from central fuselage, tilted forward 70°

Iain Wyllie

Savoia-Marchetti S.M.79-I

Specification
Savoia-Marchetti S.M.79-I
Type: four/five-crew medium bomber/torpedo-bomber
Powerplant: three 582-kW (780-hp) Alfa Romeo 126 RC.34 9-cylinder air-cooled radial piston engines
Performance: maximum speed 430 km/h (267 mph) at 4000 m (13,125 ft); climb to 4000 m (13,125 ft) in 13 minutes 15 seconds; service ceiling 6500 m (21,325 ft); maximum range at 340 km/h (211 mph) 3300 km (2,050 miles)
Weights: empty 6950 kg (15,322 lb); maximum take-off 10730 kg (23,655 lb)
Dimensions: span 21.20 m (69 ft 6¾ in); length 15.60 m (51 ft 2 in); height 4.60 m (15 ft 1 in); wing area 61.70 m² (664.2 sq ft)
Armament: one fixed 12.7-mm (0.5-in) machine-gun firing forward over cabin roof, guns of the same calibre in dorsal position and in rear of ventral position, one 7.7-mm (0.303-in) machine-gun for beam defence, plus a maximum bomb-load of five 250-kg (551-lb) bombs or one 45-cm (17.7-in) naval torpedo

Savoia-Marchetti S.M.79 variants

S.M.79P: commercial prototype (I-MAGO); originally with Piaggio P.IX Stella RC.2, later with Alfa Romeo 125 RC.35, and Alfa Romeo 126 RC.34 engines
S.M.79C: five racing aircraft; 746-kW (1,000-hp) Piaggio P.XI RC.40 engines
S.M.79T: 11 transatlantic aircraft, plus three S.M.79-1 (BISE, I-BRUN and I-MONI) modified to S.M.79T standard; Piaggio P.XI RC.40 engines
S.M.79B: twin-engine variant; prototype with 768-kW (1,030-hp) Fiat A.80 RC.41 radials; four similar aircraft to Iraq in 1938, and three to Brazil with 694-kW (930-hp) Alfa Romeo 128 RC.18 radials
S.M.79B: (Romanian): 24 Italian-built aircraft with 746-kW (1,000-hp) Gnome-Rhône K-14 Mistral Major radials, and 24 Italian-built aircraft with 910-kW (1,220-hp) Junkers 211 Da inline engines
S.M.79-JR: (Romanian): licence-built (by IAR in Bucharest) aircraft with Junkers Jumo 211Da inverted V-12 engines
S.M.79-I: military protoype for Regia Aeronautica; Piaggio P.IX Stella RC.2 radials
S.M.79-I: production version with Alfa Romeo 126 RC.34 radials for Regia Aeronautica and Aerosiluranti; also 45 aircraft to Yugoslavia; some late-series aircraft with 642-kW (860-hp) Alfa Romeo 128 RC.18 radials; in production 1936-40
S.M.79-II: production version (bombers and torpedo-bombers) with 746-kW (1,000-hp) Piaggio P.XI RC.40 radials; in production 1940-43
S.M.79-III: (sometimes designated **S.579**): production version (bombers and torpedo-bombers) with increased armament; most aircraft without ventral gondola; alternative engines were 746-kW (1,000-hp) Fiat A.80 RC.41 or 1007-kW (1,350-hp) Alfa Romeo 135 RC.32 radials

Savoia-Marchetti S.M.79-II of the 205ª Squadriglia, displaying the Sorci Verdi (Green Mice) emblem adopted from the pre-war S.M.79 record-breaking Sparviero flight led by Colonel Attilio Biseo. Although early in the war Italian bombers tended to be deployed and operated in gruppo strength, battle losses during the final stages of the North African campaign resulted in many such units being disbanded. The 205ª Squadriglia was, however, re-formed as an autonomous unit at Milis, Sardinia, on the eve of the invasion of Sicily in July 1943, albeit with only four serviceable Sparvieri.

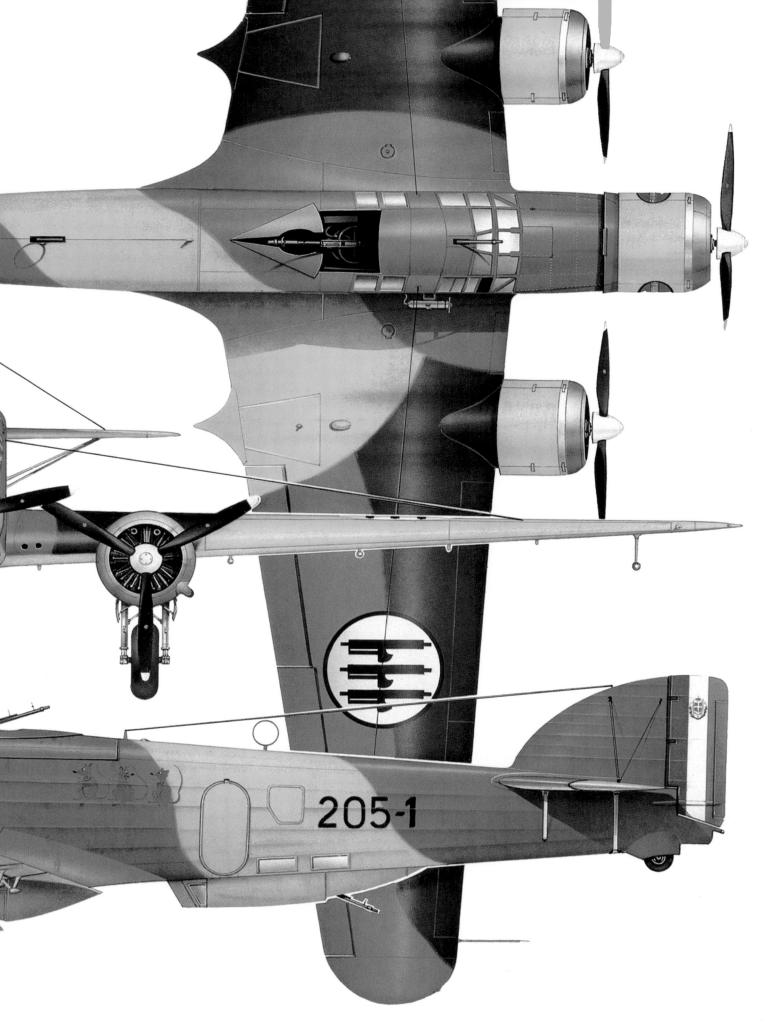

Macchi MC.202 Series VIII Folgore

Specification
Macchi MC.202 Series VIII Folgore

Type: single-seat fighter

Powerplant: one 802-kW (1,075-hp) Alfa Romeo R.A.1000 RC.41-1 Monsoni (Monsoon) inverted V-12

Performance: maximum speed 600 km/h (373 mph) at 5600 m (18,375 ft); climb to 5000 m (16,405 ft) in 4 minutes 40 seconds; service ceiling 11500 m (37,730 ft); range at maximum take-off weight 765 km (475 miles)

Weights: empty 2490 kg (5,489 lb); maximum take-off 3010 kg (6,636 lb)

Dimensions: span 10.58 m (34 ft 8⅔ in); length 8.85 m (29 ft 0½ in); height 3.50 m (11 ft 5¾ in); wing area 16.82 m² (180.83 sq ft)

Armament: two 12.7-mm (0.5-in) Breda-SAFAT machine-guns in nose, each with 360 rounds, and two 7.7-mm (0.303-in) Breda-SAFAT guns in wings, each with 500 rounds

Identified as an aircraft of the 22° Gruppo by the Spauracchio (scarecrow) device on the fuselage band, and by the numerals as belonging to the 369ª Squadriglia, this mid-series MC.202 was based at Capodichino, Naples as part of the 53° Stormo CT at the time of the invasion of Sicily in July 1943. Although its maximum speed of 600 km/h (373 mph) was adequate to match Allied fighters of the Spitfire Mk V's generation, the purpose of deploying aircraft such as the MC.202 to defend Italian cities from attacks by Allied bombers was questionable, as their light armament was quite inadequate for the role of bomber-destroyer.

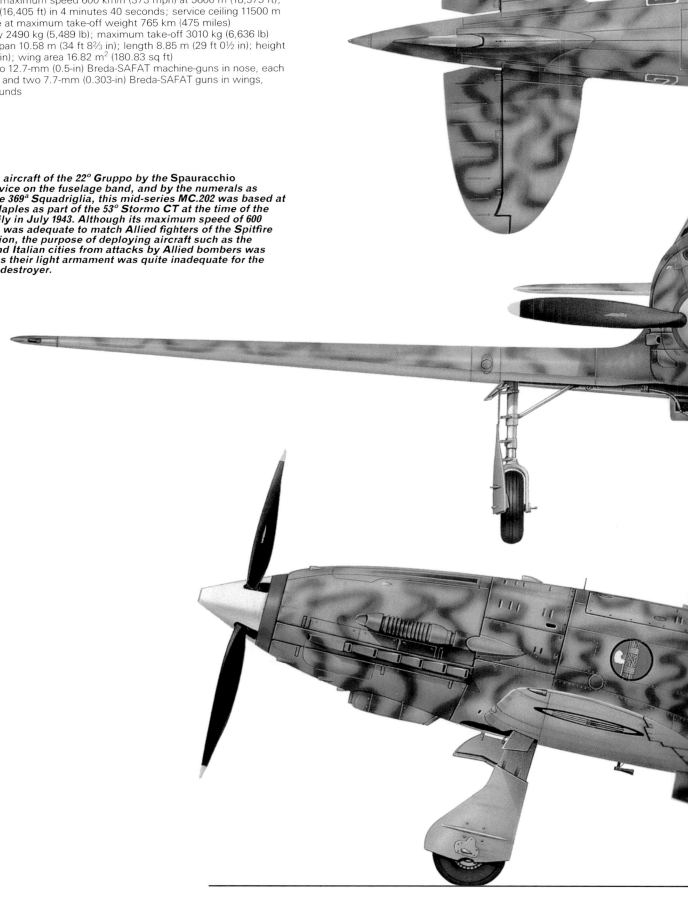

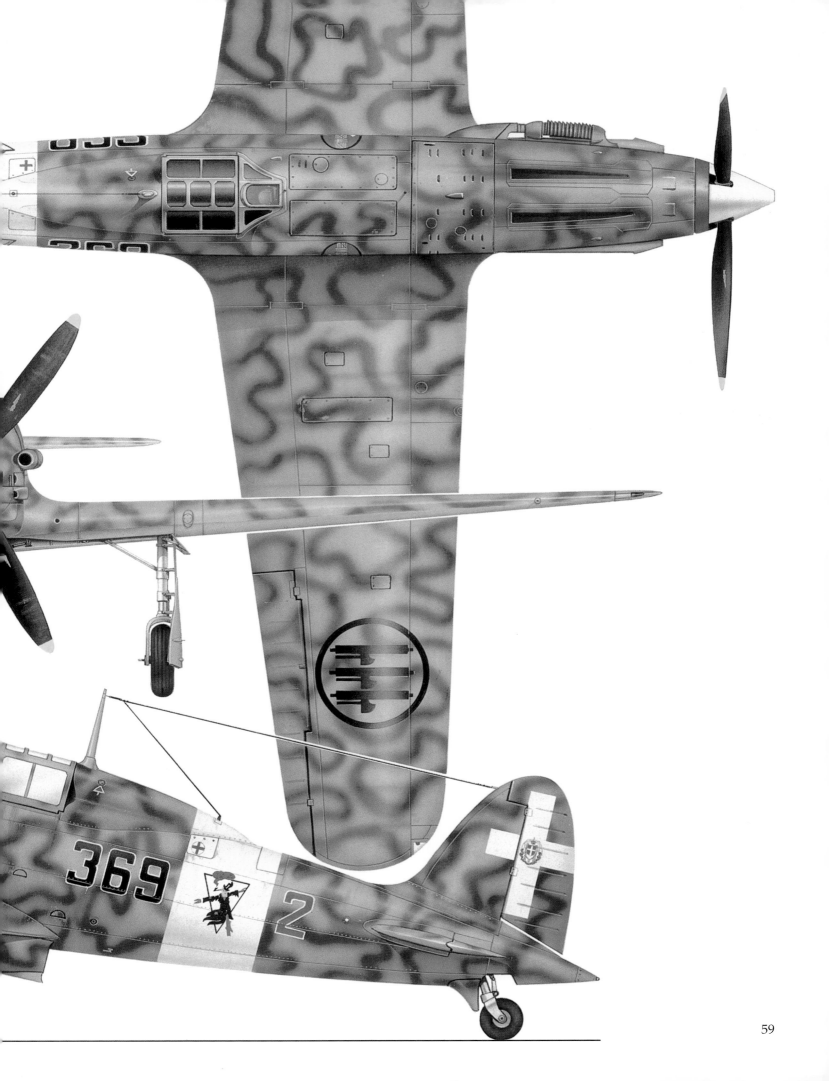

Douglas A-20G Havoc

Specification
Douglas A-20G Havoc

Type: two/three-seat light attack bomber

Powerplant: two 1193-kW (1,600-hp) Wright R-2600-23 Double Cyclone radial piston engines

Performance: maximum speed 546 km/h (339 mph) at 3780 m (12,400 ft); cruising speed 410 km/h (255 mph); initial climb rate 887 m (2,910 ft) per minute; service ceiling 7865 m (25,800 ft); range 1754 km (1,090 miles) with normal bomb load

Weights: empty 7303 kg (16,100 lb); maximum take-off 12338 kg (27,200 lb)

Dimensions: span 18.69 m (61 ft 4 in); length 14.63 m (48 ft 0 in); height 5.36 m (17 ft 7 in); wing area 43.11 m² (464.0 sq ft)

Armament: six fixed forward-firing 12.7-mm (0.5-in) machine-guns in the nose, two 12.7-mm (0.5-in) machine-guns in the power-operated dorsal turret and one manually-operated 12.7-mm (0.5-in) machine-gun in the ventral position, plus up to 1814 kg (4,000 lb) of bombs

USAAF 43-10195 was one of a sub-block of 93 A-20G-35s built in 1943 at the main Douglas plant at Santa Monica. The A-20G-35 had the rear fuselage 152-mm (6 in) wider behind the Martin electric turret, and also had underwing hardpoints which doubled the bomb load from 907 to 1814 kg (2,000 to 4,000 lb). Queen Julia served with the 646th Bomb Squadron, 410th Bomb Group, flying intensively from Gosfield, Essex, England, with the IX Bomber Command. Operations began in early May 1944 against every kind of surface target. By chance, the squadron rudder marking was the same as the 'invasion stripes' applied to all Allied aircraft in the theatre on 5 June 1944. By late September the Allied armies were getting out of range, and the whole group moved to Coulommiers, at Toulouse, to continue the fight against German units retreating in southern France.

Focke-Wulf Fw 190D-9

A standard Fw 190D-9 of JG 77. Although seen as an interim aircraft to fill in before the definitive Ta 152 could enter service, the Fw 190D was itself an excellent aircraft, blessed with good speed and climb performance. Most German pilots were sceptical of the new variant, but when they had a chance to fly it were most surprised, finding it better than the BMW 801-powered Fw 190A in most respects apart from roll-rate. The Fw 190D-9 put the Luftwaffe fighter units on a par with the later-model Spitfires and Mustangs being flown by the Allies.

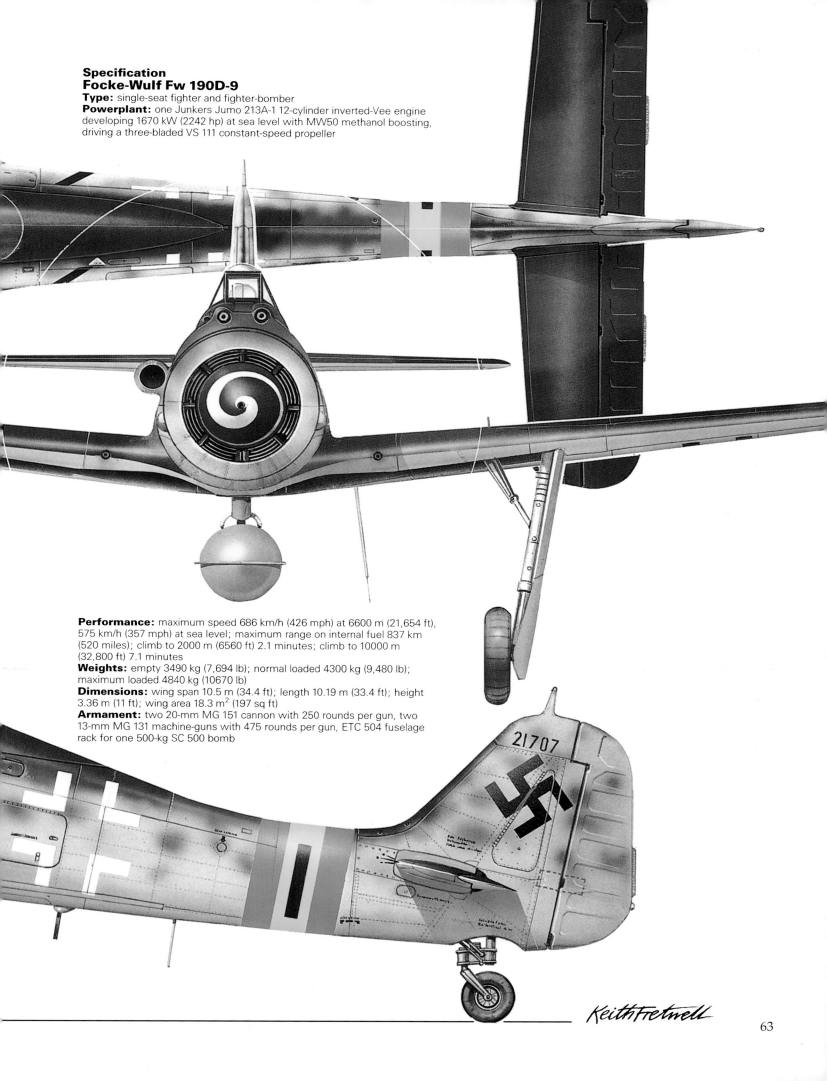

Specification
Focke-Wulf Fw 190D-9
Type: single-seat fighter and fighter-bomber
Powerplant: one Junkers Jumo 213A-1 12-cylinder inverted-Vee engine developing 1670 kW (2242 hp) at sea level with MW50 methanol boosting, driving a three-bladed VS 111 constant-speed propeller

Performance: maximum speed 686 km/h (426 mph) at 6600 m (21,654 ft), 575 km/h (357 mph) at sea level; maximum range on internal fuel 837 km (520 miles); climb to 2000 m (6560 ft) 2.1 minutes; climb to 10000 m (32,800 ft) 7.1 minutes
Weights: empty 3490 kg (7,694 lb); normal loaded 4300 kg (9,480 lb); maximum loaded 4840 kg (10670 lb)
Dimensions: wing span 10.5 m (34.4 ft); length 10.19 m (33.4 ft); height 3.36 m (11 ft); wing area 18.3 m^2 (197 sq ft)
Armament: two 20-mm MG 151 cannon with 250 rounds per gun, two 13-mm MG 131 machine-guns with 475 rounds per gun, ETC 504 fuselage rack for one 500-kg SC 500 bomb

Keith Fretwell

Nakajima Ki-43-II-Otsu

Specification
Nakajima Ki-43-II-Otsu
Type: single-seat fighter and fighter-bomber
Powerplant: one 858-kW (1,150-hp) Nakajima Ha-115 14-cylinder air-cooled radial piston engine
Performance: maximum speed 530 km/h (329 mph) at 4000 m (13,125 ft); climb to 5000 m (16,405 ft) in 5 minutes 49 seconds; service ceiling 11200 m (36,750 ft); normal range 1760 km (1,095 miles)
Weights: empty 1910 kg (4,211 lb); maximum take-off 2925 kg (6,450 lb)
Dimensions: span 10.84 m (35 ft 6¾ in); length 8.92 m (29 ft 3⁵⁄₁₆ in); height 3.27 m (10 ft 8¾ in); wing area 21.4 m^2 (230.4 sq ft)
Armament: two 12.7-mm (0.5-in) Type 1 (Ho-103) machine-guns in the upper fuselage decking, plus two 30-kg (66-lb) or 250-kg (551-lb) bombs

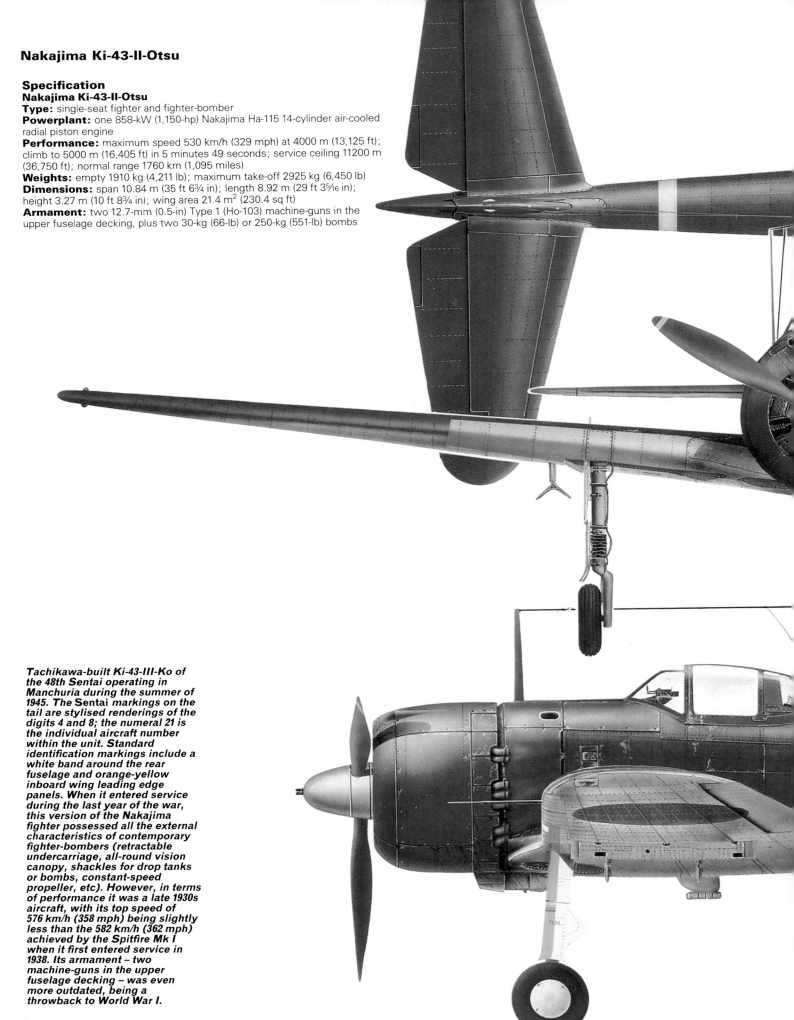

Tachikawa-built Ki-43-III-Ko of the 48th Sentai operating in Manchuria during the summer of 1945. The Sentai markings on the tail are stylised renderings of the digits 4 and 8; the numeral 21 is the individual aircraft number within the unit. Standard identification markings include a white band around the rear fuselage and orange-yellow inboard wing leading edge panels. When it entered service during the last year of the war, this version of the Nakajima fighter possessed all the external characteristics of contemporary fighter-bombers (retractable undercarriage, all-round vision canopy, shackles for drop tanks or bombs, constant-speed propeller, etc). However, in terms of performance it was a late 1930s aircraft, with its top speed of 576 km/h (358 mph) being slightly less than the 582 km/h (362 mph) achieved by the Spitfire Mk I when it first entered service in 1938. Its armament – two machine-guns in the upper fuselage decking – was even more outdated, being a throwback to World War I.

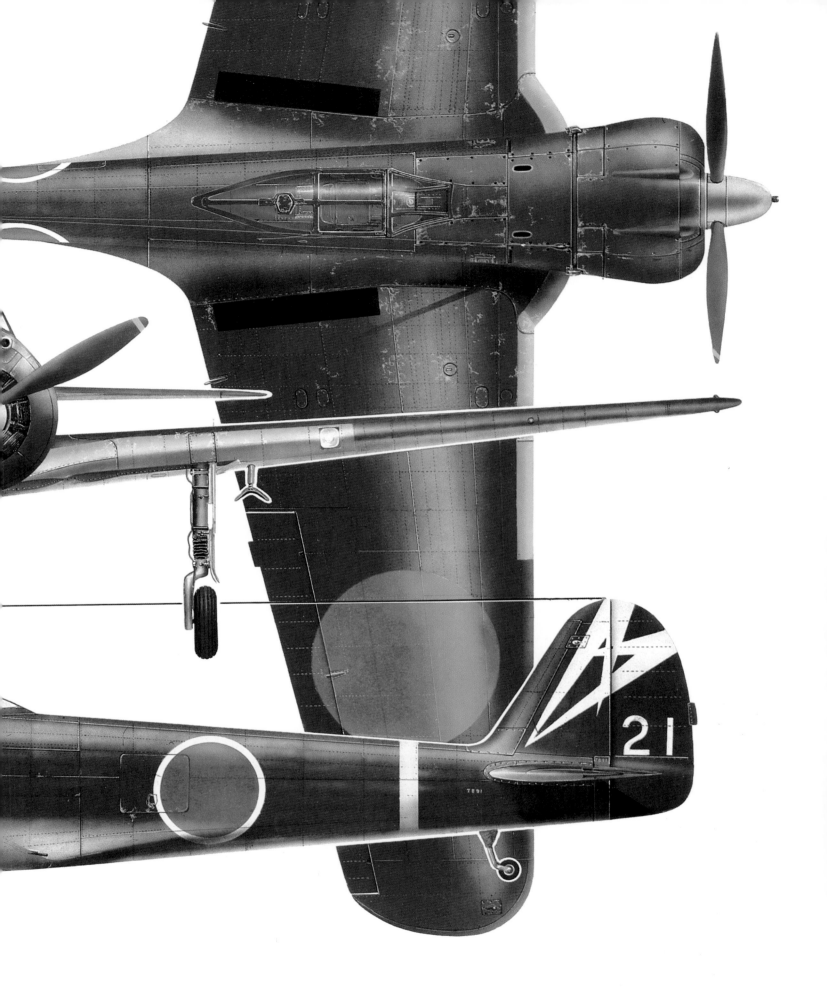

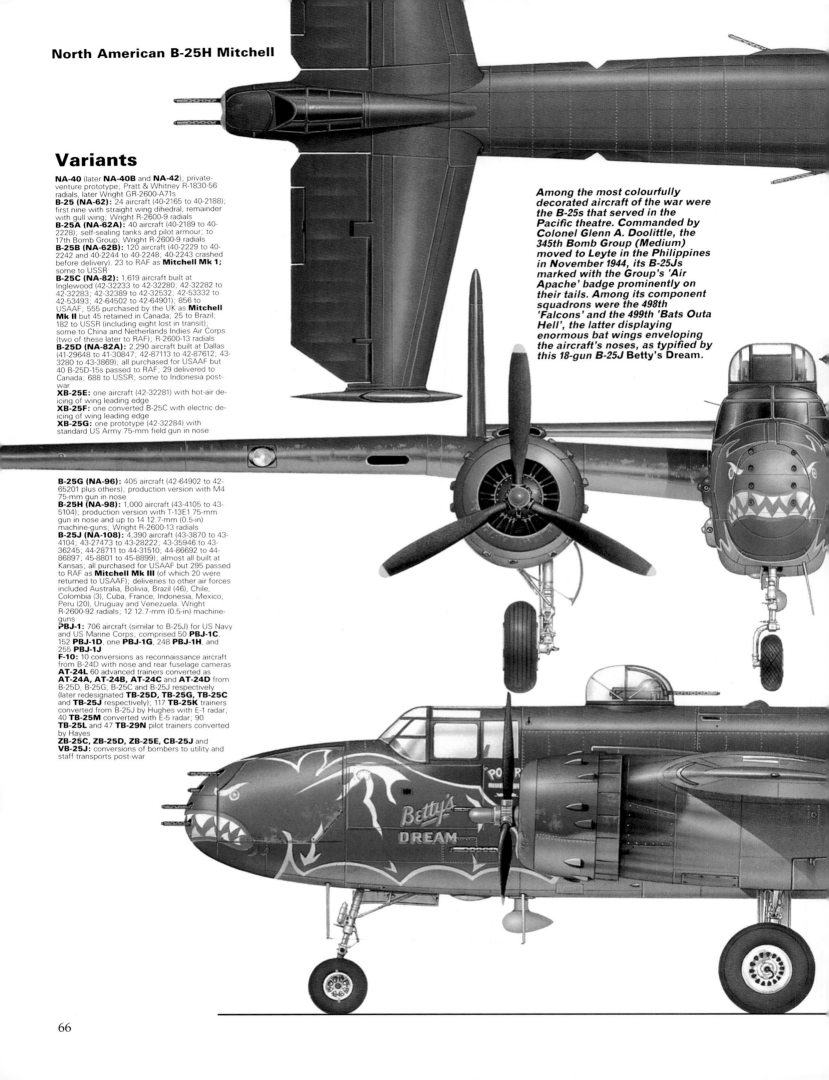

North American B-25H Mitchell

Variants

NA-40 (later **NA-40B** and **NA-42**); private-venture prototype; Pratt & Whitney R-1830-56 radials, later Wright GR-2600-A71s
B-25 (NA-62): 24 aircraft (40-2165 to 40-2188); first nine with straight wing dihedral, remainder with gull wing; Wright R-2600-9 radials
B-25A (NA-62A): 40 aircraft (40-2189 to 40-2228); self-sealing tanks and pilot armour; to 17th Bomb Group; Wright R-2600-9 radials
B-25B (NA-62B): 120 aircraft (40-2229 to 40-2242 and 40-2244 to 40-2248; 40-2243 crashed before delivery). 23 to RAF as **Mitchell Mk 1**; some to USSR
B-25C (NA-82): 1,619 aircraft built at Inglewood (42-32233 to 42-32280; 42-32282 to 42-32283; 42-32389 to 42-32532; 42-53332 to 42-53493; 42-64502 to 42-64901); 856 to USAAF; 555 purchased by the UK as **Mitchell Mk II** but 45 retained in Canada; 25 to Brazil; 182 to USSR (including eight lost in transit); some to China and Netherlands Indies Air Corps (two of these later to RAF); R-2600-13 radials
B-25D (NA-82A): 2,290 aircraft built at Dallas (41-29648 to 41-30847; 42-87113 to 42-87612; 43-3280 to 43-3869); all purchased for USAAF but 40 B-25D-15s passed to RAF; 29 delivered to Canada; 688 to USSR; some to Indonesia postwar
XB-25E: one aircraft (42-32281) with hot-air de-icing of wing leading edge
XB-25F: one converted B-25C with electric de-icing of wing leading edge
XB-25G: one prototype (42-32284) with standard US Army 75-mm field gun in nose

B-25G (NA-96): 405 aircraft (42-64902 to 42-65201 plus others); production version with M4 75-mm gun in nose
B-25H (NA-98): 1,000 aircraft (43-4105 to 43-5104); production version with T-13E1 75-mm gun in nose and up to 14 12.7-mm (0.5-in) machine-guns; Wright R-2600-13 radials
B-25J (NA-108): 4,390 aircraft (43-3870 to 43-4104; 43-27473 to 43-28222; 43-35946 to 43-36245; 44-28711 to 44-31510; 44-86692 to 44-86897; 45-8801 to 45-8899); almost all built at Kansas; all purchased for USAAF but 295 passed to RAF as **Mitchell Mk III** (of which 20 were returned to USAAF); deliveries to other air forces included Australia, Bolivia, Brazil (46), Chile, Colombia (3), Cuba, France, Indonesia, Mexico, Peru (20), Uruguay and Venezuela. Wright R-2600-92 radials; 12 12.7-mm (0.5-in) machine-guns
PBJ-1: 706 aircraft (similar to B-25J) for US Navy and US Marine Corps; comprised 50 **PBJ-1C**, 152 **PBJ-1D**, one **PBJ-1G**, 248 **PBJ-1H**, and 255 **PBJ-1J**
F-10: 10 conversions as reconnaissance aircraft from B-24D with nose and rear fuselage cameras
AT-24L 60 advanced trainers converted as **AT-24A, AT-24B, AT-24C** and **AT-24D** from B-25D, B-25G, B-25C and B-25J respectively (later redesignated **TB-25D, TB-25G, TB-25C** and **TB-25J** respectively); 117 **TB-25K** trainers converted from B-25J by Hughes with E-1 radar; 40 **TB-25M** converted with E-5 radar; 90 **TB-25L** and 47 **TB-29N** pilot trainers converted by Hayes
ZB-25C, ZB-25D, ZB-25E, CB-25J and **VB-25J:** conversions of bombers to utility and staff transports post-war

Among the most colourfully decorated aircraft of the war were the B-25s that served in the Pacific theatre. Commanded by Colonel Glenn A. Doolittle, the 345th Bomb Group (Medium) moved to Leyte in the Philippines in November 1944, its B-25Js marked with the Group's 'Air Apache' badge prominently on their tails. Among its component squadrons were the 498th 'Falcons' and the 499th 'Bats Outa Hell', the latter displaying enormous bat wings enveloping the aircraft's noses, as typified by this 18-gun B-25J Betty's Dream.

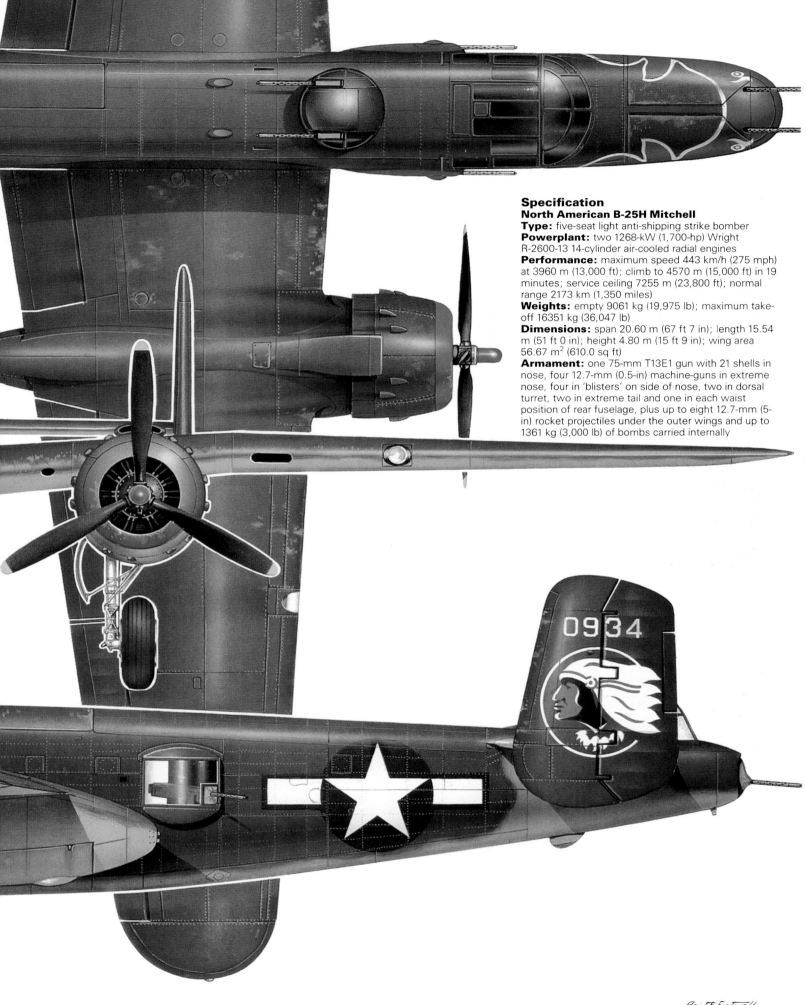

Specification
North American B-25H Mitchell
Type: five-seat light anti-shipping strike bomber
Powerplant: two 1268-kW (1,700-hp) Wright
R-2600-13 14-cylinder air-cooled radial engines
Performance: maximum speed 443 km/h (275 mph)
at 3960 m (13,000 ft); climb to 4570 m (15,000 ft) in 19
minutes; service ceiling 7255 m (23,800 ft); normal
range 2173 km (1,350 miles)
Weights: empty 9061 kg (19,975 lb); maximum take-
off 16351 kg (36,047 lb)
Dimensions: span 20.60 m (67 ft 7 in); length 15.54
m (51 ft 0 in); height 4.80 m (15 ft 9 in); wing area
56.67 m² (610.0 sq ft)
Armament: one 75-mm T13E1 gun with 21 shells in
nose, four 12.7-mm (0.5-in) machine-guns in extreme
nose, four in 'blisters' on side of nose, two in dorsal
turret, two in extreme tail and one in each waist
position of rear fuselage, plus up to eight 12.7-mm (5-
in) rocket projectiles under the outer wings and up to
1361 kg (3,000 lb) of bombs carried internally

Douglas C-47 Skytrain

Specification
Douglas C-47 Skytrain
Type: cargo, supply or 28-seat troop transport, 14-litter ambulance, or glider tug
Powerplant: two 895-kW (1,200-hp) Pratt & Whitney R-1830-92 radial piston engines
Performance: maximum speed 365 km/h (227 mph) at 2285 m (7,500 ft); initial climb rate 287 m (940 ft) per minute; service ceiling 7315 m (24,000 ft); range 2575 km (1,600 miles)
Weights: empty 8256 kg (18,200 lb); maximum take-off 11794 kg (26,000 lb)
Dimensions: span 29.11 m (95 ft 6 in); length 19.43 m (63 ft 9 in); height 5.18 m (17 ft 0 in); wing area 91.69 m² (987 sq ft)
Payload: 3629 kg (8,000 lb) to 4536 kg (10,000 lb) of military cargo (depending on aircraft variant)

General Eisenhower is on record as having stated that the C-47 was one of the four principal instruments of Allied victory in World War II (the others being the bazooka, Jeep and atom bomb). A typical example of the Skytrain was this C-47A-65-DL of the 81st Troop Carrier Squadron, 436th Troop Carrier Group, based at Membury in England between 3 March 1944 and February 1945 (it also took part in the airborne assault on Southern France, based at Voltone, Italy, during July and August 1944). The mission tally on 'Buzz Buggy', together with invasion stripes, suggests participation in the Normandy, Southern France, Nijmegen and Bastogne operations, both as a paratrooper and glider tug.

Junkers Ju 87G-1

Specification
Junkers Ju 87G-1

Type: anti-tank aircraft

Powerplant: one 1044-kW (1,400-hp) Junkers Jumo 211J-1 inline piston engine

Performance: maximum speed about 314 km/h (195 mph); cruising speed normally about 190 km/h (118 mph); rate of climb and service ceiling not known, but extremely poor; combat radius about 320 km (199 miles)

Weights: empty about 4400 kg (9,700 lb); maximum take-off about 6600 kg (14,550 lb)

Dimensions: span 15.00 m (49 ft 2½ in); length 11.50 m (37 ft 8¾ in); height 3.90 m (12 ft 9¼ in); wing area 33.69 m^2 (362.6 sq ft)

Armament: two 37-mm BK 3.7 cannon and one flexible 7.92-mm (0.331-in) MG 81 machine-gun, plus a useful bombload when the underwing cannon were not being carried

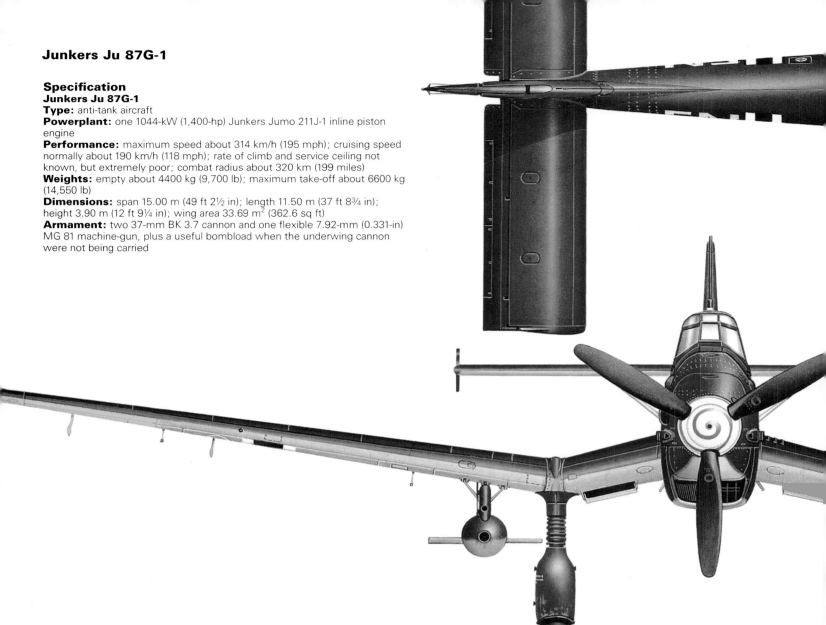

Variants

Junkers Ju 87 V1: first prototype, with 477-kW (640-hp) Rolls-Royce Kestrel

Junkers Ju 87 V2: second prototype 455-kW (610-hp) Jumo 210Aa, hurriedly fitted single-fin tail unit

Junkers Ju 87 V3: third prototype, properly designed tail, engine lowered to improve pilot view

Junkers Ju 87A: first production series, 477-kW (640-hp) Jumo 210Ca or (A-2) 507-kW (680-hp) Jumo 210Da about 200 built (1937-8)

Junkers Ju 87B: 895-kW (1,200-hp) Jumo 211Da, redesigned canopy and fuselage, larger vertical tail, spatted instead of trousered landing gears, bombloads up to 1000 kg (2,205 lb) (total deliveries in various sub-types about 1,300)

Junkers Ju 87C: navalised version intended for use from aircraft-carrier, folding wings, hook, catapult hooks, jettisonable landing gear, flotation gear and extra tankage; operated from land bases

Junkers Ju 87D: major production version, 1044-kW (1,400-hp) Jumo 211J-1 or 1119-kW (1,500-hp) Jumo 211P-1, redesigned airframe with lower drag, bombload up to 1800 kg (3,968-lb), D-2 glider tug, D-3 increased armour, D-4 for torpedo-carrying, D-5 with extended wingtips, D-7 twin MG 151 cannon and night equipment, D-8 as D-7 without night equipment

Junkers Ju 87G-1: conversion of D-3 to attack armoured vehicles with two 37-mm BK 3.7 (Flak 18) guns

Junkers Ju 87H: dual-control trainers without armament, kinked rear canopy with side blisters

Junkers Ju 87R: derivative of Ju 87B-2 with augmented tankage and provision for drop tanks to increase range, normally with single SC250 (551-lb) bomb

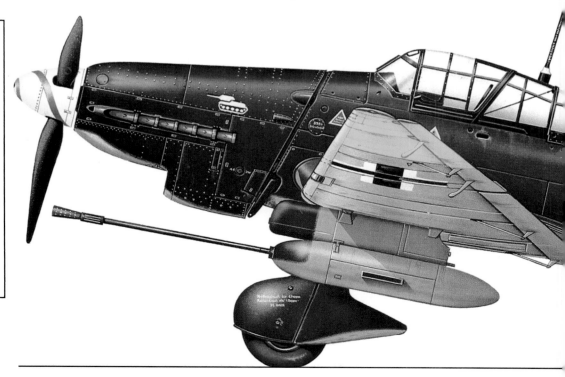

The last variant of the Ju 87 to become operational, apart from the Ju 87H trainer, was the Ju 87G-1 anti-tank model. This was not built as such, but rather converted from Ju 87D-5 airframes. The concept was the brainchild of the extraordinary Hans-Ulrich Rudel, who despite being shot down 30 times flew no fewer than 2,530 combat sorties and destroyed 519 Russian tanks: the basic Ju 87D-5 was adapted to carry a pair of massive Flak 18 (BK 3,7) 37-mm cannon pods under its outer wing panels. The aircraft illustrated was on the strength of II/Schlachtgeschwader 3, more specifically the unit's 5. Staffel, serving on the Eastern Front in late 1944. The Ju 87G-1 could carry bombs instead of guns, but had no dive-brakes.

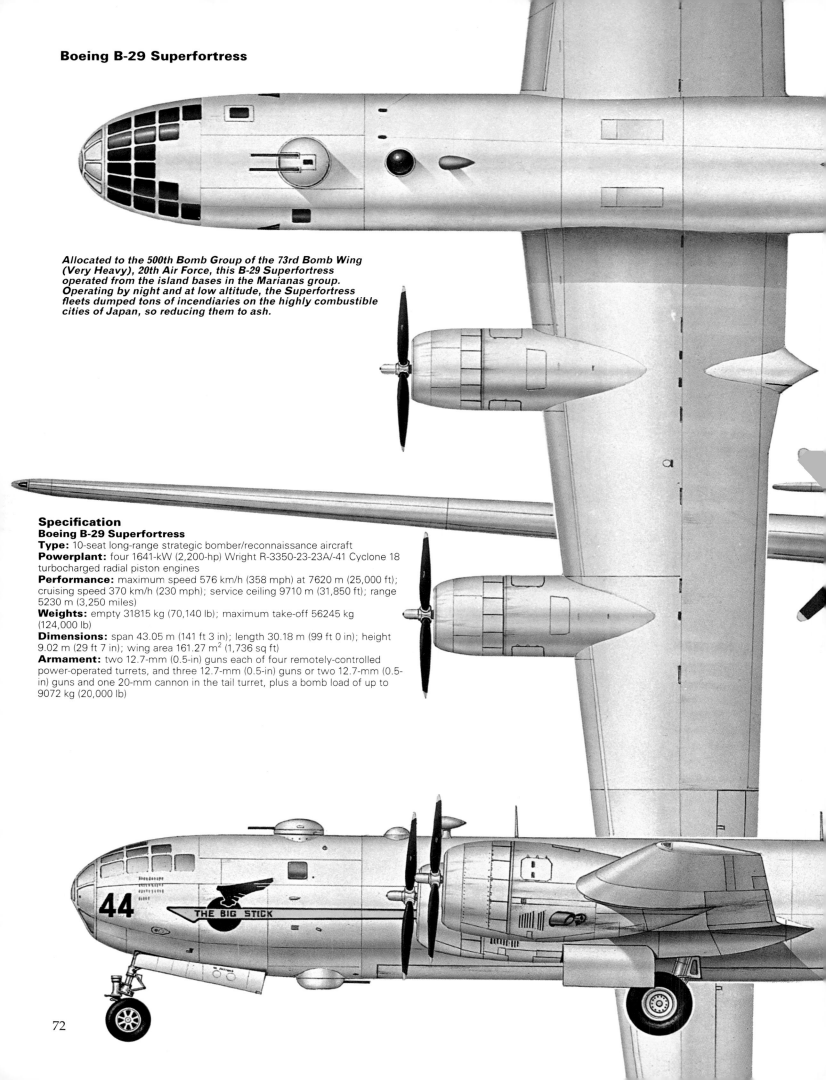

Boeing B-29 Superfortress

Allocated to the 500th Bomb Group of the 73rd Bomb Wing (Very Heavy), 20th Air Force, this B-29 Superfortress operated from the island bases in the Marianas group. Operating by night and at low altitude, the Superfortress fleets dumped tons of incendiaries on the highly combustible cities of Japan, so reducing them to ash.

Specification
Boeing B-29 Superfortress

Type: 10-seat long-range strategic bomber/reconnaissance aircraft

Powerplant: four 1641-kW (2,200-hp) Wright R-3350-23-23A/-41 Cyclone 18 turbocharged radial piston engines

Performance: maximum speed 576 km/h (358 mph) at 7620 m (25,000 ft); cruising speed 370 km/h (230 mph); service ceiling 9710 m (31,850 ft); range 5230 m (3,250 miles)

Weights: empty 31815 kg (70,140 lb); maximum take-off 56245 kg (124,000 lb)

Dimensions: span 43.05 m (141 ft 3 in); length 30.18 m (99 ft 0 in); height 9.02 m (29 ft 7 in); wing area 161.27 m² (1,736 sq ft)

Armament: two 12.7-mm (0.5-in) guns each of four remotely-controlled power-operated turrets, and three 12.7-mm (0.5-in) guns or two 12.7-mm (0.5-in) guns and one 20-mm cannon in the tail turret, plus a bomb load of up to 9072 kg (20,000 lb)

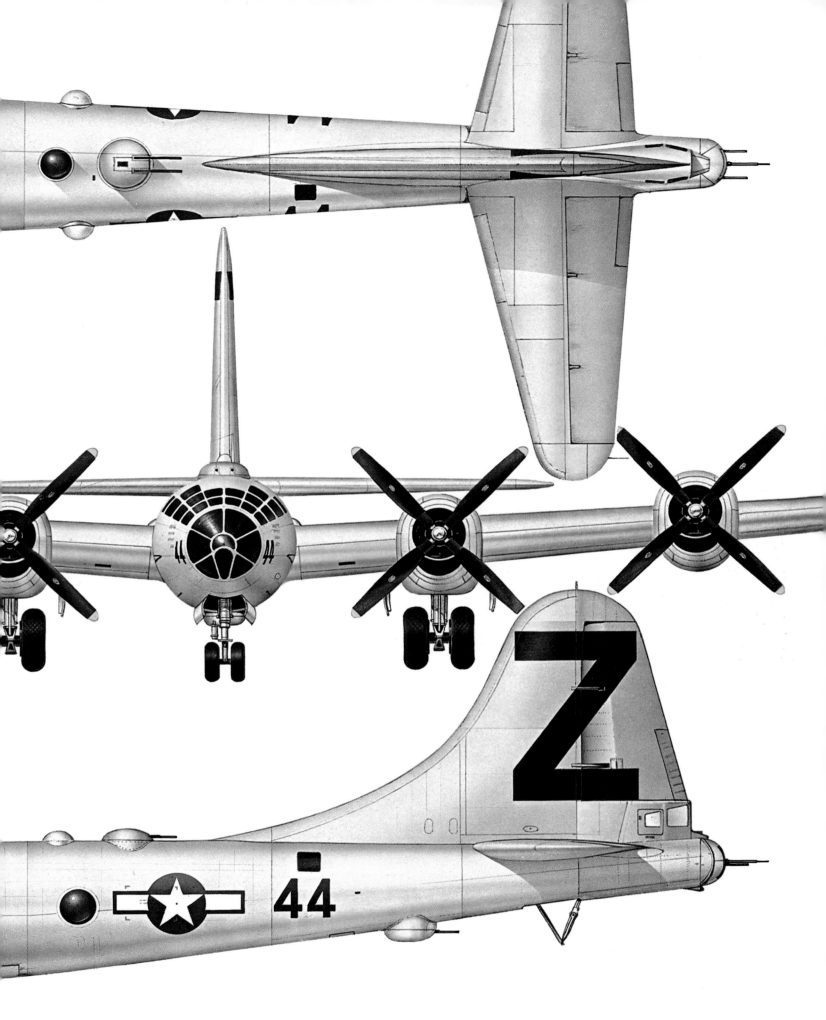

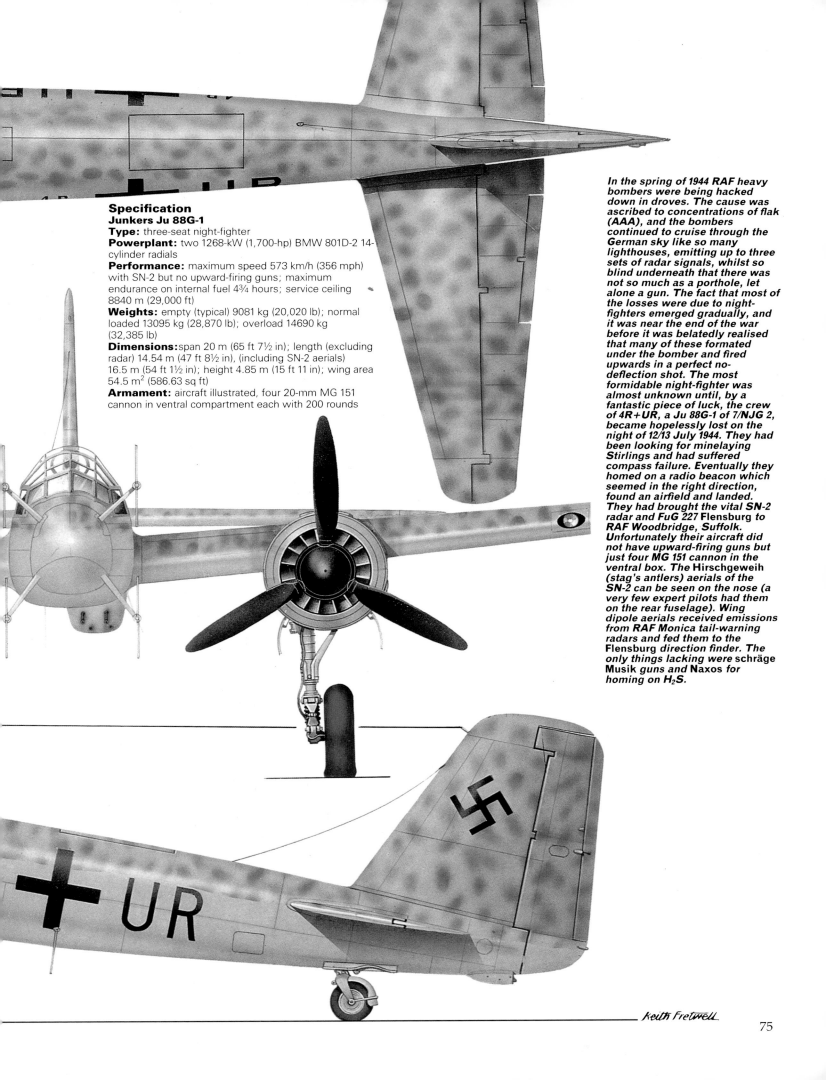

Specification
Junkers Ju 88G-1
Type: three-seat night-fighter

Powerplant: two 1268-kW (1,700-hp) BMW 801D-2 14-cylinder radials

Performance: maximum speed 573 km/h (356 mph) with SN-2 but no upward-firing guns; maximum endurance on internal fuel 4¾ hours; service ceiling 8840 m (29,000 ft)

Weights: empty (typical) 9081 kg (20,020 lb); normal loaded 13095 kg (28,870 lb); overload 14690 kg (32,385 lb)

Dimensions: span 20 m (65 ft 7½ in); length (excluding radar) 14.54 m (47 ft 8½ in), (including SN-2 aerials) 16.5 m (54 ft 1½ in); height 4.85 m (15 ft 11 in); wing area 54.5 m² (586.63 sq ft)

Armament: aircraft illustrated, four 20-mm MG 151 cannon in ventral compartment each with 200 rounds

In the spring of 1944 RAF heavy bombers were being hacked down in droves. The cause was ascribed to concentrations of flak (AAA), and the bombers continued to cruise through the German sky like so many lighthouses, emitting up to three sets of radar signals, whilst so blind underneath that there was not so much as a porthole, let alone a gun. The fact that most of the losses were due to night-fighters emerged gradually, and it was near the end of the war before it was belatedly realised that many of these formated under the bomber and fired upwards in a perfect no-deflection shot. The most formidable night-fighter was almost unknown until, by a fantastic piece of luck, the crew of 4R+UR, a Ju 88G-1 of 7/NJG 2, became hopelessly lost on the night of 12/13 July 1944. They had been looking for minelaying Stirlings and had suffered compass failure. Eventually they homed on a radio beacon which seemed in the right direction, found an airfield and landed. They had brought the vital SN-2 radar and FuG 227 Flensburg to RAF Woodbridge, Suffolk. Unfortunately their aircraft did not have upward-firing guns but just four MG 151 cannon in the ventral box. The Hirschgeweih (stag's antlers) aerials of the SN-2 can be seen on the nose (a very few expert pilots had them on the rear fuselage). Wing dipole aerials received emissions from RAF Monica tail-warning radars and fed them to the Flensburg direction finder. The only things lacking were schräge Musik guns and Naxos for homing on H₂S.

Keith Fretwell

Supermarine Spitfire F.Mk XIVE

MV349 was a Spitfire F.Mk XIVE built by Supermarine and delivered in late 1944. As the markings show it immediately went out to the Far East Air Force, being shipped to Bombay and flown to Burma, where it operated with RAF No. 28 Sqn on the Malayan front until the end of the war. The actual end of fighting came just as No. 28 Sqn, with the other squadrons, was being readied to go aboard carriers from where they were to fly off to Malayan airfields during the final assault in that theatre. As can be seen, MV349 was fitted with a low-level oblique camera aft of the cockpit, as in the FR.Mk XIVE, but did not have the latter's clipped wings. Standard E armament was fitted: two 20-mm Hispano Mk II cannon and two 12.7-mm (0.5-in) Browning machine-guns. The vertical tail had had to be increased in area to counter the longer nose, and the rear-view hood and cut-down rear fuselage ideally needed even greater fin area in compensation.

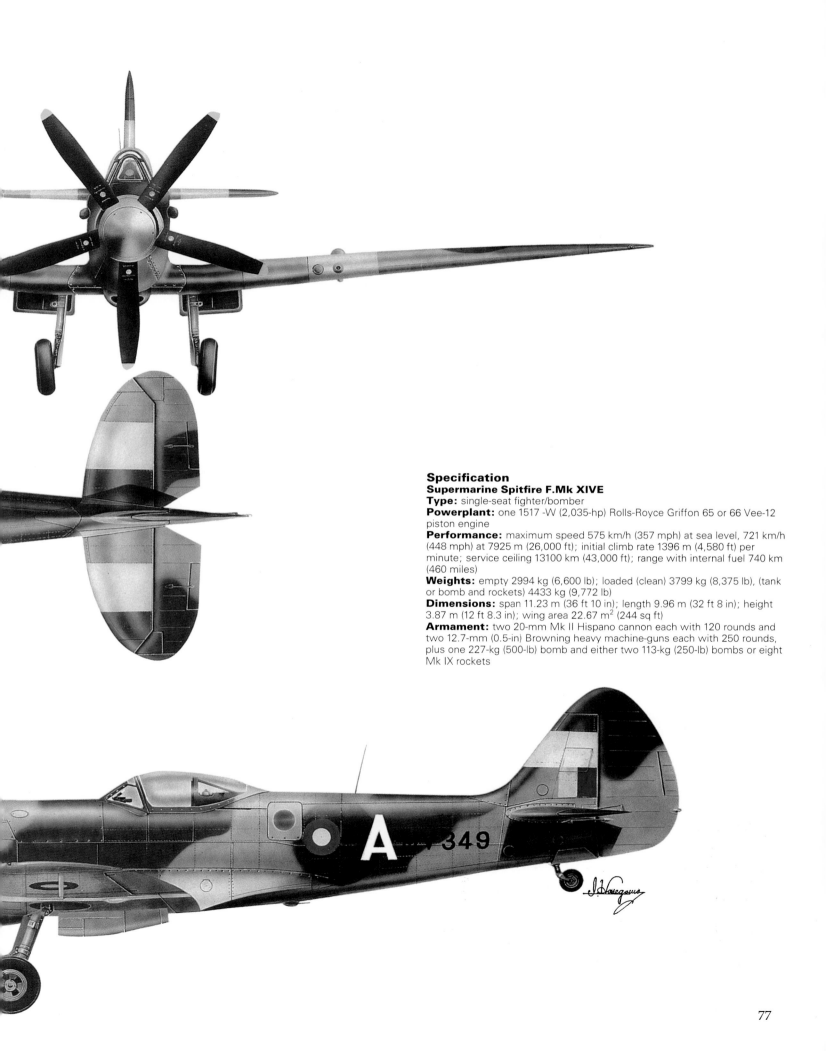

Specification
Supermarine Spitfire F.Mk XIVE

Type: single-seat fighter/bomber

Powerplant: one 1517 -W (2,035-hp) Rolls-Royce Griffon 65 or 66 Vee-12 piston engine

Performance: maximum speed 575 km/h (357 mph) at sea level, 721 km/h (448 mph) at 7925 m (26,000 ft); initial climb rate 1396 m (4,580 ft) per minute; service ceiling 13100 km (43,000 ft); range with internal fuel 740 km (460 miles)

Weights: empty 2994 kg (6,600 lb); loaded (clean) 3799 kg (8,375 lb), (tank or bomb and rockets) 4433 kg (9,772 lb)

Dimensions: span 11.23 m (36 ft 10 in); length 9.96 m (32 ft 8 in); height 3.87 m (12 ft 8.3 in); wing area 22.67 m^2 (244 sq ft)

Armament: two 20-mm Mk II Hispano cannon each with 120 rounds and two 12.7-mm (0.5-in) Browning heavy machine-guns each with 250 rounds, plus one 227-kg (500-lb) bomb and either two 113-kg (250-lb) bombs or eight Mk IX rockets

Petlyakov Pe-2FT

Specification
Petlyakov Pe-2FT

Type: three-seat tactical bomber

Powerplant: two 939-kW (1,260-hp) Klimov VK-105PF vee 12-cylinder piston engines

Performance: maximum speed 449 km/h (279 mph) at sea level and 580 km/h (360 mph) at 4000 m (13,125 ft); service ceiling 8800 m (28,870 ft); range with 1000-kg (2,205-lb) bombload 1315 km (817 miles)

Weights: empty 6200 kg (13,668 lb); maximum 8520 kg (18,783 lb)

Dimensions: span 17.11 m (56 ft 1⅔ in); length 12.78 m (41 ft 11 in); height 3.42 m (11 ft 2⅔ in); wing area 40.5 m² (436 sq ft)

Armament: provision for four FAB-100 (220.5-lb) bombs in internal bomb bay, two FAB-100 bombs in rear of engine nacelles and four FAB-250 (551-lb) bombs on external racks under centre section; two 7.62-mm (0.31-in) ShKAS machine-guns firing ahead aimed by pilot, MV-3 dorsal turret with single 12.7-mm (0.5-in) UBT, one ShKAS aimed by hand from rear ventral position (drawing shows UBS, very unusual) and one ShKAS aimed through left or right rear beam position

This Pe-2FT served with an unknown bomber regiment on the Eastern Front in 1944; after 1942 the 'British style' camouflage was very unusual. Also depicted is the original VK-105 engine installation with a separate supercharger air inlet just behind the spinner, and with the oil-cooler inlet smaller and further aft than in the VK-105PF, which was used in the Pe-2FT. All aircraft of this series had the main coolant radiators inside the wing, fed by leading-edge inlets and exhausting through the upper surface. Note the small wind vane on the MV-3 turret (a product of the Mozharovskii-Venyevidov bureau) which assisted the gunner to slew it rapidly. The square hatch in the roof of the radio operator's compartment was normally closed by left/right-hinged doors.

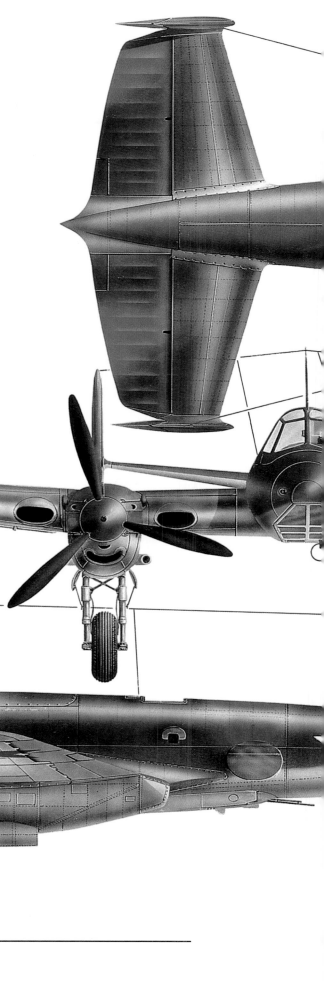

Yakovlev Yak-9

This Yak-9 was one of those equipping the Free French Normandie-Niémen regiment in 1944. It can be seen to be normal in all visible features, with armament of one ShVAK and one BS and with the blunt wingtips introduced early in production at the same time that the wing ribs were changed to aluminium. Many colour schemes were used by VVS front-line regiments, and in winter it was usual to add a rough coat of white on the upper surfaces.

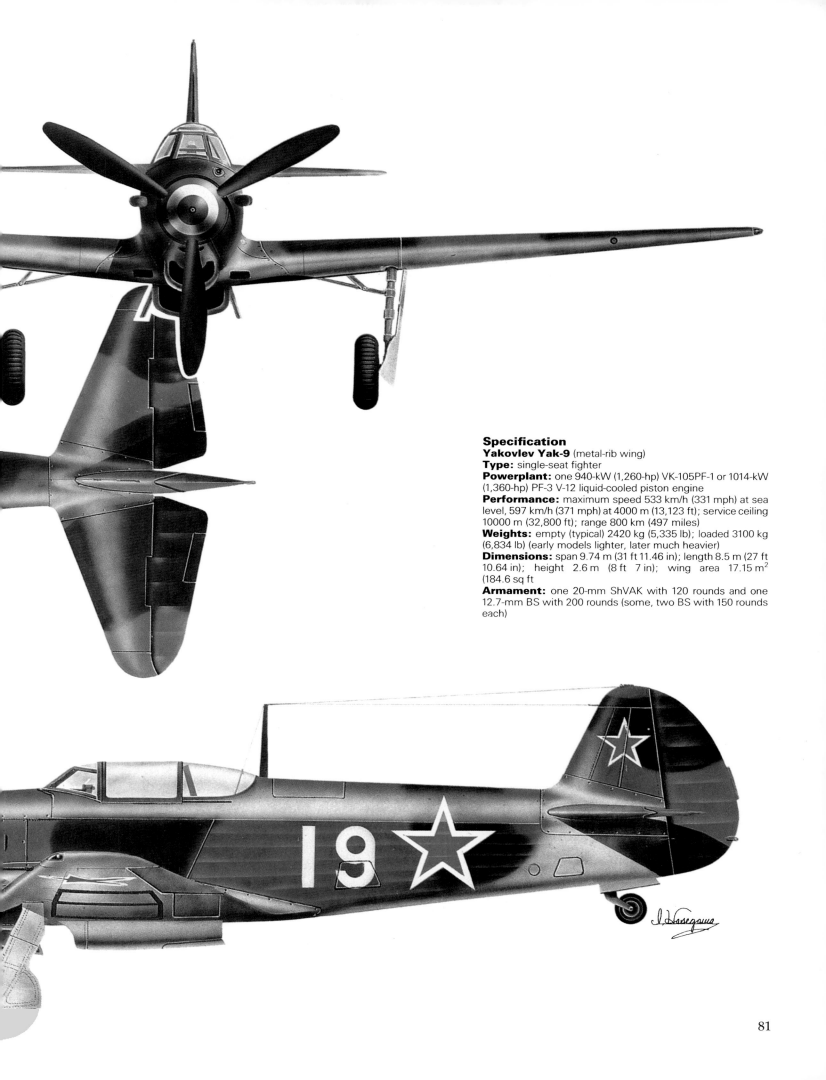

Specification
Yakovlev Yak-9 (metal-rib wing)
Type: single-seat fighter
Powerplant: one 940-kW (1,260-hp) VK-105PF-1 or 1014-kW (1,360-hp) PF-3 V-12 liquid-cooled piston engine
Performance: maximum speed 533 km/h (331 mph) at sea level, 597 km/h (371 mph) at 4000 m (13,123 ft); service ceiling 10000 m (32,800 ft); range 800 km (497 miles)
Weights: empty (typical) 2420 kg (5,335 lb); loaded 3100 kg (6,834 lb) (early models lighter, later much heavier)
Dimensions: span 9.74 m (31 ft 11.46 in); length 8.5 m (27 ft 10.64 in); height 2.6 m (8 ft 7 in); wing area 17.15 m² (184.6 sq ft
Armament: one 20-mm ShVAK with 120 rounds and one 12.7-mm BS with 200 rounds (some, two BS with 150 rounds each)

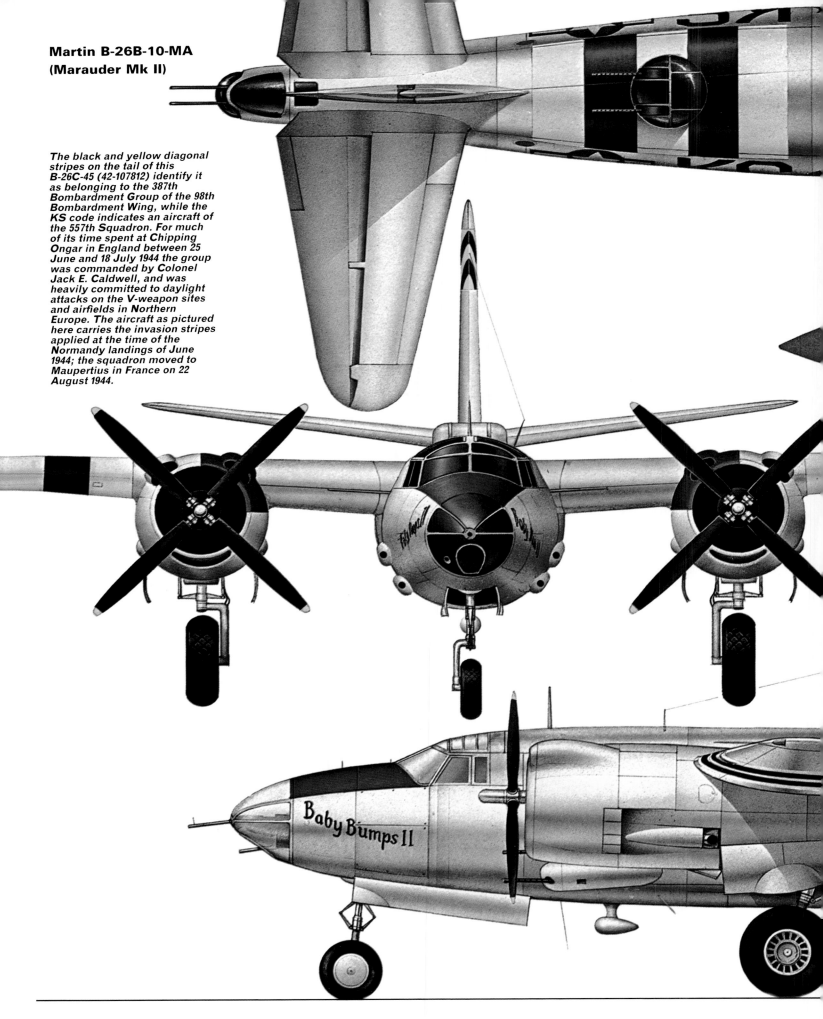

**Martin B-26B-10-MA
(Marauder Mk II)**

The black and yellow diagonal stripes on the tail of this B-26C-45 (42-107812) identify it as belonging to the 387th Bombardment Group of the 98th Bombardment Wing, while the KS code indicates an aircraft of the 557th Squadron. For much of its time spent at Chipping Ongar in England between 25 June and 18 July 1944 the group was commanded by Colonel Jack E. Caldwell, and was heavily committed to daylight attacks on the V-weapon sites and airfields in Northern Europe. The aircraft as pictured here carries the invasion stripes applied at the time of the Normandy landings of June 1944; the squadron moved to Maupertius in France on 22 August 1944.

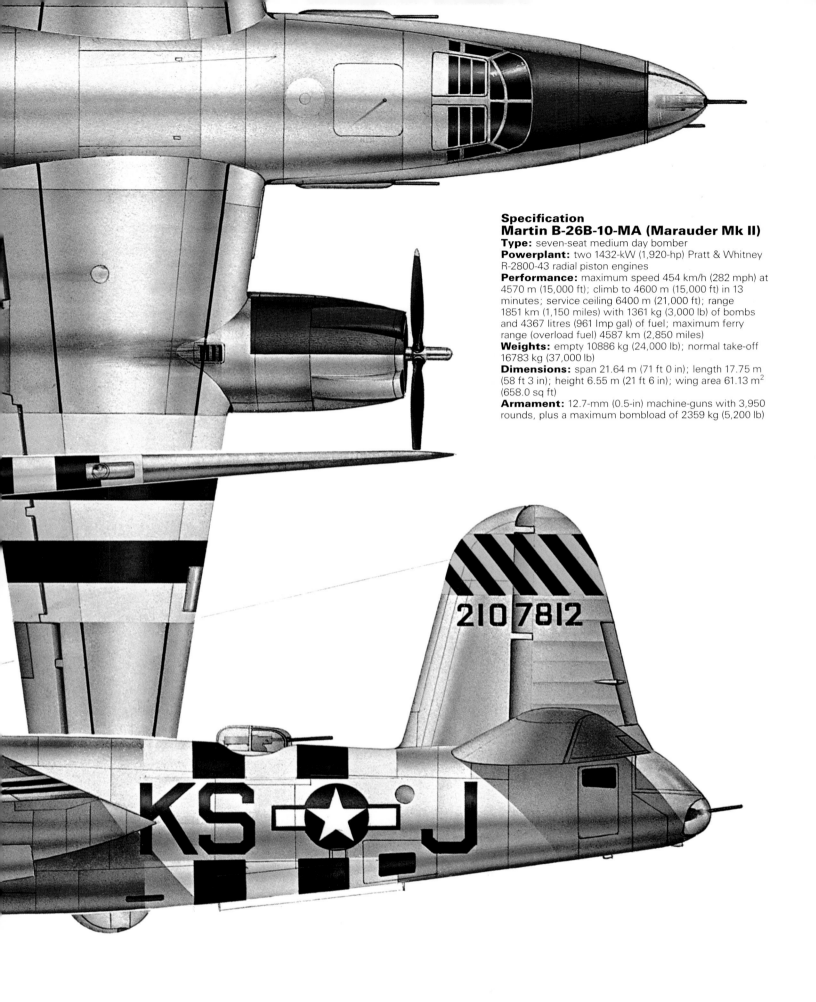

Specification
Martin B-26B-10-MA (Marauder Mk II)
Type: seven-seat medium day bomber
Powerplant: two 1432-kW (1,920-hp) Pratt & Whitney R-2800-43 radial piston engines
Performance: maximum speed 454 km/h (282 mph) at 4570 m (15,000 ft); climb to 4600 m (15,000 ft) in 13 minutes; service ceiling 6400 m (21,000 ft); range 1851 km (1,150 miles) with 1361 kg (3,000 lb) of bombs and 4367 litres (961 Imp gal) of fuel; maximum ferry range (overload fuel) 4587 km (2,850 miles)
Weights: empty 10886 kg (24,000 lb); normal take-off 16783 kg (37,000 lb)
Dimensions: span 21.64 m (71 ft 0 in); length 17.75 m (58 ft 3 in); height 6.55 m (21 ft 6 in); wing area 61.13 m^2 (658.0 sq ft)
Armament: 12.7-mm (0.5-in) machine-guns with 3,950 rounds, plus a maximum bombload of 2359 kg (5,200 lb)

North American P-51D Mustang

Though it was in service only in the final 18 months of World War II, the P-51D and basically identical K (different propeller) have since hogged almost all the Mustang limelight and also accounted for most of the 15,586 of all models produced. This aircraft, USAAF 1944-13926, served with the 361st Fighter Group of the 8th Air Force, at Bottisham (England) and in late 1944 at St Dizier (France).

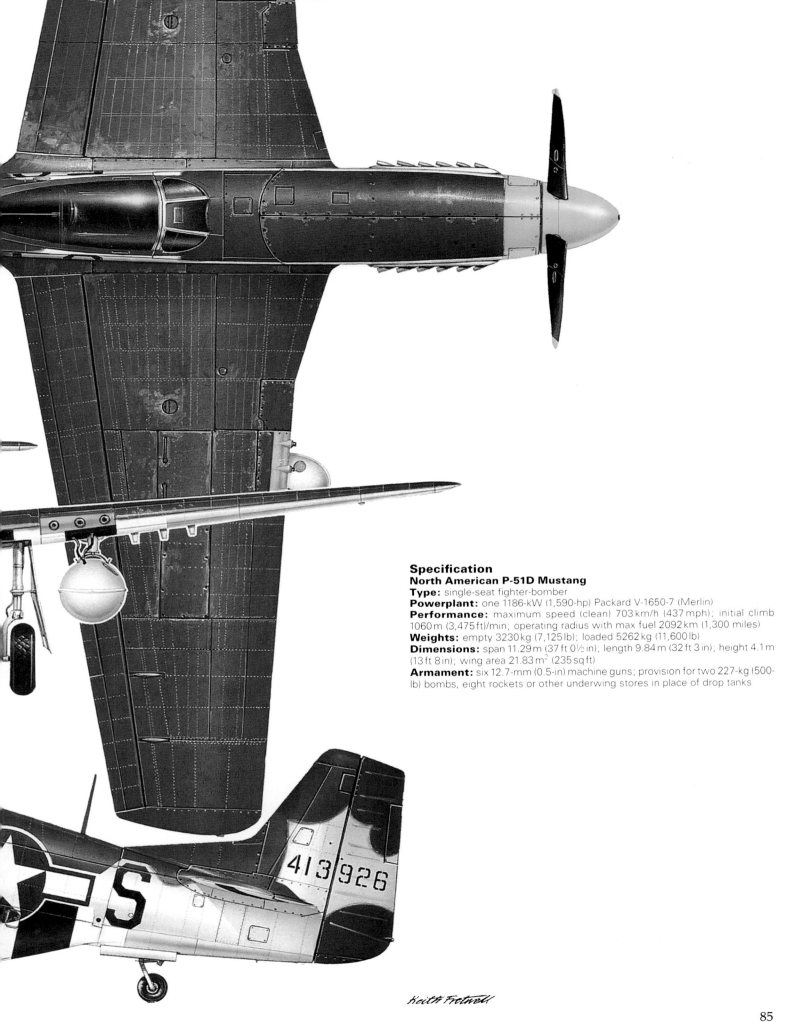

Specification
North American P-51D Mustang
Type: single-seat fighter-bomber
Powerplant: one 1186-kW (1,590-hp) Packard V-1650-7 (Merlin)
Performance: maximum speed (clean) 703 km/h (437 mph); initial climb 1060 m (3,475 ft)/min; operating radius with max fuel 2092 km (1,300 miles)
Weights: empty 3230 kg (7,125 lb); loaded 5262 kg (11,600 lb)
Dimensions: span 11.29 m (37 ft 0½ in); length 9.84 m (32 ft 3 in); height 4.1 m (13 ft 8 in); wing area 21.83 m² (235 sq ft)
Armament: six 12.7-mm (0.5-in) machine guns; provision for two 227-kg (500-lb) bombs, eight rockets or other underwing stores in place of drop tanks

Keith Fretwell

Lavochkin La-5FN

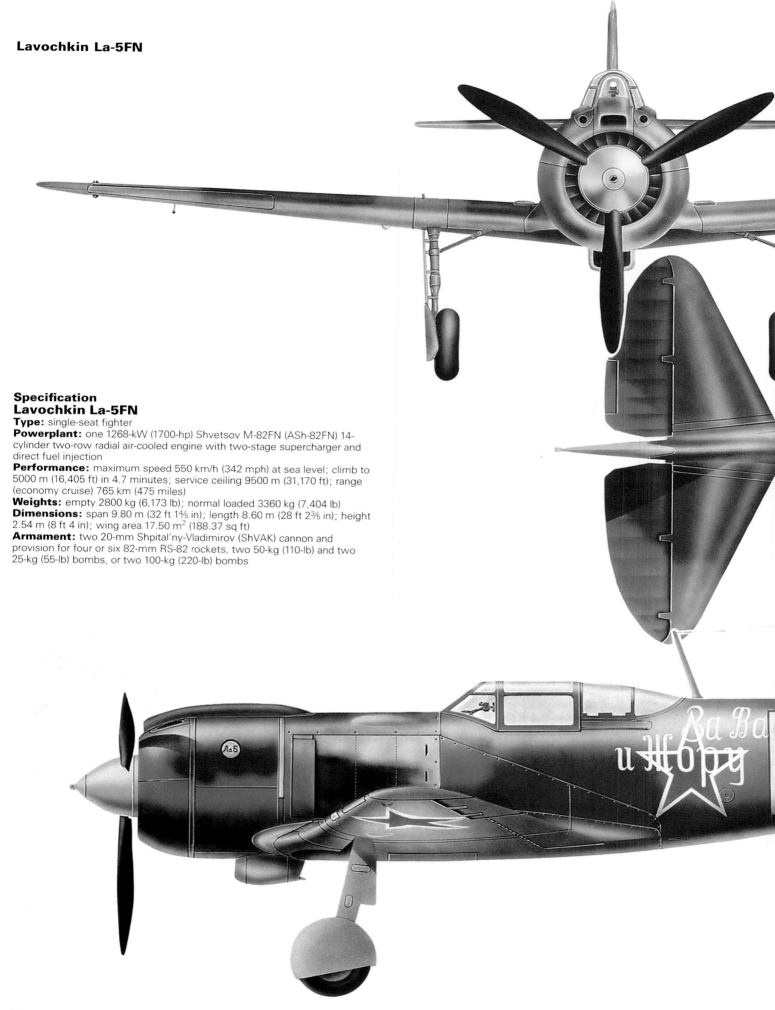

Specification
Lavochkin La-5FN
Type: single-seat fighter
Powerplant: one 1268-kW (1700-hp) Shvetsov M-82FN (ASh-82FN) 14-cylinder two-row radial air-cooled engine with two-stage supercharger and direct fuel injection
Performance: maximum speed 550 km/h (342 mph) at sea level; climb to 5000 m (16,405 ft) in 4.7 minutes; service ceiling 9500 m (31,170 ft); range (economy cruise) 765 km (475 miles)
Weights: empty 2800 kg (6,173 lb); normal loaded 3360 kg (7,404 lb)
Dimensions: span 9.80 m (32 ft 1⅘ in); length 8.60 m (28 ft 2⅗ in); height 2.54 m (8 ft 4 in); wing area 17.50 m² (188.37 sq ft)
Armament: two 20-mm Shpital'ny-Vladimirov (ShVAK) cannon and provision for four or six 82-mm RS-82 rockets, two 50-kg (110-lb) and two 25-kg (55-lb) bombs, or two 100-kg (220-lb) bombs

Illustrating one of several camouflage schemes applied to the La-5 during World War II, this La-5FN was flown by Captain P. J. Linkholetov of the 159th Gv IAP from Leningrad during the summer of 1944. Fuselage slogans proclaiming victory over the Germans and loyalty to the state were common on Soviet fighters, as were the outsize fuselage numbers. Although officially translated as 'directly boosted', the FN designation was dubbed by pilots as meaning Frontu Nado, 'frontal need'.

Northrop P-61B-1-NO

Specification
Northrop P-61B-1-NO

Type: three-seat night-fighter

Powerplant: two 1491-kW (2,000-hp) Pratt & Whitney R-2800-65 Double Wasp 18-cylinder radials

Performance: maximum speed (1678-kW/2,250-hp war emergency power) 589 km/h (366 mph) at 6096 m (20,000 ft); initial climb (military power 1491-kW/2,000-hp) 637 m (2,090 ft) per minute; range (long-range cruise power) 2172 km (1,350 miles) at 368 km/h (229 mph)

Weights: empty 10637 kg (23,450 lb); maximum overload 16420 kg (36,200 lb)

Dimensions: span 20.11 m (66 ft 0¾ in); length 15.11 m (49 ft 7 in); height 4.47 m (14 ft 8 in); wing area 61.53 m² (662.36 sq ft)

Armament: four 20-mm (0.78-in) M2 cannon each with 200 rounds; dorsal barbette with four 12.7-mm (0.5-in) Colt-Browning machine-guns each with 560 rounds; four external pylons each rated at up to 726 kg (1,600 lb) and able to carry bombs or other stores of up to this weight

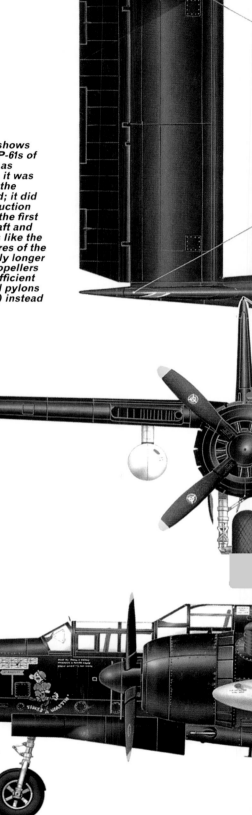

This superb illustration shows one of the most famous P-61s of the Pacific theatre. Built as P-61B-1-NO, no. 42-39403, it was almost unique in having the dorsal gun barbette fitted; it did not come back into production until the P-61B-15 block, the first 200 (except for this aircraft and 42-39419) being turretless like the later P-61As. Other features of the B-model include a slightly longer nose, Curtiss Electric propellers with broader and more efficient blades, and four external pylons (here occupied by tanks) instead of two.

Northrop P-61 variants

XP-61: two prototypes, with R-2800-10 engines (41-19509/10)

YP-61: service-test aircraft (13), with Dash-10 engines (41-18876-88)

P-61A: production aircraft (200), from 38th without dorsal turret (often restored later); from 46th with water-injection Dash-65 engine (42-5485/5634 and -39348/39397)

P-61B: production aircraft (450), with Dash-65 engines; most with turret and four pylons, various equipment fits (42-39398/39757 and 43-8231/8320)

P-61C: production aircraft, with Dash-73 engines and CH-5 turbochargers, wet emergency rating 2089 kW (2,800 hp), Curtiss Electric paddle-blade hollow steel propellers, 692 km/h (430 mph) at high altitude (476 cancelled at VJ-Day and only 41, 43-8321/8361, delivered)

XP-61D: P-61As 42-5559 and 42-5587 re-engined with Dash-77 turbocharged engines

XP-61E: P-61Bs 42-39549 and 42-39557 rebuilt with slim nacelle, four 12.7-mm (0.5-in) guns in nose in place of radar, pilot and navigator under bubble hood (then largest piece of moulded Plexiglas ever attempted), 4382 litres (1,158 US gal) of internal fuel; first became XF-15

XP-61F: P-61C 43-8338 to be modified as P-61E but never completed

P-61G: production weather-reconnaissance aircraft modified from P-61Bs in 1945 (various numbers)

XF-15 Reporter: first XP-61E rebuilt as unarmed reconnaissance aircraft with six cameras in modified nose

XF-15A: P-61C (43-8335) modified with same nacelle as F-15 (visually distinguished from F-15 by large turbocharger ducts under engines)

F-15A Reporter: production aircraft (originally 175, only 36 actually built), based on part-complete P-61C airframes (45-59300/35)

F2T-1N: surplus P-61As (12) used as night-fighter trainers by US Marine Corps (Bu. Nos 52750/61)

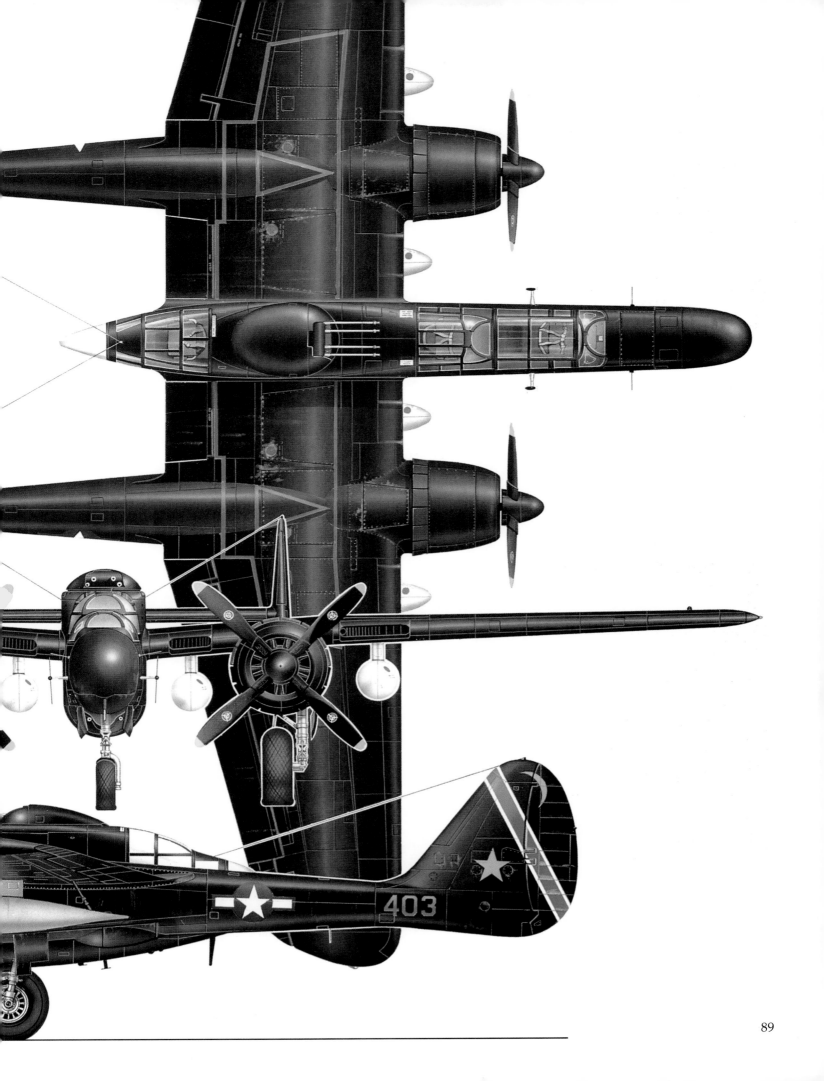

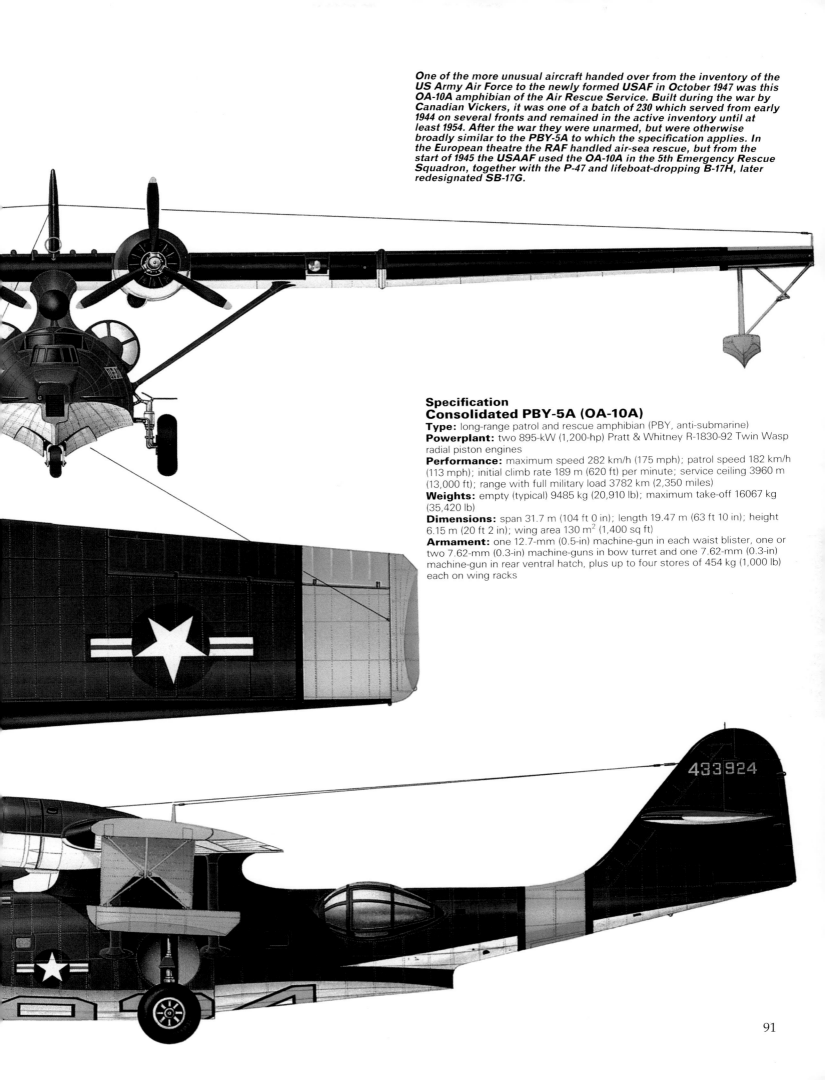

One of the more unusual aircraft handed over from the inventory of the *US Army Air Force* to the newly formed *USAF* in October 1947 was this *OA-10A* amphibian of the Air Rescue Service. Built during the war by Canadian Vickers, it was one of a batch of 230 which served from early 1944 on several fronts and remained in the active inventory until at least 1954. After the war they were unarmed, but were otherwise broadly similar to the *PBY-5A* to which the specification applies. In the European theatre the RAF handled air-sea rescue, but from the start of 1945 the USAAF used the OA-10A in the 5th Emergency Rescue Squadron, together with the P-47 and lifeboat-dropping *B-17H*, later redesignated *SB-17G*.

Specification
Consolidated PBY-5A (OA-10A)
Type: long-range patrol and rescue amphibian (PBY, anti-submarine)
Powerplant: two 895-kW (1,200-hp) Pratt & Whitney R-1830-92 Twin Wasp radial piston engines
Performance: maximum speed 282 km/h (175 mph); patrol speed 182 km/h (113 mph); initial climb rate 189 m (620 ft) per minute; service ceiling 3960 m (13,000 ft); range with full military load 3782 km (2,350 miles)
Weights: empty (typical) 9485 kg (20,910 lb); maximum take-off 16067 kg (35,420 lb)
Dimensions: span 31.7 m (104 ft 0 in); length 19.47 m (63 ft 10 in); height 6.15 m (20 ft 2 in); wing area 130 m² (1,400 sq ft)
Armament: one 12.7-mm (0.5-in) machine-gun in each waist blister, one or two 7.62-mm (0.3-in) machine-guns in bow turret and one 7.62-mm (0.3-in) machine-gun in rear ventral hatch, plus up to four stores of 454 kg (1,000 lb) each on wing racks

Messerschmitt Me 262A-1a

*Messerschmitt Me 262A-1a fighter in the colours of the 9.Staffel
Jagdgeschwader Nr 7, based at Parchim in early 1945 under
1.Jagddivision of I Jagdkorps in the defence of the Reich. After
capture at the end of the war this particular aircraft, Nr 500491, was
given the code FE-111 by the technical branch of the USAAF for
evaluation. In the course of 1979 the aircraft was stripped down,
refurbished and rebuilt in over 6,000 hours of work, and placed on
display at the National Air and Space Museum, Washington DC,
where it remains to this day. The illustration accentuates the Me 262's
sleek lines: the airframe alone, in particular the wing design, was
considered by the Allies to be far ahead of their own attainments in
the field of high-speed flight.*

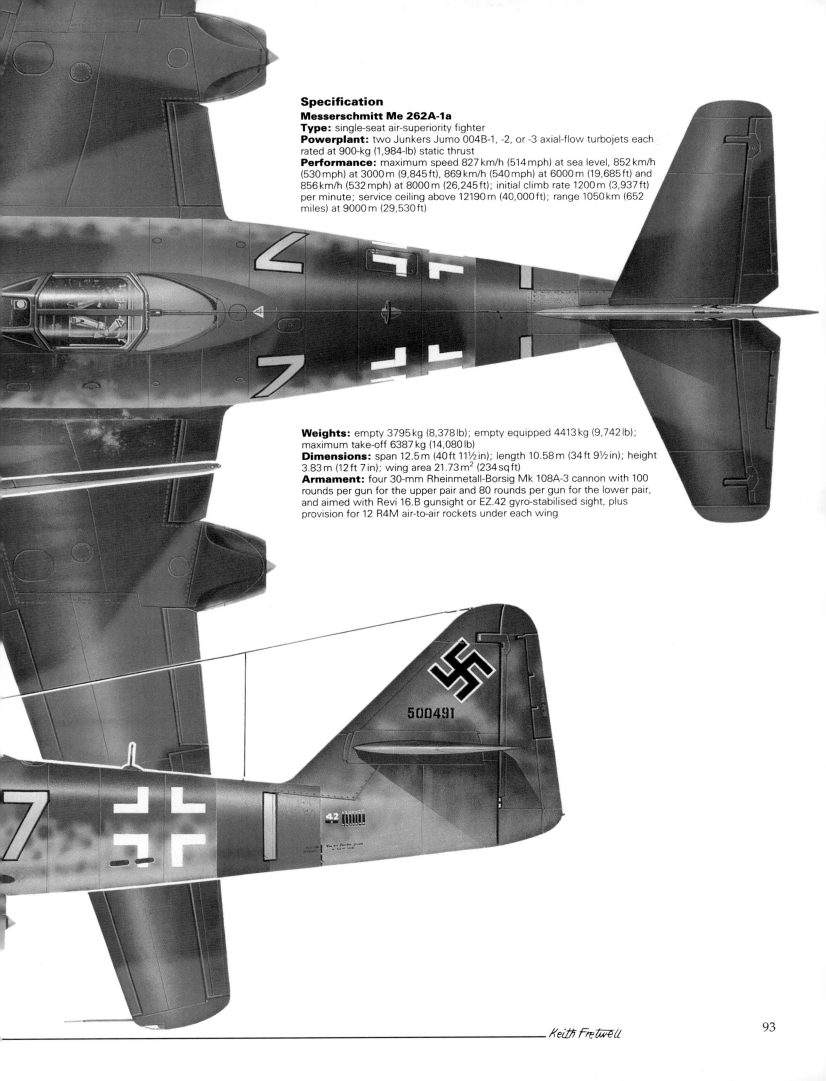

Specification
Messerschmitt Me 262A-1a
Type: single-seat air-superiority fighter
Powerplant: two Junkers Jumo 004B-1, -2, or -3 axial-flow turbojets each rated at 900-kg (1,984-lb) static thrust
Performance: maximum speed 827 km/h (514 mph) at sea level, 852 km/h (530 mph) at 3000 m (9,845 ft), 869 km/h (540 mph) at 6000 m (19,685 ft) and 856 km/h (532 mph) at 8000 m (26,245 ft); initial climb rate 1200 m (3,937 ft) per minute; service ceiling above 12190 m (40,000 ft); range 1050 km (652 miles) at 9000 m (29,530 ft)

Weights: empty 3795 kg (8,378 lb); empty equipped 4413 kg (9,742 lb); maximum take-off 6387 kg (14,080 lb)
Dimensions: span 12.5 m (40 ft 11½ in); length 10.58 m (34 ft 9½ in); height 3.83 m (12 ft 7 in); wing area 21.73 m² (234 sq ft)
Armament: four 30-mm Rheinmetall-Borsig Mk 108A-3 cannon with 100 rounds per gun for the upper pair and 80 rounds per gun for the lower pair, and aimed with Revi 16.B gunsight or EZ.42 gyro-stabilised sight, plus provision for 12 R4M air-to-air rockets under each wing

Keith Fretwell

Gloster Meteor F.Mk 8

Specification
Gloster Meteor F.Mk 8

Type: single-seat interceptor fighter

Powerplant: two 15.5-kN (3,500-lb) thrust Rolls-Royce Derwent 8 turbojets

Performance: maximum speed 953 km/h (592 mph) at sea level, and 885 km/h (550 mph) at 9145 m (30,000 ft); climb to 9180 m (30,000 ft) in 6 minutes 30 seconds; service ceiling 13410 m (44,000 ft); range without wing drop tanks 1111 km (690 miles)

Weights: empty 4846 kg (10,684 lb); maximum take-off 7122 kg (15,700 lb)

Dimensions: span 11.33 m (37 ft 2 in); length 13.59 m (44 ft 7 in); height 3.96 m (13 ft 0 in); wing area 32.515 m² (350.0 sq ft)

Armament: four 20-mm Hispano cannon in the nose with 195 rounds per gun

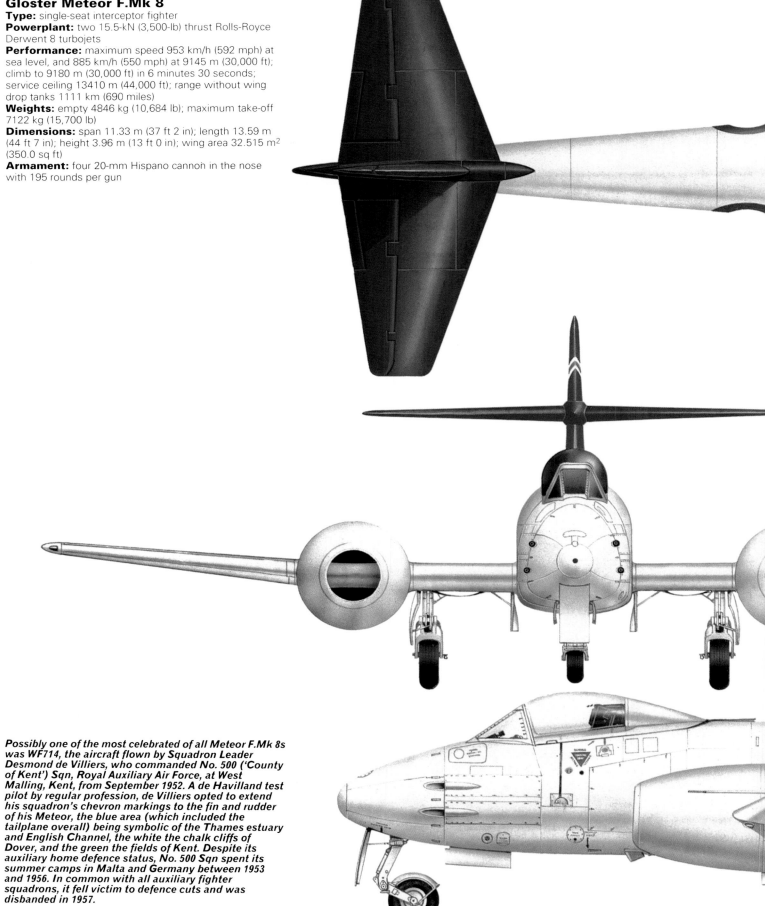

Possibly one of the most celebrated of all Meteor F.Mk 8s was WF714, the aircraft flown by Squadron Leader Desmond de Villiers, who commanded No. 500 ('County of Kent') Sqn, Royal Auxiliary Air Force, at West Malling, Kent, from September 1952. A de Havilland test pilot by regular profession, de Villiers opted to extend his squadron's chevron markings to the fin and rudder of his Meteor, the blue area (which included the tailplane overall) being symbolic of the Thames estuary and English Channel, the white the chalk cliffs of Dover, and the green the fields of Kent. Despite its auxiliary home defence status, No. 500 Sqn spent its summer camps in Malta and Germany between 1953 and 1956. In common with all auxiliary fighter squadrons, it fell victim to defence cuts and was disbanded in 1957.

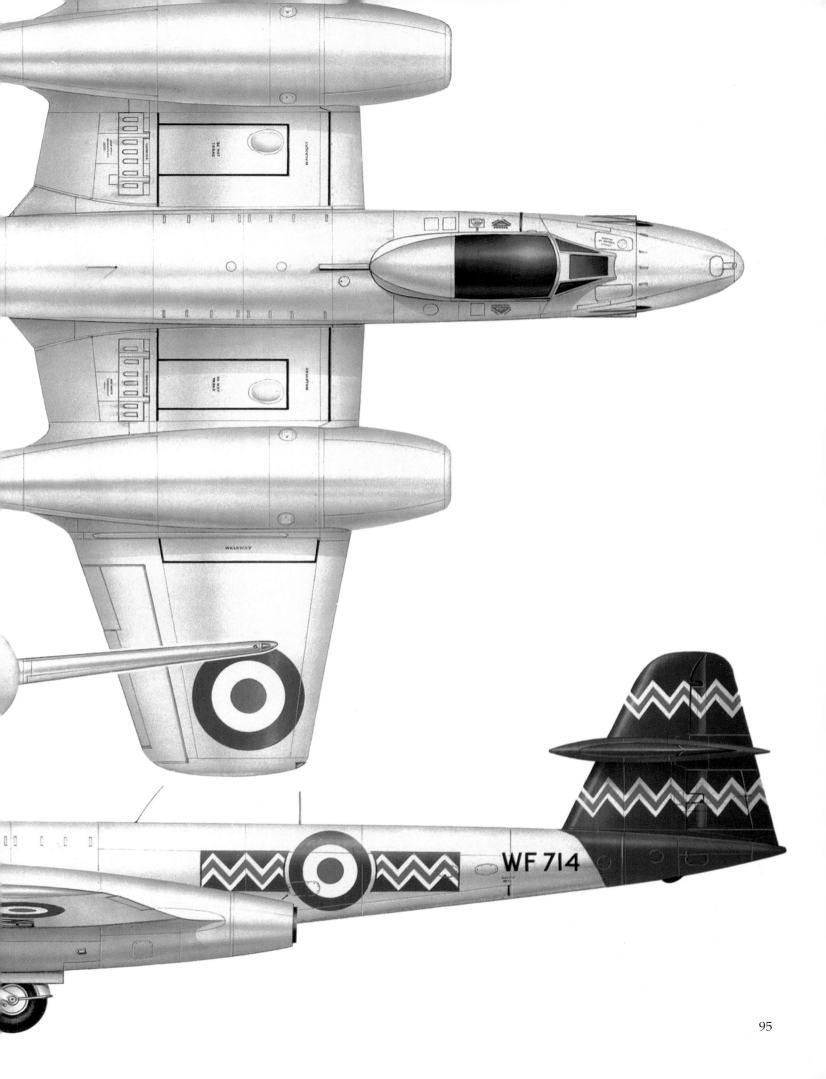

WF 714

Republic F-84F-45-RE

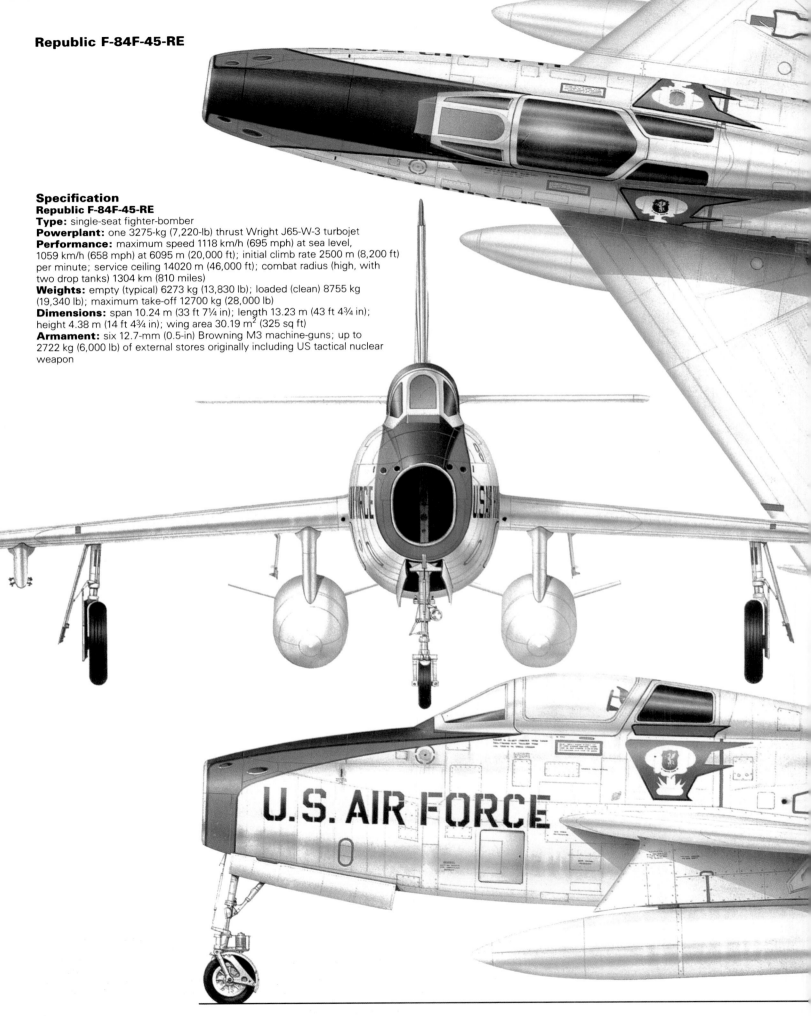

Specification
Republic F-84F-45-RE
Type: single-seat fighter-bomber
Powerplant: one 3275-kg (7,220-lb) thrust Wright J65-W-3 turbojet
Performance: maximum speed 1118 km/h (695 mph) at sea level, 1059 km/h (658 mph) at 6095 m (20,000 ft); initial climb rate 2500 m (8,200 ft) per minute; service ceiling 14020 m (46,000 ft); combat radius (high, with two drop tanks) 1304 km (810 miles)
Weights: empty (typical) 6273 kg (13,830 lb); loaded (clean) 8755 kg (19,340 lb); maximum take-off 12700 kg (28,000 lb)
Dimensions: span 10.24 m (33 ft 7¼ in); length 13.23 m (43 ft 4¾ in); height 4.38 m (14 ft 4¾ in); wing area 30.19 m² (325 sq ft)
Armament: six 12.7-mm (0.5-in) Browning M3 machine-guns; up to 2722 kg (6,000 lb) of external stores originally including US tactical nuclear weapon

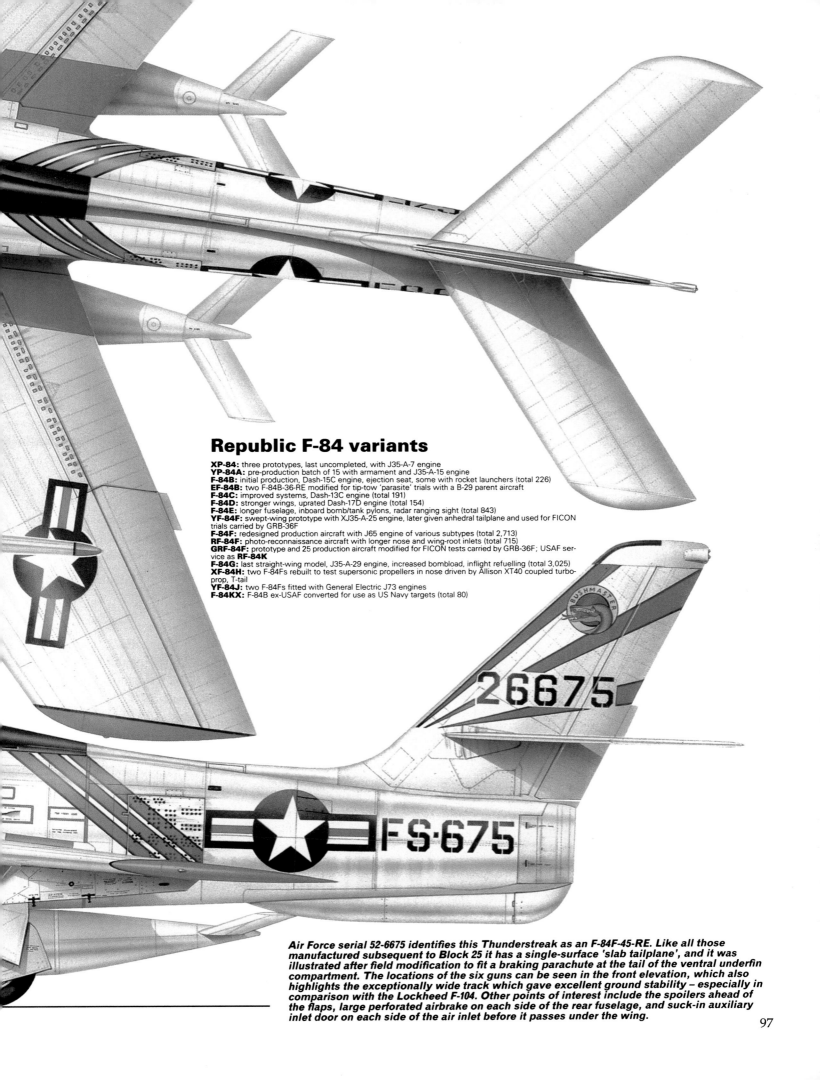

Republic F-84 variants

XP-84: three prototypes, last uncompleted, with J35-A-7 engine
YP-84A: pre-production batch of 15 with armament and J35-A-15 engine
F-84B: initial production, Dash-15C engine, ejection seat, some with rocket launchers (total 226)
EF-84B: two F-84B-36-RE modified for tip-tow 'parasite' trials with a B-29 parent aircraft
F-84C: improved systems, Dash-13C engine (total 191)
F-84D: stronger wings, uprated Dash-17D engine (total 154)
F-84E: longer fuselage, inboard bomb/tank pylons, radar ranging sight (total 843)
YF-84F: swept-wing prototype with XJ35-A-25 engine, later given anhedral tailplane and used for FICON trials carried by GRB-36F
F-84F: redesigned production aircraft with J65 engine of various subtypes (total 2,713)
RF-84F: photo-reconnaissance aircraft with longer nose and wing-root inlets (total 715)
GRF-84F: prototype and 25 production aircraft modified for FICON tests carried by GRB-36F; USAF service as **RF-84K**
F-84G: last straight-wing model, J35-A-29 engine, increased bombload, inflight refuelling (total 3,025)
XF-84H: two F-84Fs rebuilt to test supersonic propellers in nose driven by Allison XT40 coupled turbo-prop, T-tail
YF-84J: two F-84Fs fitted with General Electric J73 engines
F-84KX: F-84B ex-USAF converted for use as US Navy targets (total 80)

Air Force serial 52-6675 identifies this Thunderstreak as an F-84F-45-RE. Like all those manufactured subsequent to Block 25 it has a single-surface 'slab tailplane', and it was illustrated after field modification to fit a braking parachute at the tail of the ventral underfin compartment. The locations of the six guns can be seen in the front elevation, which also highlights the exceptionally wide track which gave excellent ground stability – especially in comparison with the Lockheed F-104. Other points of interest include the spoilers ahead of the flaps, large perforated airbrake on each side of the rear fuselage, and suck-in auxiliary inlet door on each side of the air inlet before it passes under the wing.

97

de Havilland Vampire variants

D.H.100 (Spidercrab): three prototype aircraft (LZ548/G, LZ551/G and MP838/G); Goblin I engine; first flight 20 September 1943
Vampire Mk I: total of 244 aircraft (including 70 for Sweden and 4 for Switzerland) TG and VF serials; Goblin 2 engine; production by English Electric (TG281, TG283 and TG306 modified as D.H.108; TG283 became VW120); some ex-Swedish aircraft sold to Austria and Dominican Republic
Vampire Mk II: one prototype (TX807) and two Mk I conversions (TG276 and TG280): Nene 1 engine
Vampire F.Mk 3: two prototypes converted from Mk I (TG275 and VF317); production totalled 202 aircraft (including 83 for Canada and 4 for Norway); 15 ex-RAF aircraft to Mexico in 1961; VF, VG, VT and VV serials
Vampire Mk IV: not built as such; project using Nene in Vampire Mk 3 became Vampire Mk 30
Vampire FB.Mk 5: Goblin 2; underwing store provision; 930 for RAF (including 30 later exported to France, 5 to Italy and others to India, Egypt and Venezuela); 41 to Australia, 47 to New Zealand and 17 to South Africa; 67 assembled plus 183 built under licence in France; VV, VX, VZ, WA and WG serials
Vampire FB.Mk 6: Goblin 3 engine; Swiss version, with 75 exported to and 100 licence-built in Switzerland
Vampire Mk 8: Ghost-powered Mk 1 conversion (TG278); one only
Vampire FB.Mk 9: Goblin 3 and tropicalisation modifications; 324 for RAF (including 15 later to Rhodesia and 10 to Jordan), and 2 for Ceylon (but repossessed); WG, WL, WP, WR and WX serials
Vampire Mk 10: two-seater; two prototypes (G-5-2, later WP256, and G-5-5); Goblin 3
Vampire NF.Mk 10: two-seat night-fighter; total of 95 built (62 at Chester, 33 at Hatfield), including 29 (designated **Vampire NF.Mk 54**) for Italy; WM, WP and VV serials
Sea Vampire Mk X: prototype (LZ551) converted for deck trials in 1945
Vampire Mk 11: one prototype (G-5-7); Goblin 3; private-venture two-seat trainer
Vampire T.Mk 11: two-seat trainer; Goblin 35 engine; total of 731 built with WZ, XD, XE, XH and XK serials; 427 built at Chester, remainder at Hatfield; some aircraft assembled by Hindustan Aircraft, India
'Hooked Vampire': three converted Vampire Mk I and Mk 3 (TG328, TG426 and VF315) as prototypes for naval version

Sea Vampire F.Mk 20: 18 aircraft for Fleet Air Arm; VG, VT and VV serials
Sea Vampire Mk 21: three aircraft converted for belly deck-landing trials
Sea Vampire T.Mk 22: 73 aircraft (two-seaters) built for Fleet Air Arm; XA and XG serials
Vampire FB.Mk 25: designation covered 47 Vampire Mk 5s exported to New Zealand (included above)
Vampire F.Mk 30: Australian production; Nene engine; 80 aircraft built
Vampire FB.Mk 31: Australian production; Nene engine; Vampire Mk 5 modification; 29 aircraft built
Vampire F.Mk 32: Australian; one Vampire F.Mk 30 converted with air conditioning
Vampire T.Mk 33: Australian production; Goblin engine; 36 aircraft built
Vampire T.Mk 34: Australian production; five navalised aircraft built
Vampire T.Mk 34A: Australian T.Mk 34s converted to include ejector seats
Vampire T.Mk 35: Australian production; 68 built with increased fuel capacity and revised canopy
Vampire T.Mk 35A: Australian Vampire T.Mk 33s converted to full or partial T.Mk 35 standard
Vampire FB.Mk 50: 143 new-built aircraft exported to Sweden (as **J28**)
Vampire FB.Mk 51: export prototype converted from Vampire Mk 5 (VV658); delivered as pattern aircraft to France
Vampire FB.Mk 52: export version based on Vampire Mk 6; production totalled 101, including 25 for Norway, 50 for Egypt, 6 for Finland, 12 for Iraq and 8 for Lebanon; 7 ex-Egyptian aircraft later went to Jordan
Vampire FB.Mk 52A: 80 aircraft licence-built by Macchi and Fiat in Italy
Vampire FB.Mk 53: 250 aircraft licence-built by SNCASE (France) with Nene engine, and named **Mistral**
Vampire NF.Mk 54: designation covered 29 Vampire Mk 10s (included above) for Italy, then sold to India
Vampire T.Mk 55: 216 new aircraft built for export (Austria 5, Burma 8, Ceylon 5 – repossessed, Chile 5, Egypt 12, Ireland 6, Finland 5, India 55, Indonesia 8, Iraq 6, Lebanon 3, New Zealand 6, Norway 4, Portugal 3, South Africa 21, Sweden 57 as **J28C**, Syria 2 and Venezuela 6); 6 other ex-RAF Vampire T.Mk 11s modified to T.Mk 55 standard for New Zealand, plus 2 to Jordan and 4 to Southern Rhodesia

Specification
de Havilland Vampire FB.Mk 5

Type: single-seat close-support fighter-bomber
Powerplant: one 14-kN (3,100-lb) thrust de Havilland Goblin 2 centrifugal-flow turbojet
Performance: maximum speed 861 km/h (535 mph) at 10365 m (34,000 ft); initial climb rate 1235 m (4,050 ft) per minute; service ceiling 12190 m (40,000 ft); range 1883 km (1,170 miles)
Weights: empty 3290 kg (7,253 lb); maximum take-off 5606 kg (12,360 lb)
Dimensions: span 11.58 m (38 ft 0 in); length 9.37 m (30 ft 9 in); height 2.69 m (8 ft 10 in); wing area 24.34 m² (262.0 sq ft)
Armament: gun armament of four 20-mm Hispano cannon in nose, plus an underwing warload of either two 227-kg (500-lb) bombs or eight 27-kg (60-lb) rocket projectiles

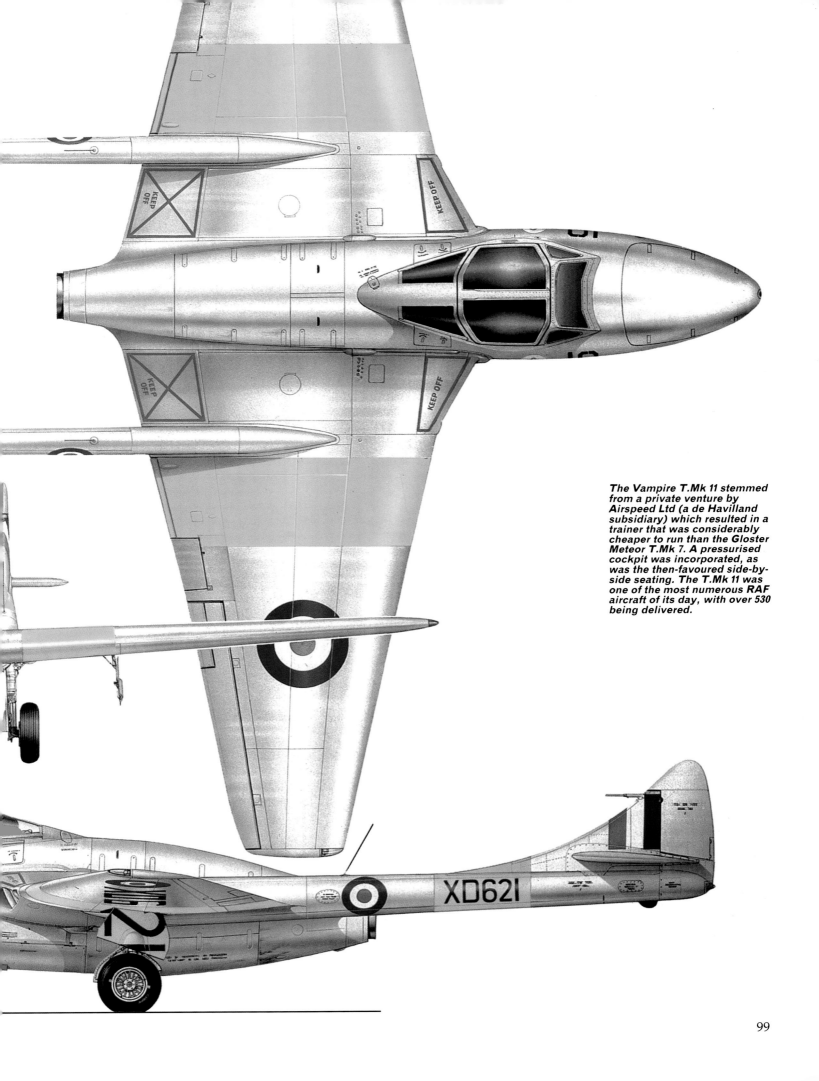

The Vampire T.Mk 11 stemmed from a private venture by Airspeed Ltd (a de Havilland subsidiary) which resulted in a trainer that was considerably cheaper to run than the Gloster Meteor T.Mk 7. A pressurised cockpit was incorporated, as was the then-favoured side-by-side seating. The T.Mk 11 was one of the most numerous RAF aircraft of its day, with over 530 being delivered.

XD621

Douglas A-1H Skyraider

Douglas Skyraider variants

XBT2D: first version with 1716-kW (2,300-hp) R-3350-24W; included prototypes of five other versions; total 25
AD-1: redesignation of **BT2D-1**, with 1865-kW (2,500-hp) R-3350-24W engine and strengthened structure; total 242
AD-1Q: ECM platform with jammer pod on left wing and ECM operator in fuselage cabin; total 35
AD-2: further strengthening, more fuel, 2014-kW (2,700-hp) R-3350-26W engine, mainwheel doors added; total 156
AD-2D: conversion to drone (RPV) directors
AD-2Q: ECM version; total 22
AD-2Q(U): further rebuild to tow Mk 22 target
AD-3: further strengthening, long-stroke main gears, Aeroproducts propeller and new canopy; total 124
AD-3E: conversion for ASW search
AD-3N: night attack version; total 15
AD-3Q: ECM version; total 23
AD-3S: anti-submarine attack, partner to AD-3E; all conversions
AD-3W: AEW version with improved APS-20 surveillance radar and two operators in fuselage cabin, plus auxiliary fins; total 31
AD-4: refined structure, cleared for great increase in gross weight from 8392 kg (18,500 lb) to 10886 kg (24,000 lb), P-1 autopilot, modified windscreen, improved radar (APS-19A) option; total 344

AD-4B: four cannon, provision for nuclear bombs; total 194
AD-4L: conversion for winter (Arctic)
AD-4N: night attack version with APS-19A; total 248
AD-4NA: night version stripped for day attack; total 23 plus conversions; redesignated **A-1D** from 1962
AD-4NL: winterised night version; total 36
AD-4Q: ECM version; total 39
AD-4W: AEW version as AD-3W; total 168
AD-5(A-1E): redesigned multi-role model with wide forward fuselage, side-by-side cockpit, longer fuselage, taller fin, side dive brakes removed (leaving ventral brake), four guns standard, provision for quick role conversions; cleared to 11340 kg (25,000 lb); total 212
AD-5N(A-1G): night attack version; total 239
AD-5Q(EA-1F): ECM conversions of 54 aircraft
AD-5S: (no 1962 designation) anti-submarine conversion
AD-5U(UA-1E): conversions as target tow/transport for 12 seats or 1361 kg (3,000 lb) of freight
AD-5W(EA-1E): AEW version; total 156
AD-6(A-1H): new standard close-support single-seater, LABS toss-bombing avionics and reinforced wing as AD-4B; total 713
AD-7(A-1J): further reinforced wing and main gear, 2275-kW (3,050-hp) R-3350-26WB engine; total 72

Specification
Douglas A-1H Skyraider
Type: carrierborne attack aircraft
Powerplant: one 2013-kW (2,700-hp) Wright R-3350-26WA 18-cylinder two-row radial piston engine
Performance: maximum speed 518 km/h (322 mph) at 5485 m (18,000 ft); cruising speed 319 km/h (198 mph); initial climb rate 870 m (2,850 ft) per minute; service ceiling 8685 m (28,500 ft); normal range 2116 km (1,315 miles)
Weights: empty 5429 kg (11,968 lb); normal take-off 8213 kg (18,106 lb); maximum take-off 11340 kg (25,000 lb)
Dimensions: wing span 15.25 m (50 ft 0¼ in); length 11.84 m (38 ft 10 in); height 4.78 m (15 ft 8¼ in); wing area 37.192 m² (400.33 s1 ft)
Armament: four wing-mounted 20-mm cannon, plus up to 3629 kg (8,000 lb) of external stores on one underfuselage and 14 underwing hardpoints

The exceptionally colourful and high-quality decoration of this A-1H (originally designated as an AD-6) shows that it was the personal mount of a commanding officer; in this case Commander Bill Phillips of US Navy attack squadron VA-52, the attack element of Carrier Air Wing 19, then embarked aboard USS Ticonderoga. The period was 1961-66, when on one mission against a Vietnam ground transport convoy they had to use depth bombs fitted with impact fuses (with devastating effect). Phillips' successor, Commander Gordon Smith Jr, had to bail out on a pitch-black night just above the sea while upside down.

COM ATK CAR AIR WING NINETEEN

COM ATK CAR AIR WING NINETEEN
USS TICONDEROGA
NAVY
VA-52
NM
34569
A-1H
134569

Keith Fretwell

North American F-86F Sabre

'Dottie' was a North American F-86F-30-NA Sabre, serial number 52-4701, flown by Captain D. R. Hall during the Korean War. The aircraft carries the markings of the 336th Fighter Interceptor Squadron of the 4th Fighter Interceptor Wing, based at K-14, the air base at Kimpo, about 40 km (25 miles) north-west of Seoul. The yellow wing and fuselage bands were an ordered identification marking on all F-86s of the Far East Air Forces. The F-86Fs were considerably improved in comparison with the F-86As that had been taking the Korean air war to 'MiG Alley': the later model had more power, increased range capability and a large non-slatted wing enabling the Sabre to turn with the MiG-15.

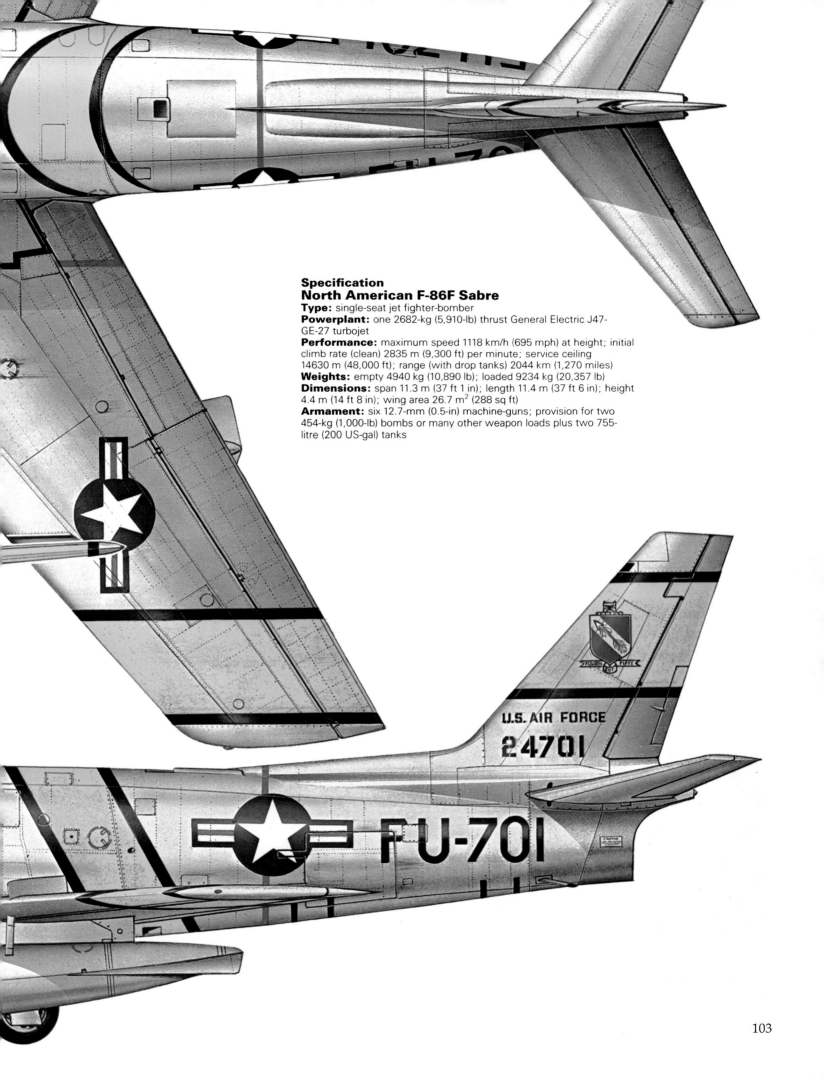

Specification
North American F-86F Sabre
Type: single-seat jet fighter-bomber
Powerplant: one 2682-kg (5,910-lb) thrust General Electric J47-GE-27 turbojet
Performance: maximum speed 1118 km/h (695 mph) at height; initial climb rate (clean) 2835 m (9,300 ft) per minute; service ceiling 14630 m (48,000 ft); range (with drop tanks) 2044 km (1,270 miles)
Weights: empty 4940 kg (10,890 lb); loaded 9234 kg (20,357 lb)
Dimensions: span 11.3 m (37 ft 1 in); length 11.4 m (37 ft 6 in); height 4.4 m (14 ft 8 in); wing area 26.7 m² (288 sq ft)
Armament: six 12.7-mm (0.5-in) machine-guns; provision for two 454-kg (1,000-lb) bombs or many other weapon loads plus two 755-litre (200 US-gal) tanks

Mikoyan-Gurevich MiG-15UTI

Specification
Mikoyan-Gurevich MiG-15UTI

Type: two-seat advanced, weapons and conversion trainer

Powerplant: one 26.47-kN (5,952-lb) thrust Klimov VK-1 centrifugal-flow turbojet

Performance: maximum speed 1015 km/h (630 mph) at sea level; service ceiling 15625 m (47,980 ft); range (with either slipper or pylon tanks) 1424 km (885 miles)

Weights: empty 4000 kg (8,820 lb); normal take-off 4850 kg (10,692 lb) clean, 5400 kg (11,905 lb) with guns and drop tanks

Dimensions: wing span 10.08 m (33 ft ¾ in); length 10.04 m (32 ft 11¼ in); height 3.74 m (12 ft 1½ in); wing area 20.6 m² (221.74 sq ft)

Armament: often not fitted; one 23-mm cannon with 80 rounds or one 12.7-mm (0.5-in) machine-gun with 150 rounds; option for two underwing pylons carrying up to 500 kg (1,102 lb) of stores as alternative to drop tanks

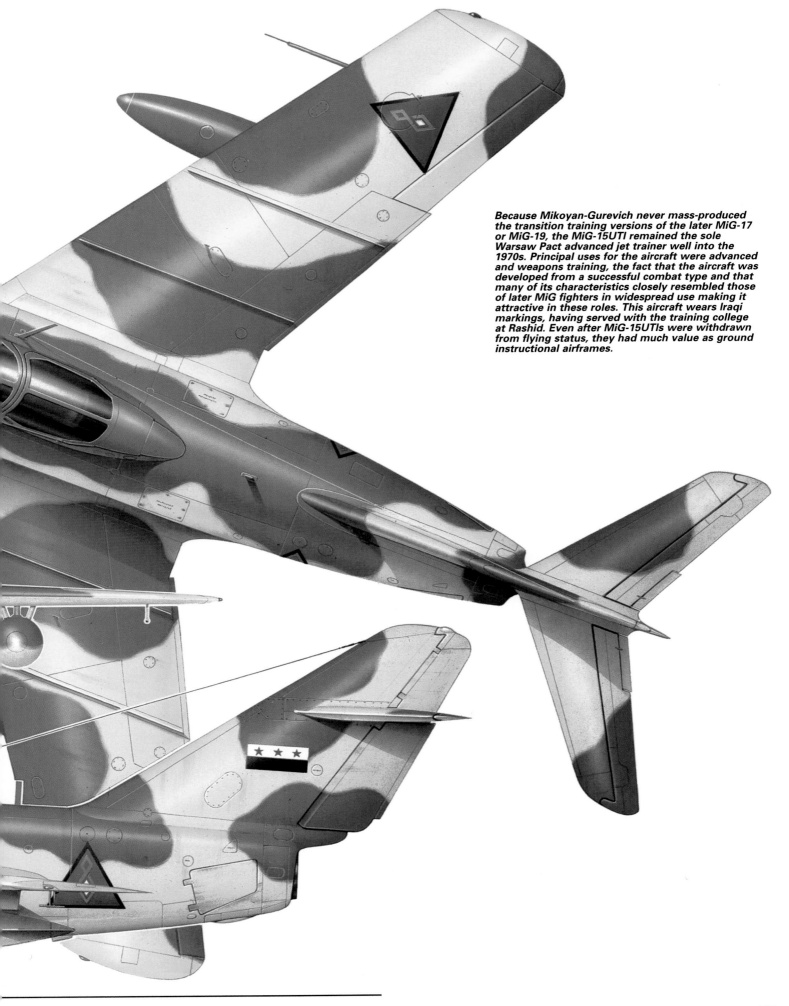

Because Mikoyan-Gurevich never mass-produced the transition training versions of the later MiG-17 or MiG-19, the MiG-15UTI remained the sole Warsaw Pact advanced jet trainer well into the 1970s. Principal uses for the aircraft were advanced and weapons training, the fact that the aircraft was developed from a successful combat type and that many of its characteristics closely resembled those of later MiG fighters in widespread use making it attractive in these roles. This aircraft wears Iraqi markings, having served with the training college at Rashid. Even after MiG-15UTIs were withdrawn from flying status, they had much value as ground instructional airframes.

Identified by its bulbous nose radome, this aircraft is a Canberra T.Mk 17, wearing the Druse Moth insignia of No. 360 Squadron, Royal Air Force. From its base at RAF Wyton, No. 360 Sqn undertook electronic warfare training missions, supplying jamming to recreate the type of electronic environment that might be experienced in wartime. This gave realistic training for defence systems operators, notably aboard ships of the Royal Navy. The T.Mk 17 was based on the B.Mk 2 airframe, as distinguished at a glance by the short intake centre-bodies. No 360 Squadron disbanded in 1994 and the RAF retired its last Canberras (PR.9s) in July 2007.

WJ 633

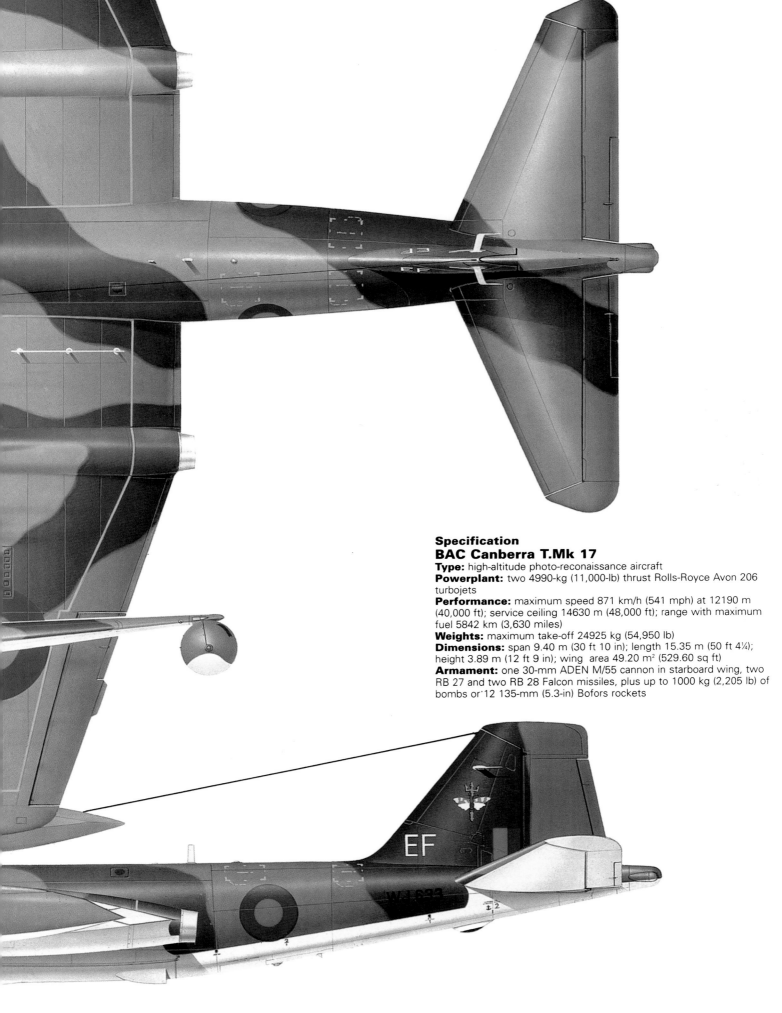

Specification
BAC Canberra T.Mk 17

Type: high-altitude photo-reconaissance aircraft
Powerplant: two 4990-kg (11,000-lb) thrust Rolls-Royce Avon 206
turbojets
Performance: maximum speed 871 km/h (541 mph) at 12190 m
(40,000 ft); service ceiling 14630 m (48,000 ft); range with maximum
fuel 5842 km (3,630 miles)
Weights: maximum take-off 24925 kg (54,950 lb)
Dimensions: span 9.40 m (30 ft 10 in); length 15.35 m (50 ft 4¼);
height 3.89 m (12 ft 9 in); wing area 49.20 m² (529.60 sq ft)
Armament: one 30-mm ADEN M/55 cannon in starboard wing, two
RB 27 and two RB 28 Falcon missiles, plus up to 1000 kg (2,205 lb) of
bombs or 12 135-mm (5.3-in) Bofors rockets

Hawker Hunter F.Mk 1

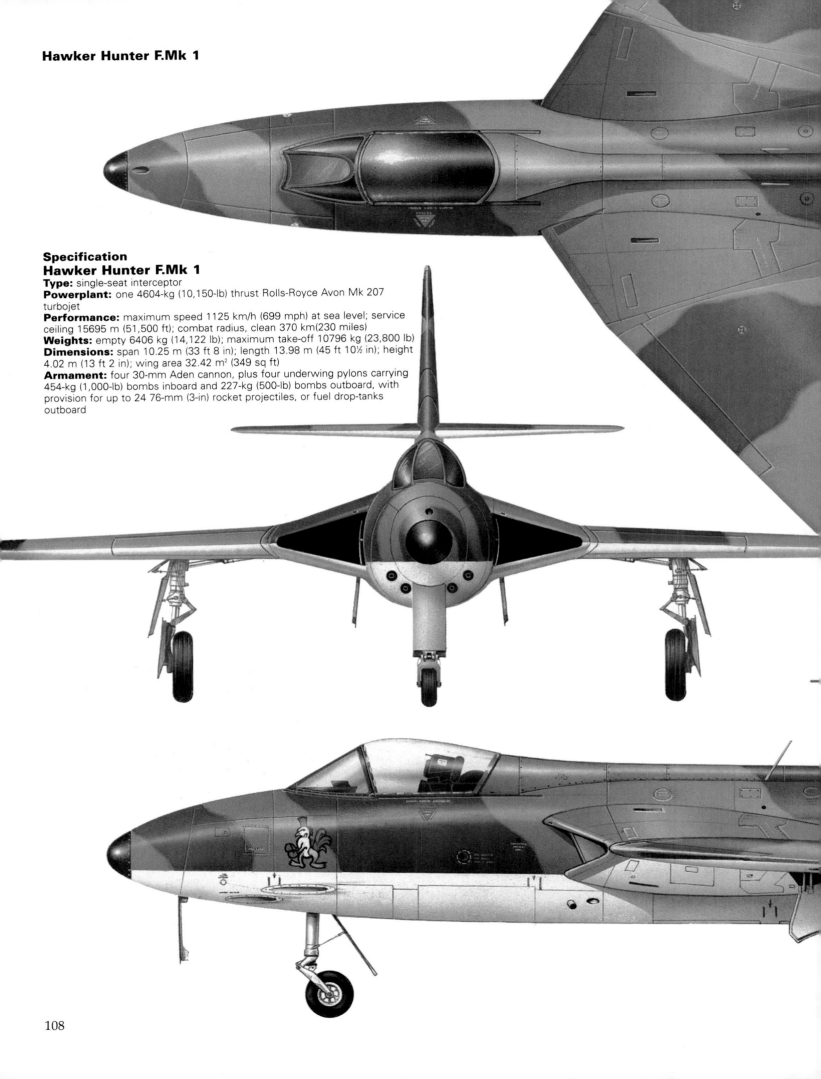

Specification
Hawker Hunter F.Mk 1

Type: single-seat interceptor

Powerplant: one 4604-kg (10,150-lb) thrust Rolls-Royce Avon Mk 207 turbojet

Performance: maximum speed 1125 km/h (699 mph) at sea level; service ceiling 15695 m (51,500 ft); combat radius, clean 370 km(230 miles)

Weights: empty 6406 kg (14,122 lb); maximum take-off 10796 kg (23,800 lb)

Dimensions: span 10.25 m (33 ft 8 in); length 13.98 m (45 ft 10½ in); height 4.02 m (13 ft 2 in); wing area 32.42 m² (349 sq ft)

Armament: four 30-mm Aden cannon, plus four underwing pylons carrying 454-kg (1,000-lb) bombs inboard and 227-kg (500-lb) bombs outboard, with provision for up to 24 76-mm (3-in) rocket projectiles, or fuel drop-tanks outboard

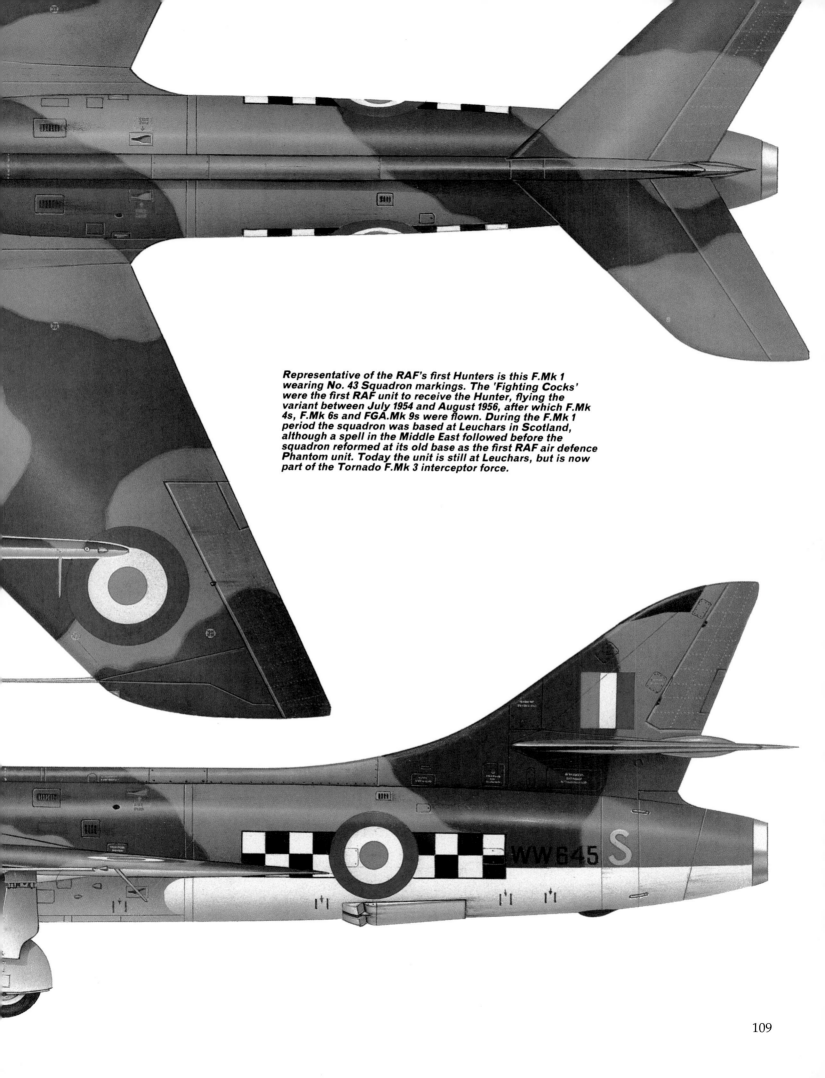

Representative of the RAF's first Hunters is this F.Mk 1 wearing No. 43 Squadron markings. The 'Fighting Cocks' were the first RAF unit to receive the Hunter, flying the variant between July 1954 and August 1956, after which F.Mk 4s, F.Mk 6s and FGA.Mk 9s were flown. During the F.Mk 1 period the squadron was based at Leuchars in Scotland, although a spell in the Middle East followed before the squadron reformed at its old base as the first RAF air defence Phantom unit. Today the unit is still at Leuchars, but is now part of the Tornado F.Mk 3 interceptor force.

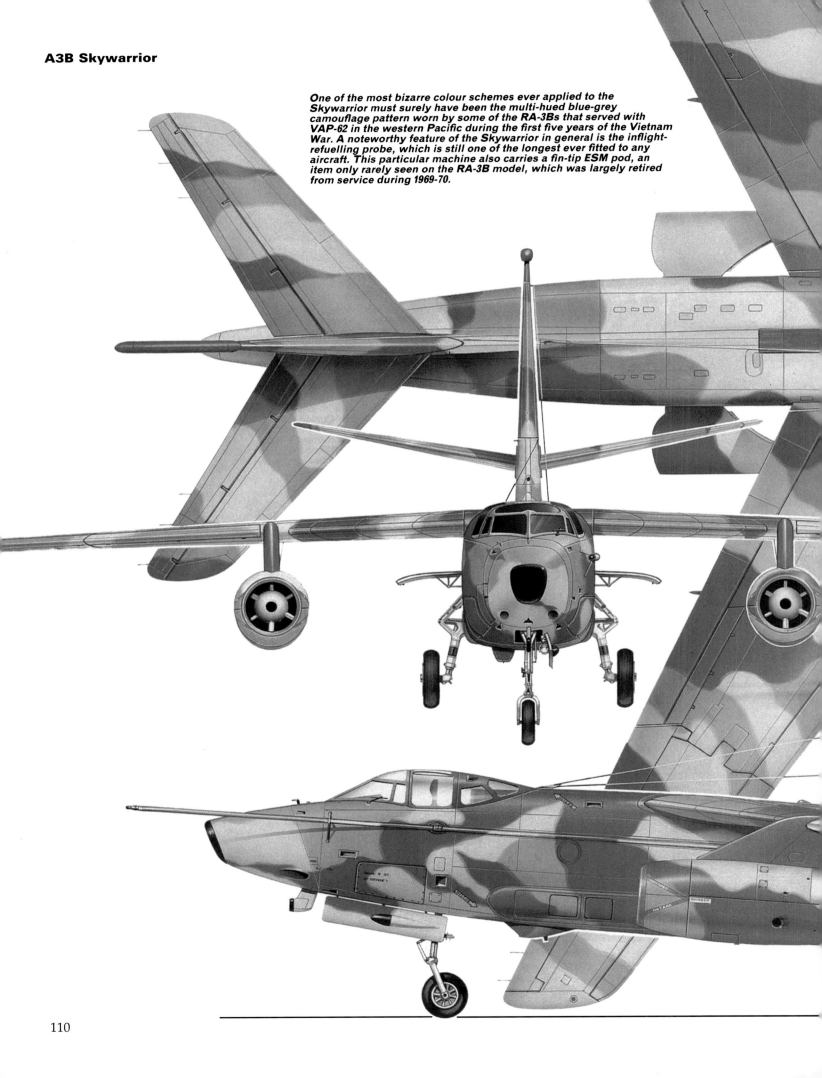

A3B Skywarrior

One of the most bizarre colour schemes ever applied to the Skywarrior must surely have been the multi-hued blue-grey camouflage pattern worn by some of the RA-3Bs that served with VAP-62 in the western Pacific during the first five years of the Vietnam War. A noteworthy feature of the Skywarrior in general is the inflight-refuelling probe, which is still one of the longest ever fitted to any aircraft. This particular machine also carries a fin-tip ESM pod, an item only rarely seen on the RA-3B model, which was largely retired from service during 1969-70.

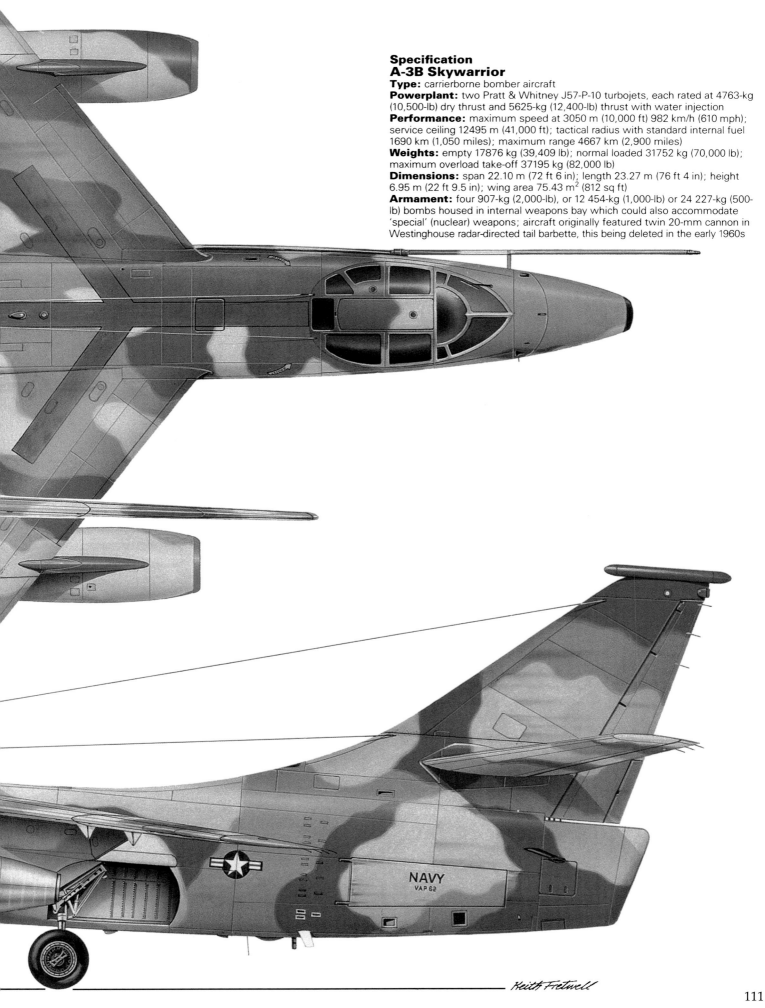

Specification
A-3B Skywarrior

Type: carrierborne bomber aircraft
Powerplant: two Pratt & Whitney J57-P-10 turbojets, each rated at 4763-kg (10,500-lb) dry thrust and 5625-kg (12,400-lb) thrust with water injection
Performance: maximum speed at 3050 m (10,000 ft) 982 km/h (610 mph); service ceiling 12495 m (41,000 ft); tactical radius with standard internal fuel 1690 km (1,050 miles); maximum range 4667 km (2,900 miles)
Weights: empty 17876 kg (39,409 lb); normal loaded 31752 kg (70,000 lb); maximum overload take-off 37195 kg (82,000 lb)
Dimensions: span 22.10 m (72 ft 6 in); length 23.27 m (76 ft 4 in); height 6.95 m (22 ft 9.5 in); wing area 75.43 m² (812 sq ft)
Armament: four 907-kg (2,000-lb), or 12 454-kg (1,000-lb) or 24 227-kg (500-lb) bombs housed in internal weapons bay which could also accommodate 'special' (nuclear) weapons; aircraft originally featured twin 20-mm cannon in Westinghouse radar-directed tail barbette, this being deleted in the early 1960s

Keith Fretwell

North American F-100 variants

YF-100A: two prototypes (52-5754/5755) with tall tail and XJ57-P-7 engine
F-100A: initial production day fighter (with unused offensive stores capability), with cut-down vertical tail but original design restored at 71st aircraft and wingspan extended; J57-7 engine; total 203 (52-5766/5778 and 53-1529/1708)
RF-100A: post-1960 rebuild of F-100As as unarmed photo aircraft
YF-100B: redesignated **F-107A**, new design with Y175 engine
F-100C: first fighter-bomber version, eight pylons, FR probe, major systems revision and J57-21 engine; total 476 (451 at Inglewood: 53-1709/1778, 54-1740/2120; and 25 at Columbus: 552709/2733)
TF-100C: redesignated **F-100F**
F-100D: dedicated attack version with full equipment for delivery of increased underwing load including nuclear bombs and Bullpup missiles, modified wing with flaps, revised vertical tail, better avionics and P-21A engine; most stressed for Zell launch; total 1,274 (940 at Inglewood: 54-2121/2303, 55-3502/3814, 56-2903/3346; and 334 at Columbus: 55-2734/2954, 56-3351/3463)
F-100F: tandem dual trainer with reduced armament; total 339, all at Inglewood (56-3725/4019, 58-1205/1233, 58-6975/6983, 59-2558/2563)
DF-100F: conversion as drone (RPV) director
NF-100F: conversions for trials and research
TF-100F: interim Danish F-100F from US stocks

Specification
North American F-100D-75-NA
Type: single-seat fighter-bomber
Powerplant: one Pratt & Whitney J57-P-21A afterburning turbojet with maximum augmenting rating of 7689 kg (16,950 lb)
Performance: maximum speed, clean 1239 km/h (770 mph) or Mach 1.013 at low level, and 1390 km/h (864 mph) or Mach 1.3 at high altitude; initial climb rate, clean 5045 m (16,550 ft) per minute; service ceiling 14020 m (46,000 ft); range at high altitude 966 km (600 miles), or 2492 km (1,500 miles) with two drop tanks
Weights: empty 9526 kg (21,000 lb); clean take-off 13500 kg (29,762 lb); maximum take-off 15800 kg (34,832 lb)
Dimensions: span 11.82 m (38 ft 9½ in); length excluding probe 14.36 m (47 ft 1¼ in); height 4.945 m (16 ft 2⅔ in); wing area 35.77 m² (385.0 sq ft)
Armament: four M39E 20-mm cannon each with 200 rounds, plus up to 3402 kg (7,500 lb) externally carried on eight pylons, including up to six 454-kg (1,000-lb) bombs, four Bullpup air/surface missiles or two AIM-9B Sidewinder AAMs

This illustration shows a North American F-100D-75-NA, company number NA-235-282, USAF serial originally 56-3184 but later prefixed by an O (obsolete) indicating an aircraft over 10 years old. The serial style with black AF63 (actually meaning 1956-63) was introduced in 1968; five years later all numbers were repainted white. On application of camouflage most aircraft lost the red stripes previously used to warn of the potentially dangerous location of the turbine wheels, as well as the black 'buzz number' painted amidships in earlier days. This particular aircraft was assigned to the 416th TFS at Phu Cat AB.

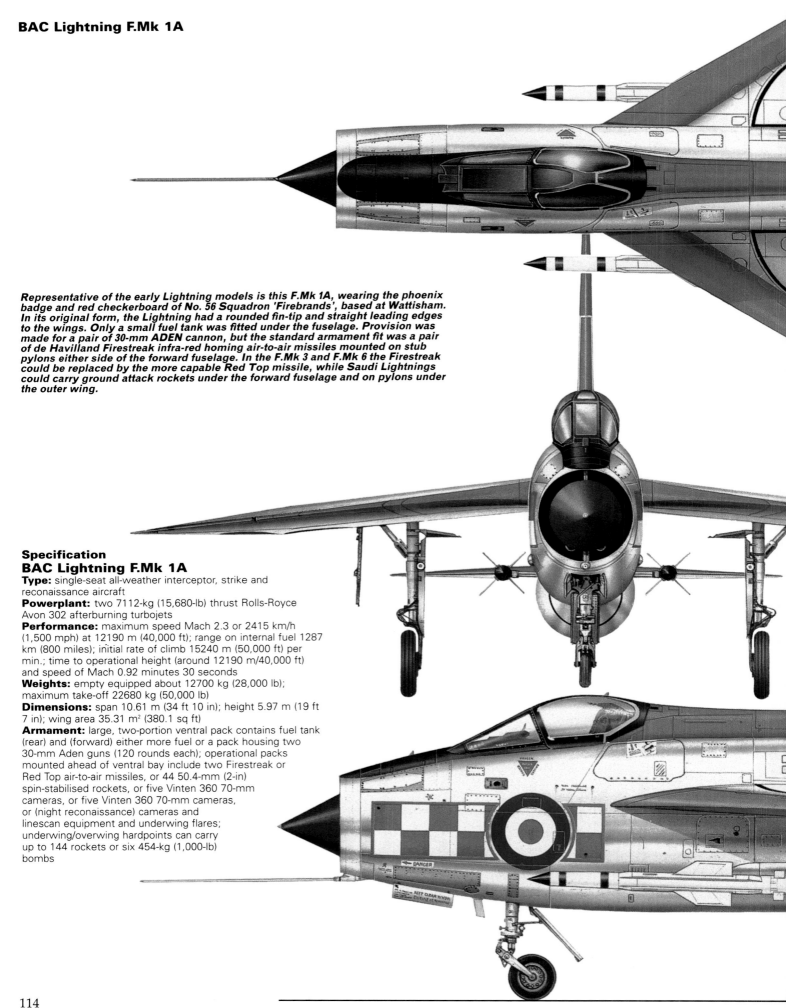

Representative of the early Lightning models is this F.Mk 1A, wearing the phoenix badge and red checkerboard of No. 56 Squadron 'Firebrands', based at Wattisham. In its original form, the Lightning had a rounded fin-tip and straight leading edges to the wings. Only a small fuel tank was fitted under the fuselage. Provision was made for a pair of 30-mm ADEN cannon, but the standard armament fit was a pair of de Havilland Firestreak infra-red homing air-to-air missiles mounted on stub pylons either side of the forward fuselage. In the F.Mk 3 and F.Mk 6 the Firestreak could be replaced by the more capable Red Top missile, while Saudi Lightnings could carry ground attack rockets under the forward fuselage and on pylons under the outer wing.

Specification
BAC Lightning F.Mk 1A

Type: single-seat all-weather interceptor, strike and reconaissance aircraft

Powerplant: two 7112-kg (15,680-lb) thrust Rolls-Royce Avon 302 afterburning turbojets

Performance: maximum speed Mach 2.3 or 2415 km/h (1,500 mph) at 12190 m (40,000 ft); range on internal fuel 1287 km (800 miles); initial rate of climb 15240 m (50,000 ft) per min.; time to operational height (around 12190 m/40,000 ft) and speed of Mach 0.92 minutes 30 seconds

Weights: empty equipped about 12700 kg (28,000 lb); maximum take-off 22680 kg (50,000 lb)

Dimensions: span 10.61 m (34 ft 10 in); height 5.97 m (19 ft 7 in); wing area 35.31 m² (380.1 sq ft)

Armament: large, two-portion ventral pack contains fuel tank (rear) and (forward) either more fuel or a pack housing two 30-mm Aden guns (120 rounds each); operational packs mounted ahead of ventral bay include two Firestreak or Red Top air-to-air missiles, or 44 50.4-mm (2-in) spin-stabilised rockets, or five Vinten 360 70-mm cameras, or five Vinten 360 70-mm cameras, or (night reconaissance) cameras and linescan equipment and underwing flares; underwing/overwing hardpoints can carry up to 144 rockets or six 454-kg (1,000-lb) bombs

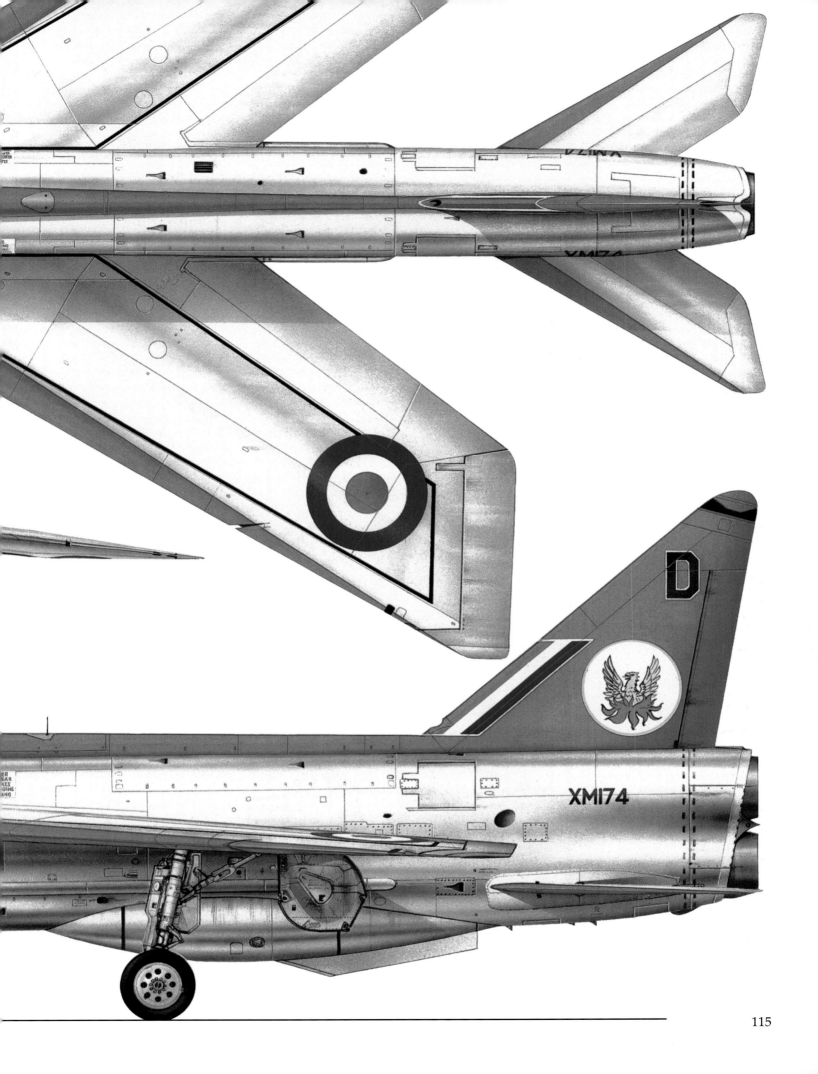

XM174

Douglas F4D-1 Skyray

Nicknamed the 'Hunters', VF-162 was in fact the shortest-lived US Navy Skyray-equipped squadron, being commissioned at **NAS Cecil Field, Florida, on 1 September 1960.** It received its first 'Ford' during the following month and retained this type until early April 1962, when it moved to Miramar and began to convert to the F8U-1 variant of the Crusader. Whilst equipped with the F4D-1, VF-162 made just one major deployment, operating in the Mediterranean as part of Carrier Air Group Six aboard **USS** Intrepid between August 1961 and March 1962. The Skyray depicted here features the markings which were applied to VF-162's aircraft during the course of this cruise.

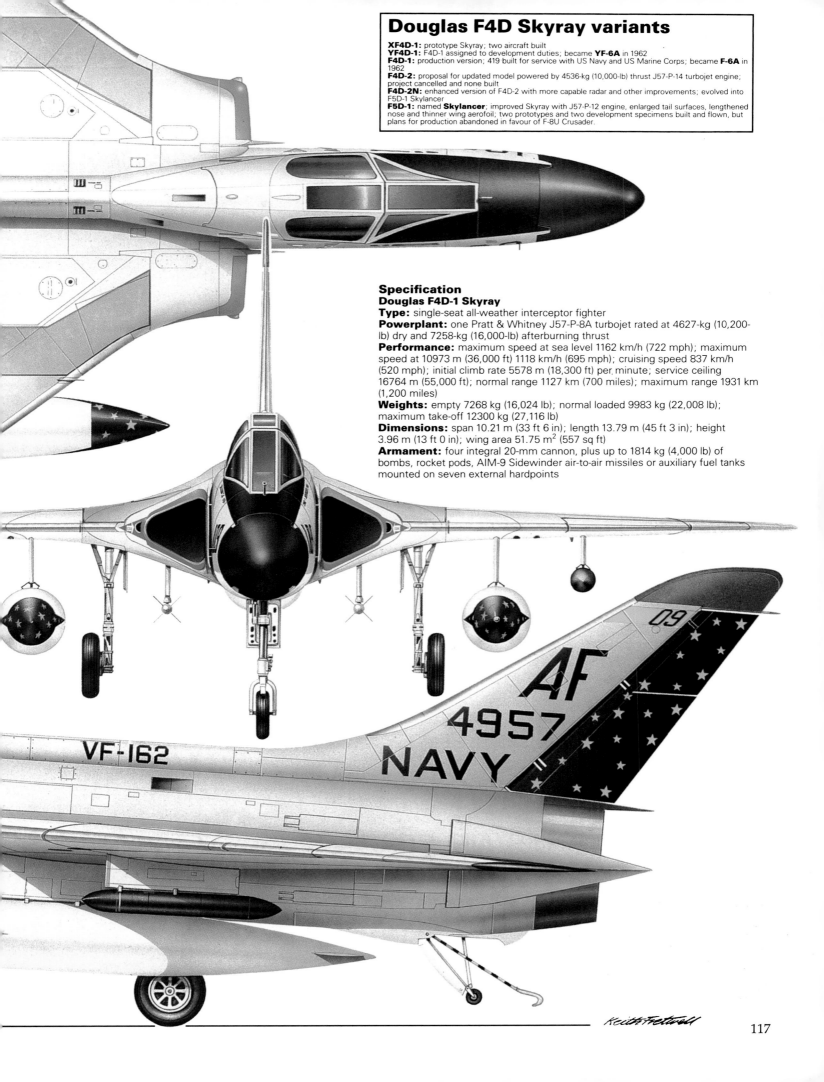

Douglas F4D Skyray variants

XF4D-1: prototype Skyray; two aircraft built
YF4D-1: F4D-1 assigned to development duties; became **YF-6A** in 1962
F4D-1: production version; 419 built for service with US Navy and US Marine Corps; became **F-6A** in 1962
F4D-2: proposal for updated model powered by 4536-kg (10,000-lb) thrust J57-P-14 turbojet engine; project cancelled and none built
F4D-2N: enhanced version of F4D-2 with more capable radar and other improvements; evolved into F5D-1 Skylancer
F5D-1: named **Skylancer**; improved Skyray with J57-P-12 engine, enlarged tail surfaces, lengthened nose and thinner wing aerofoil; two prototypes and two development specimens built and flown, but plans for production abandoned in favour of F-8U Crusader.

Specification
Douglas F4D-1 Skyray
Type: single-seat all-weather interceptor fighter
Powerplant: one Pratt & Whitney J57-P-8A turbojet rated at 4627-kg (10,200-lb) dry and 7258-kg (16,000-lb) afterburning thrust
Performance: maximum speed at sea level 1162 km/h (722 mph); maximum speed at 10973 m (36,000 ft) 1118 km/h (695 mph); cruising speed 837 km/h (520 mph); initial climb rate 5578 m (18,300 ft) per minute; service ceiling 16764 m (55,000 ft); normal range 1127 km (700 miles); maximum range 1931 km (1,200 miles)
Weights: empty 7268 kg (16,024 lb); normal loaded 9983 kg (22,008 lb); maximum take-off 12300 kg (27,116 lb)
Dimensions: span 10.21 m (33 ft 6 in); length 13.79 m (45 ft 3 in); height 3.96 m (13 ft 0 in); wing area 51.75 m² (557 sq ft)
Armament: four integral 20-mm cannon, plus up to 1814 kg (4,000 lb) of bombs, rocket pods, AIM-9 Sidewinder air-to-air missiles or auxiliary fuel tanks mounted on seven external hardpoints

Prior to President de Gaulle's decision to evict US forces from French territory, the USAF maintained a number of air bases in France. Laon was one, this serving as the home for the 66th Tactical Reconnaissance Wing from July 1958 to September 1966, and one of its RF-101Cs is portrayed here in the markings it wore during September 1962. Subsequently, the star on the fin was replaced by the wing badge while the marking on the nose section related to Royal Flush, a NATO-organised reconnaissance competition which was held annually at this time. The 66th TRW remained at Laon until 1966 when it was transferred to Upper Heyford, where it eventually disbanded on 1 April 1970.

U.S. AIR FORCE

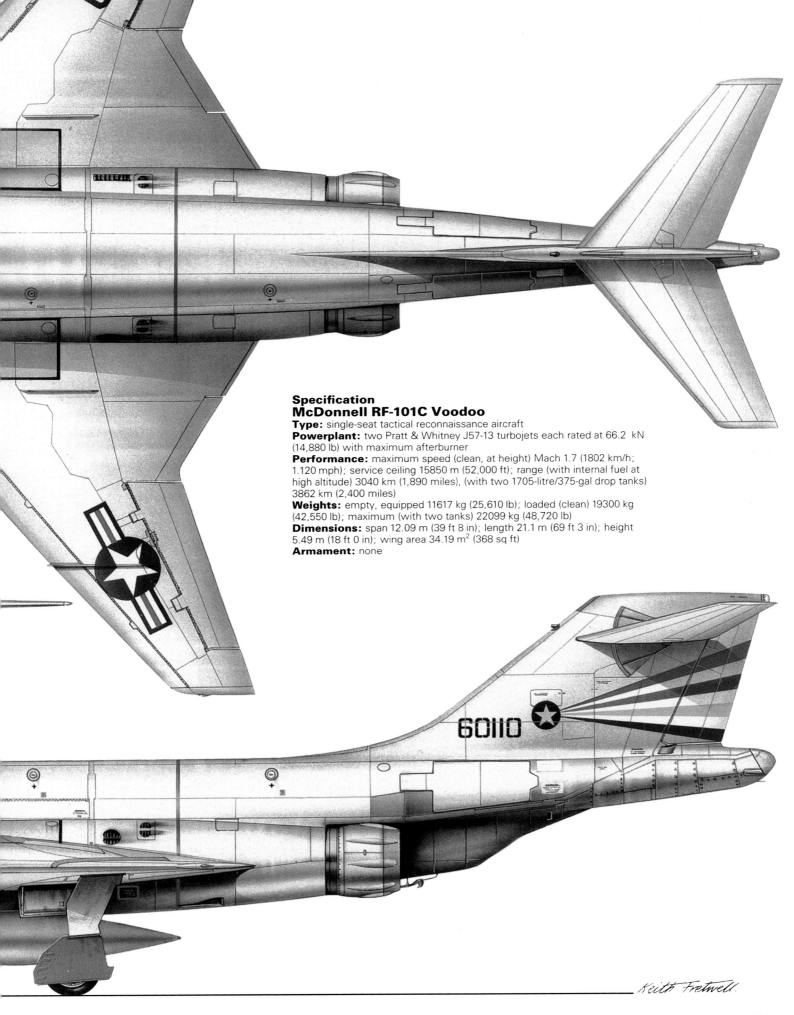

Specification
McDonnell RF-101C Voodoo
Type: single-seat tactical reconnaissance aircraft
Powerplant: two Pratt & Whitney J57-13 turbojets each rated at 66.2 kN (14,880 lb) with maximum afterburner
Performance: maximum speed (clean, at height) Mach 1.7 (1802 km/h; 1.120 mph); service ceiling 15850 m (52,000 ft); range (with internal fuel at high altitude) 3040 km (1,890 miles), (with two 1705-litre/375-gal drop tanks) 3862 km (2,400 miles)
Weights: empty, equipped 11617 kg (25,610 lb); loaded (clean) 19300 kg (42,550 lb); maximum (with two tanks) 22099 kg (48,720 lb)
Dimensions: span 12.09 m (39 ft 8 in); length 21.1 m (69 ft 3 in); height 5.49 m (18 ft 0 in); wing area 34.19 m^2 (368 sq ft)
Armament: none

Keith Fretwell

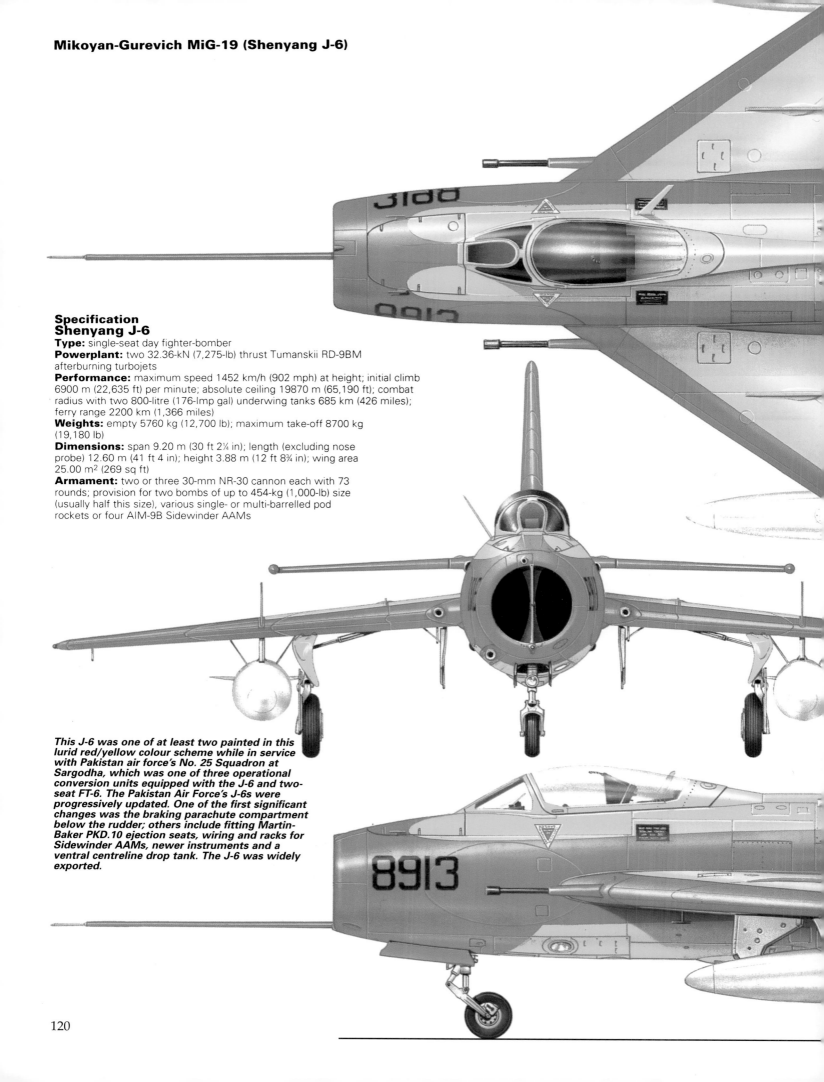

Mikoyan-Gurevich MiG-19 (Shenyang J-6)

Specification
Shenyang J-6

Type: single-seat day fighter-bomber

Powerplant: two 32.36-kN (7,275-lb) thrust Tumanskii RD-9BM afterburning turbojets

Performance: maximum speed 1452 km/h (902 mph) at height; initial climb 6900 m (22,635 ft) per minute; absolute ceiling 19870 m (65,190 ft); combat radius with two 800-litre (176-Imp gal) underwing tanks 685 km (426 miles); ferry range 2200 km (1,366 miles)

Weights: empty 5760 kg (12,700 lb); maximum take-off 8700 kg (19,180 lb)

Dimensions: span 9.20 m (30 ft 2¼ in); length (excluding nose probe) 12.60 m (41 ft 4 in); height 3.88 m (12 ft 8¾ in); wing area 25.00 m² (269 sq ft)

Armament: two or three 30-mm NR-30 cannon each with 73 rounds; provision for two bombs of up to 454-kg (1,000-lb) size (usually half this size), various single- or multi-barrelled pod rockets or four AIM-9B Sidewinder AAMs

This J-6 was one of at least two painted in this lurid red/yellow colour scheme while in service with Pakistan air force's No. 25 Squadron at Sargodha, which was one of three operational conversion units equipped with the J-6 and two-seat FT-6. The Pakistan Air Force's J-6s were progressively updated. One of the first significant changes was the braking parachute compartment below the rudder; others include fitting Martin-Baker PKD.10 ejection seats, wiring and racks for Sidewinder AAMs, newer instruments and a ventral centreline drop tank. The J-6 was widely exported.

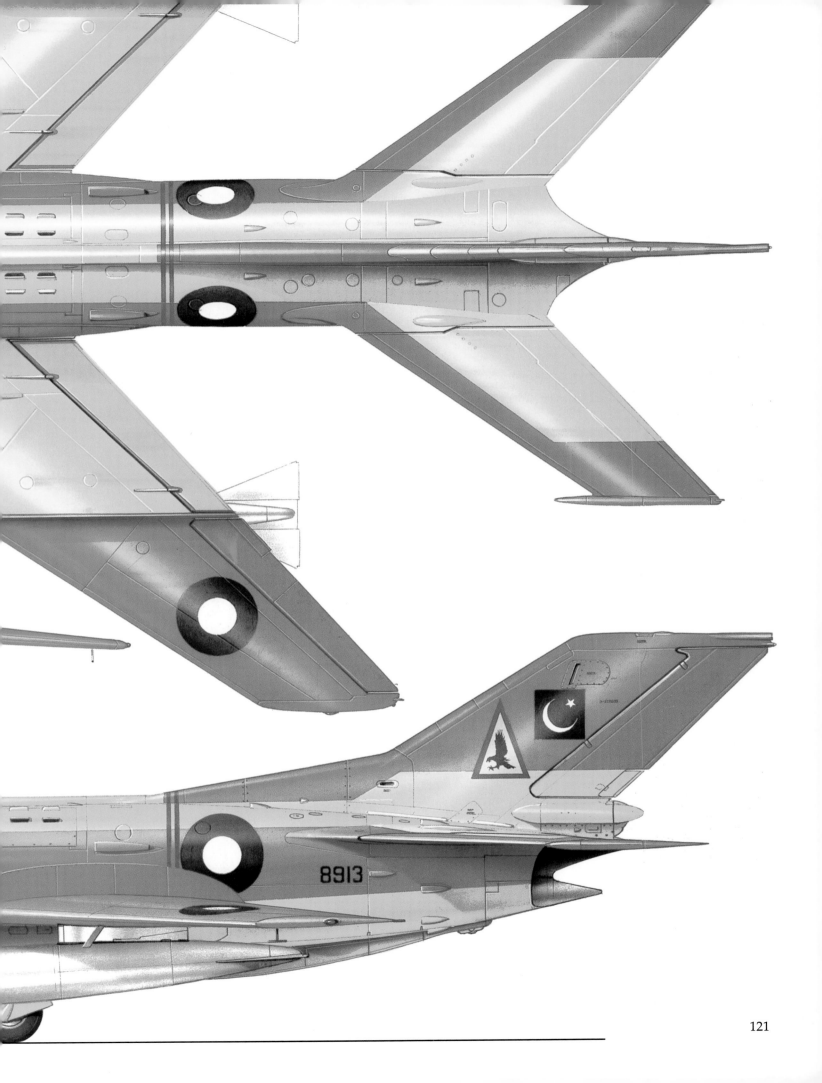

8913

Vought F-8E Crusader

Specification
Vought F-8E Crusader

Type: single-seat naval fighter

Powerplant: one 8165-kg (18,000-lb) Pratt & Whitney J57-P-20A afterburning turbojet

Performance: maximum speed (clean) 1800 km/h (1,120 mph), Mach 1.7 at 12192 m (40,000 ft); climbs to 17374 m (57,000 ft) in six minutes; service ceiling 17983 m (59,000 ft); radius at high altitude 966 km (600 miles)

Weights: empty 9038 kg (19,925 lb); maximum (with external stores) 15422 kg (34,000 lb)

Dimensions: span 10.72 m (35 ft 2 in); length 16.61 m (54 ft 6 in); height 4.80 m (15 ft 9 in); wing area 32.52 m² (350 sq ft)

Armament: four 20-mm Mk 12 cannon with 144 rounds per gun; up to four AIM-9 Sidewinder AAMs; or 12 113-kg (250-lb) or eight 227-kg (500-lb) bombs; or eight Zuni rockets; or two AGM-12A or AGM-12B Bullpup attack missiles

US Navy involvement in the Vietnam War gave the Crusader the chance to prove its worth in deadly combat, a challenge to which it responded magnificently. No less than 17 MiG-17s were downed by its Sidewinder AAMs; supersonic MiG-21s were also destroyed, and the Crusader's 20-mm forward-mounted cannon also scored victories in the air. The relatively small and light design enabled the Crusader to operate from the smaller carriers, in this instance an F-8E from USS Hancock (CVA-19) during March 1967.

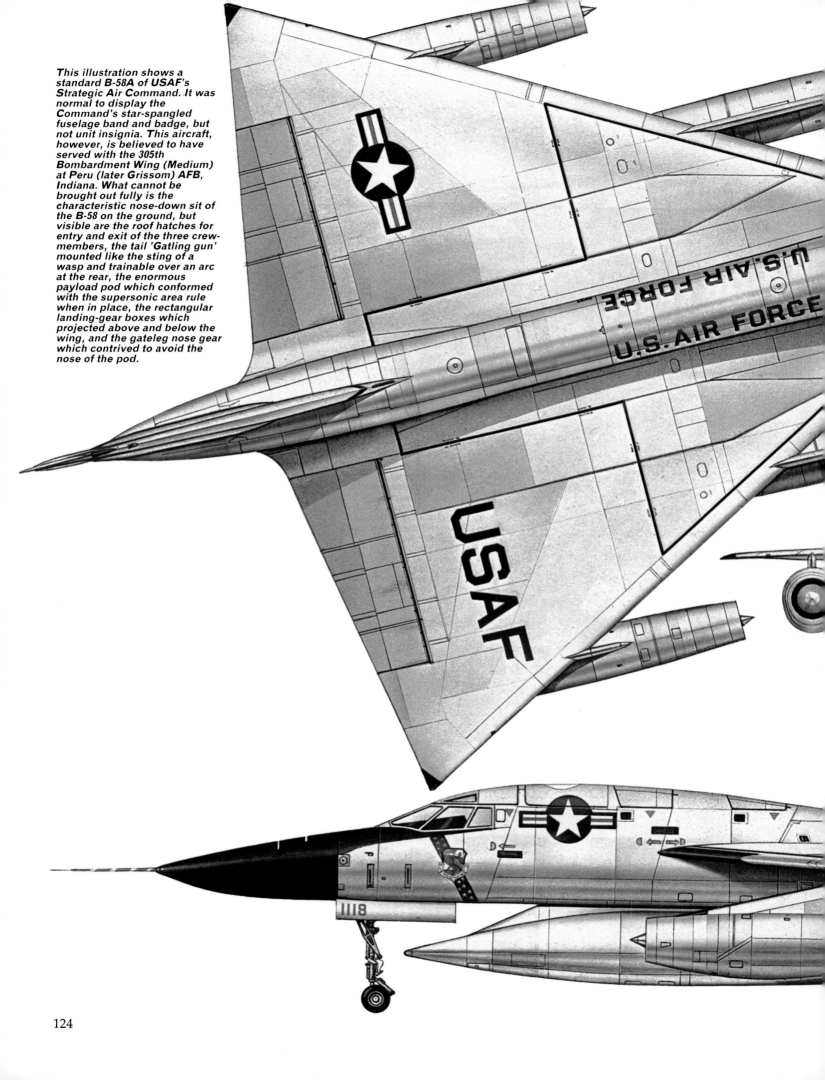

This illustration shows a standard **B-58A** of **USAF's Strategic Air Command**. It was normal to display the Command's star-spangled fuselage band and badge, but not unit insignia. This aircraft, however, is believed to have served with the 305th Bombardment Wing (Medium) at Peru (later Grissom) AFB, Indiana. What cannot be brought out fully is the characteristic nose-down sit of the B-58 on the ground, but visible are the roof hatches for entry and exit of the three crew-members, the tail 'Gatling gun' mounted like the sting of a wasp and trainable over an arc at the rear, the enormous payload pod which conformed with the supersonic area rule when in place, the rectangular landing-gear boxes which projected above and below the wing, and the gateleg nose gear which contrived to avoid the nose of the pod.

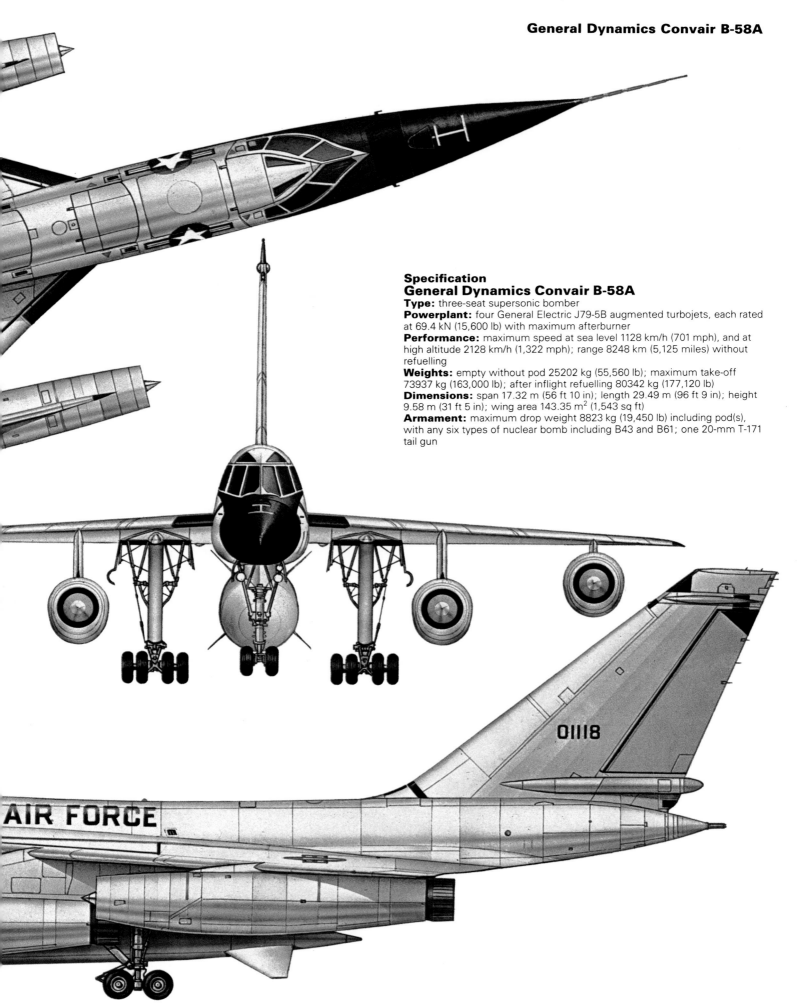

Specification
General Dynamics Convair B-58A
Type: three-seat supersonic bomber
Powerplant: four General Electric J79-5B augmented turbojets, each rated at 69.4 kN (15,600 lb) with maximum afterburner
Performance: maximum speed at sea level 1128 km/h (701 mph), and at high altitude 2128 km/h (1,322 mph); range 8248 km (5,125 miles) without refuelling
Weights: empty without pod 25202 kg (55,560 lb); maximum take-off 73937 kg (163,000 lb); after inflight refuelling 80342 kg (177,120 lb)
Dimensions: span 17.32 m (56 ft 10 in); length 29.49 m (96 ft 9 in); height 9.58 m (31 ft 5 in); wing area 143.35 m² (1,543 sq ft)
Armament: maximum drop weight 8823 kg (19,450 lb) including pod(s), with any six types of nuclear bomb including B43 and B61; one 20-mm T-171 tail gun

Convair F-106A Delta Dart

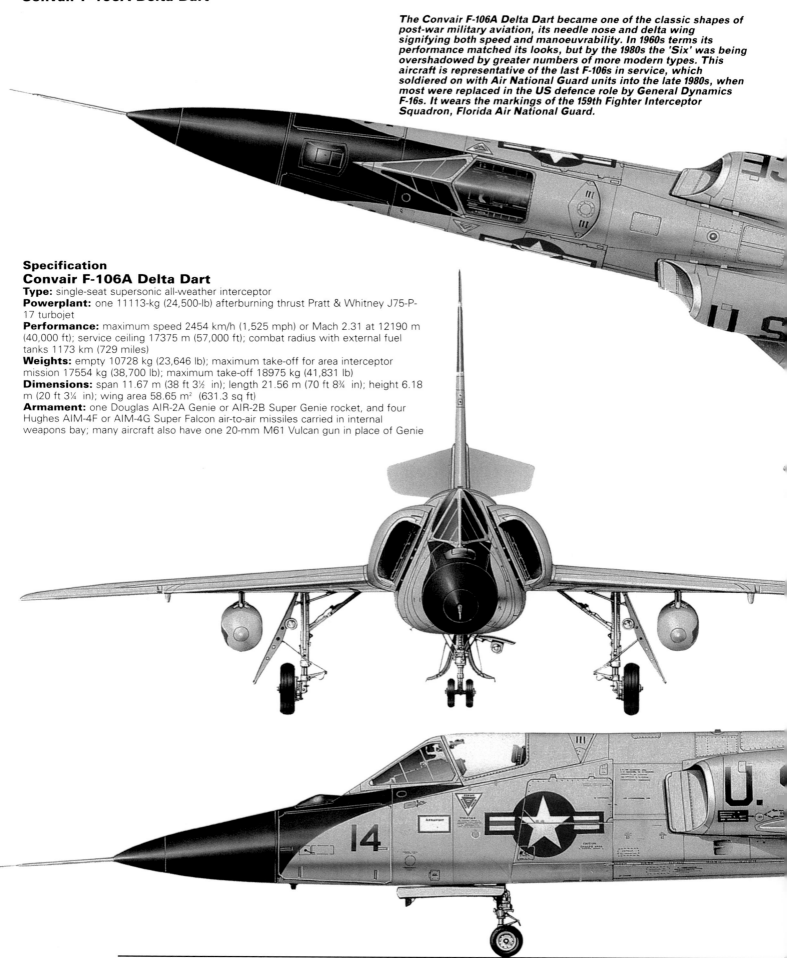

The Convair F-106A Delta Dart became one of the classic shapes of post-war military aviation, its needle nose and delta wing signifying both speed and manoeuvrability. In 1960s terms its performance matched its looks, but by the 1980s the 'Six' was being overshadowed by greater numbers of more modern types. This aircraft is representative of the last F-106s in service, which soldiered on with Air National Guard units into the late 1980s, when most were replaced in the US defence role by General Dynamics F-16s. It wears the markings of the 159th Fighter Interceptor Squadron, Florida Air National Guard.

Specification
Convair F-106A Delta Dart

Type: single-seat supersonic all-weather interceptor

Powerplant: one 11113-kg (24,500-lb) afterburning thrust Pratt & Whitney J75-P-17 turbojet

Performance: maximum speed 2454 km/h (1,525 mph) or Mach 2.31 at 12190 m (40,000 ft); service ceiling 17375 m (57,000 ft); combat radius with external fuel tanks 1173 km (729 miles)

Weights: empty 10728 kg (23,646 lb); maximum take-off for area interceptor mission 17554 kg (38,700 lb); maximum take-off 18975 kg (41,831 lb)

Dimensions: span 11.67 m (38 ft 3½ in); length 21.56 m (70 ft 8¾ in); height 6.18 m (20 ft 3¼ in); wing area 58.65 m² (631.3 sq ft)

Armament: one Douglas AIR-2A Genie or AIR-2B Super Genie rocket, and four Hughes AIM-4F or AIM-4G Super Falcon air-to-air missiles carried in internal weapons bay; many aircraft also have one 20-mm M61 Vulcan gun in place of Genie

Keith Fretwell.

F-102A Delta Dagger

Displaying the attractive blue and white fin stripes of the 525th Fighter Interceptor Squadron at Bitburg, West Germany, this F-102A Delta Dagger profile dates back to about 1962 and is typical of the type's standard configuration at that time. Noteworthy features are the open missile bays complete with AIM-4 Falcon air-to-air missiles and the underwing auxiliary fuel tanks which were a standard fitment to USAFE 'Deuces'.

Specification
Convair F-102A Delta Dagger

Type: single-seater interceptor

Powerplant: one Pratt & Whitney J57-P-23 turbojet rated at 52 kN (11,700 lb) dry and 77 kN (17,200 lb) afterburning thrust

Performance: maximum speed, clean at 12190 m (40,000 ft) 1328 km/h (825 mph); normal cruise speed at 10670 m (35,000 ft) 869 km/h (540 mph); initial climb rate 5304 m (17,400 ft) per minute; service ceiling 16460 m (54,000 ft); tactical radius with two 871-litre (230-US gal) drop tanks and full armament 805 km (500 miles) at 869 km/h (540 mph); maximum range 2173 km (1,350 miles)

Weights: normal loaded, clean 12565 kg (27,700 lb); normal loaded, point interceptor 12769 kg (28,150 lb); maximum take-off 14288 kg (31,500 lb)

Dimensions: span 11.62 m (38 ft 1.5 in); length 20.84 m (68 ft 4.6 in); height 6.46 m (21 ft 2.5 in); wing area 61.45 m^2 (661.5 sq ft)

Armament: three AIM-4C Falcon infra-red homing air-to-air missiles and one AIM-26A Nuclear Falcon, or three AIM-4A/4E beam-riding and three AIM-4C/4F infra-red homing air-to-air missiles; up to 24 unguided 70-mm (2.75-in) folding-fin aerial rockets were originally carried but these were eventually deleted

Keith Fretwell.

Avro Canada CF-105 Arrow

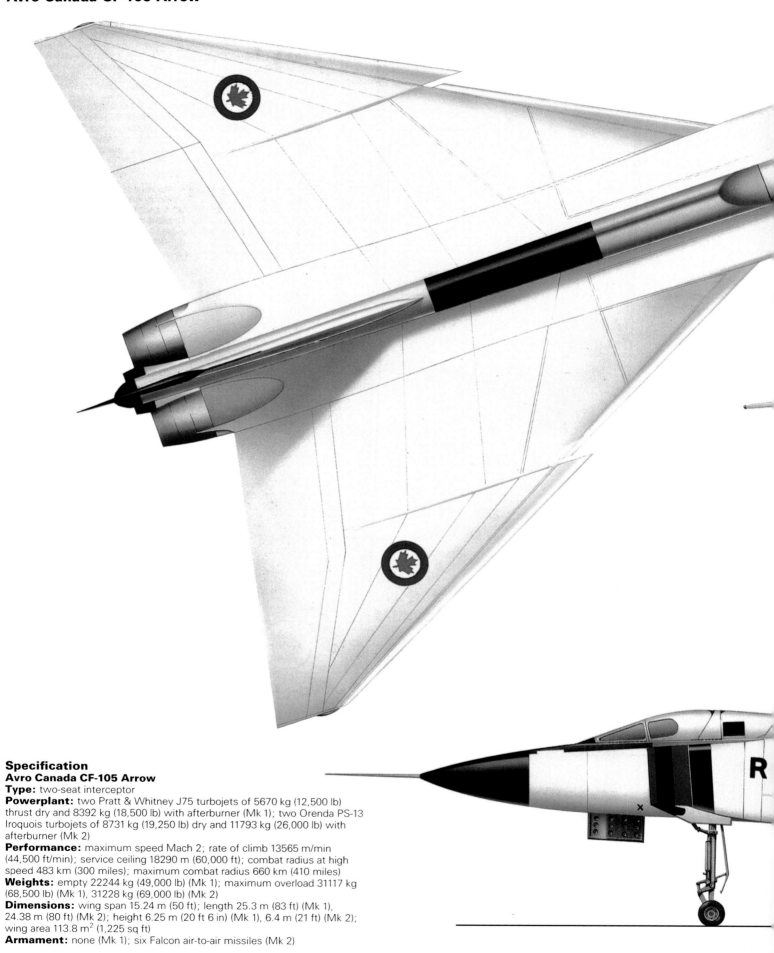

Specification
Avro Canada CF-105 Arrow

Type: two-seat interceptor

Powerplant: two Pratt & Whitney J75 turbojets of 5670 kg (12,500 lb) thrust dry and 8392 kg (18,500 lb) with afterburner (Mk 1); two Orenda PS-13 Iroquois turbojets of 8731 kg (19,250 lb) dry and 11793 kg (26,000 lb) with afterburner (Mk 2)

Performance: maximum speed Mach 2; rate of climb 13565 m/min (44,500 ft/min); service ceiling 18290 m (60,000 ft); combat radius at high speed 483 km (300 miles); maximum combat radius 660 km (410 miles)

Weights: empty 22244 kg (49,000 lb) (Mk 1); maximum overload 31117 kg (68,500 lb) (Mk 1), 31228 kg (69,000 lb) (Mk 2)

Dimensions: wing span 15.24 m (50 ft); length 25.3 m (83 ft) (Mk 1), 24.38 m (80 ft) (Mk 2); height 6.25 m (20 ft 6 in) (Mk 1), 6.4 m (21 ft) (Mk 2); wing area 113.8 m² (1,225 sq ft)

Armament: none (Mk 1); six Falcon air-to-air missiles (Mk 2)

The mighty Arrow flew for only a year before being cancelled, although five aircraft made it into the air. At the time, it was the world's most advanced interceptor, and by all accounts was a superb aircraft that would probably have still been serving today. Among many reasons, it suffered from the prevailing thought in some circles that the guided missile would render the manned aircraft obsolete, the same reasoning that killed many other splendid aircraft designs at this time.

201

JAMIE MEDLIN

Blackburn B-103 Buccaneer

Specification
Blackburn B-103 Buccaneer

Type: two-seat carrier- or land-based low-level strike aircraft

Powerplant: two 5105-kg (11,255-lb) thrust Rolls-Royce RB.168 Spey Mk101 turbofans

Performance: maximum speed 1040 km/h (646 mph) at 61 m (200 ft); service ceiling over 12190 m (40,000 ft); typical range with weapons 3701 km (2,300 miles)

Weights: empty 13608 kg (30,000 lb); maximum take-off 28123 kg (62,000 lb)

Dimensions: span 13.41 m (44 ft 0 in); length 19.33 m (63 ft 5 in); height 4.97 m (16 ft 3 in); wing area 47.82m² (514.7 sq ft)

Armament: four 454-kg (1,000-lb) bombs, fuel tank, or reconaissance pack on inside of rotary bomb door, and up to 5443 kg (12,000 lb) of bombs and/or missiles on four underwing hardpoints

XZ430 was from the final batch of Buccaneers, delivered to the RAF in 1977. Features of the last production configuration were the bulged bomb bay housing additional fuel and the fin-mounted radar warning receivers. The aircraft served with No. 208 Squadron at RAF Lossiemouth, where it partnered No. 12 Squadron in the anti-shipping role, employing the Sea Eagle and Martel missile. A secondary role was to provide laser designation for the Tornado GR.Mk 1 force, a role it performed in the 1991 Gulf War. The area-ruling of the fuselage gave the Buccaneer its distinctive shape, right down to the extended bulged tailcone, which doubled as a split airbrake. No 12 Squadron rearmed with Tornados in 1993, and No 208 became a reserve squadron, flying BAe Hawk trainers at RAF Valley, Wales.

Keith Fretwell.

A Saab Draken in the markings of *F10 wing of the Swedish air force, based at Ängelhom in the South Sweden military command. The J 35F, or 'Filip', was Saab's first attempt at a fully integrated weapons system, an approach later much refined with the Viggen. This Draken differs from earlier versions in having a more powerful Ericsson PS-01 radar, Saab S7B collision-course fire control and FH5 autopilot. It also introduced a zero-zero ejection seat and a single-piece blown hood. The left-hand cannon was deleted to provide extra avionics space.*

Specification
SAAB-35 Draken
Type: single-seat interceptor
Powerplant: one 7830-kg (17,262-lb) afterburning thrust Flygmotor RM6C (licence-built) Rolls Royce Avon 300 turbojet
Performance: maximum speed, clean Mach 2 or 2125 km/h (1,320 mph) at 11000 m (36,090 ft); service ceiling 20000 m (65,615 ft); hi-lo-hi radius on internal fuel 560 km (348 miles)
Weights: empty 7425 kg (16,369 lb); maximum take-off 12700 kg (27,998 lb)
Dimensions: span 9.40 m (30 ft 10 in); length 15.35 m (50 ft 4¾ in); height 3.89 m (12 ft 9 in); wing area 49.20 m² (529.60 sq ft)
Armament: one 30-mm ADEN M/55 cannon in starboard wing, two RB 27 and two RB 28 Falcon missiles, plus up to 1000 kg (2,205 lb) of bombs or 12 135-mm (5.3-in) Bofors rockets

Keith Fretwell.

Mikoyan-Gurevich MiG-21bis 'Fishbed-N'

Typical of many late-model MiG-21s, this is a MiG-21bis 'Fishbed-N'. The MiG-21bis introduced the uprated Tumanskii R-25-300 jet, rated at 73.6 kN (16,535 lb) thrust, the late 'Fishbed-N' version offering further improvements to avionics, as indicated by the 'Swift Rod' ILS antennae under the nose and on the fin. This aircraft is carrying a standard air-to-air load of four 'Atoll' missiles. On the inboard pylons are AA-2D infra-red guided missiles, while the weapons outboard are AA-2C semi-active radar-guided missiles. The MiG-21bis also routinely carried the far more capable AA-B 'Aphid' in place of the AA-2Ds.

Specification
Mikoyan-Gurevich MiG-21bis 'Fishbed-N'
Type: single-seat multi-role fighter
Powerplant: one Tumanskii R-25 turbojet with afterburning thrust of 73.5-kN (16,535 lb)
Performance: maximum speed 2230 km/h (1,386 mph) or Mach 2.1 above 11000 m (36,090 ft); service ceiling 15250 m (50,035 ft); maximum range with internal fuel 11000 km (684 miles)
Weights: maximum take-off 9400 kg (20,723 lb)
Dimensions: span 7.15 m (23 ft 5½ in); length 15.76 m (51 ft 8½ in); height 410 m (13 ft 5½ in); wing area 23 m² (247.58 sq ft)
Armament: one 23-mm Gsh-23 twin-barrel cannon in underbelly pack, plus about 1500 kg (3,307 lb) of stores on four underwing pylons

Specification
Republic F-105D Thunderchief

Type: single-seat strike fighter

Powerplant: one Pratt & Whitney J75-P-19W turbojet rated at 7802 kg (17,200 lb) thrust dry and 11113 kg (24,500 lb) thrust with afterburning; water injection permits 60-second rating of 12020 kg (26,500 lb) thrust in afterburner mode

Performance: maximum speed 2,237 km/h (1,390 mph) or Mach 2.1 at 10970 m (36,000 ft); initial climb rate 10485 m (34,400 ft) per minute in clean configuration; service ceiling 12560 m (41,200 ft) on a typical mission; range 1480 km (920 miles) with two 1703-litre (450-US gal) drop-tanks underwing, one 2461-litre (650-US gal) drop-tank on centreline and two AGM-12 Bullpup ASMs; ferry range 3846 km (2,390 miles) with maximum external fuel at 940 km/h (584 mph)

Weights: empty 12,474 kg (27,500 lb); maximum overload take-off 23967 kg (52,838 lb)

Dimensions: span 10.59 m (34 ft 9 in); length 19.61 m (64 ft 4 in); height 5.97 m (19 ft 7 in); wing area 35.77 m^2 (385.0 sq ft)

Armament: combinations of 340-kg (750-lb) M117 bombs, 454-kg (1,000-lb) Mk 83 bombs, 1361-kg (3,000-lb) M118 bombs, AGM-12 Bullpup ASMs, AIM-9 Sidewinder AAMs, 70-mm (2.75-in) rocket pods, napalm containers, Mk 28/43 special weapons, chemical bombs, leaflet bombs, 127-mm (5-in) rocket pods and MLU-10/B mines; also one M61 Vulcan 20-mm cannon with 1,028 rounds of ammunition

Republic F-105 Thunderchief variants

YF-105A: two prototypes each powered by Pratt & Whitney J57-P-25 engines rated at 6804-kg (15,000-lb) thrust

F-105B: initial production model; total of 75 built, including 10 for RDT & E purposes; powered by Pratt & Whitney J57-P-3 rated at 7484-kg (16,500-lb) thrust

RF-105B: proposed reconnaissance model; three prototypes ordered but completed as JF-105B RDT & E aircraft when reconnaissance variant abandoned

JF-105B: three aircraft built for systems test work using those airframes originally laid down as RF-105B prototypes

F-105C: projected tandem two-seat operational trainer derivative of F-105B; subsequently abandoned after reaching mock-up stage

F-105D: definitive single-seat

Thunderchief model, 610 being built; powered by Pratt & Whitney J75-P-19W rated at 7802 kg (17,200 lb) thrust

RF-105D: proposed reconnaissance variant of F-105D; abandoned in December 1961 in favour of RF-4C Phantom

F-105E: projected tandem two-seat operational trainer variant of F-105D; construction begun but abandoned, those aircraft on assembly line being completed as F-105Ds

F-105F: two-seat combat proficiency trainer variant based on F-105D; 143 built

EF-105F: initial designation applied to 'Wild Weasel' SAM suppression model which ultimately became the F-105G

F-105G: ultimate 'Wild Weasel' SAM suppression aircraft, approximately 60 F-105Fs being converted to this configuration

Bearing the fin-tip colours of the 4th Tactical Fighter Wing's 334th Tactical Fighter Squadron, F-105D-5-RE (59-1745) was one of the first camouflaged examples to see combat action, deploying to Da Nang, South Vietnam, during 1965 prior to the organisation of permanently-based units at Takhli and Korat in Thailand. Surviving this tour of combat duty, 59-1745's good fortune finally ran out on 31 March 1967 when it was brought down over North Vietnam while attached to the 388th TFW at Korat. Auxiliary fuel tanks and eight 340-kg (750-lb) bombs are carried on the five external stores stations, the internal weapons bay being used to accommodate additional fuel.

Republic F-105D Thunderchief

USAF
91745

Keith Fretwell.

Lockheed F-104G Starfighter

The Starfighter is best-known wearing the iron cross of West Germany. Huge numbers served with both the Luftwaffe and the Marineflieger, although they have now been replaced by Tornados. In West German service the 'Star' developed a reputation for a high attrition rate, drawing the epithet 'Widowmaker' from the popular press. In fact the type was highly regarded by its pilots, many of whom mourned its passing when they had to convert to the two-seat Tornado. Its attrition rate, while high by today's standards, was nevertheless considerably lower than many other contemporary aircraft, and it was lower than for many other Starfighter operators. This aircraft is one of the F-104Gs supplied to the German navy, wearing the badge of Marinefliegergeschwader 1 based at Schleswig. It is seen armed with MBB Kormoran anti-ship missiles on the wing pylons, and with practice bombs on the centreline. In addition to the anti-ship F-104Gs, the Marineflieger also had RF-104G tactical reconnaissance aircraft, these serving with MFG 2 and making daily flights along the Baltic coasts of East Germany and Poland.

Specification
Lockheed F-104G Starfighter
Type: single-seat multi-mission fighter
Powerplant: one General Electric J79-GE-11A turbojet of 7076 kg (15,600 lb) afterburning thrust
Performance: maximum speed 1845 km/h (1,146 mph) at 15240 m (50,000 ft); service ceiling 15240 m (50,000 ft); range 1740 km (1,081 miles)
Weights: empty 6348 kg (13,995 lb); maximum take-off 13170 kg (29,035 lb)
Dimensions: span (excluding missiles) 6.36 m (21 ft 9 in); length 16.66 m (54 ft 8 in); height 4.09 m (13 ft 5 in); wing area 18.22 m² (196.10 sq ft)
Armament: one 20-mm General Electric six-barrelled cannon, wingtip-mounted Sidewinder air-to-air missiles and up to 1814 kg (4,000 lb) of stores

MARINE

Sukhoi Su-7BMK 'Fitter-A'

In its Warsaw Pact days the Czechoslovakian air force operated large numbers of these early model 'Fitters'. This Su-7BMK 'Fitter-A' displays the features common to all these widely-exported aircraft, such as the bulged nosewheel doors, tail-mounted Sirena radar warning receiver and the additional weapons pylon outboard of the wing fence. Today, however, Czech Su-7s have been largely relegated either to museums or to the scrapheap.

Specification
Sukhoi Su-7BMK 'Fitter-A'
Type: ground-attack fighter
Powerplant: one 98-kN (22,046-lb) afterburning thrust Lyulka AL-7F-1 turbojet
Performance: maximum speed, clean, 1700 km/h (1,056 mph) or Mach 1.6 at 11000 m (36,090 ft); service ceiling, clean, 15150 m (49,700 ft); typical combat radius 320 km (199 miles)
Weights: empty 8636 kg (19,040 lb); maximum take-off 14800 kg (32,628 lb)
Dimensions: span 8.93 m (29 ft 3¾ in); length 17.37 m (57 ft 0 in); height 4.57 m (15 ft 0 in)
Armament: two 30-mm NR-30 cannon in wing roots, plus underwing pylons for two 750-kg (1653-lb) and two 500-kg (1,102-lb) bombs; limited to weapon load of 1000 kg (2204 lb) when two drop tanks are carried

This RA-5C was one of those that began life as an A-5A and subsequently underwent complete rebuild in the conversion to the hump-backed reconnaissance aircraft with much greater internal fuel capacity. It did not carry the names of its crew, but everything else is broadcast: Squadron RVAH-14, Modex 604, tail code AB of the Atlantic Fleet, embarked aboard CV-67 USS John F. Kennedy. RVAH-14 was part of Air Wing CVW-1, but after 1972 its place was taken by RVAH-11; and, because of attrition, the squadron's embarked complement was reduced from four aircraft to three.

Specification
North American (Rockwell) RA-5C Vigilante

Type: carrierborne reconnaissance aircraft

Powerplant: two General Electric J79-GE-10 turbojets each rated at 8127 kg (17,900 lb) with maximum afterburner

Performance: maximum speed Mach 2.1 (2229 km/h; 1,385 mph) at 12192 m (40,000 ft); cruising limit 2018 km/h (1,254 mph); service ceiling 14750 m (48,400 ft); combat range up to 2414 km (1,500 miles) at 10920-12993 m (35,800-42,600 ft); total internal fuel capacity 13633 litres (3,600 US gal) comprising 2708 litres (715 US gal) in each wing integral tank, 4866 litres (1,285 US gal) in four fuselage tanks and 3315 litres (885 US gal) in three tanks in armament tunnel; provision for four 1515-litre (400-US gal) underwing drop tanks

Weights: empty 17024 kg (37,498 lb); take-off with full internal fuel 29777 kg (65,589 lb); maximum take-off (field or catapult) 36133 kg (79,588 lb)

Dimensions: span 16.17 m (53 ft 0 in); length 23.35 m (76 ft 6 in); height 5.91 m (19 ft 4.75 in); wing area 70.02 m² (753.7 sq ft)

Grumman A-6A Intruder

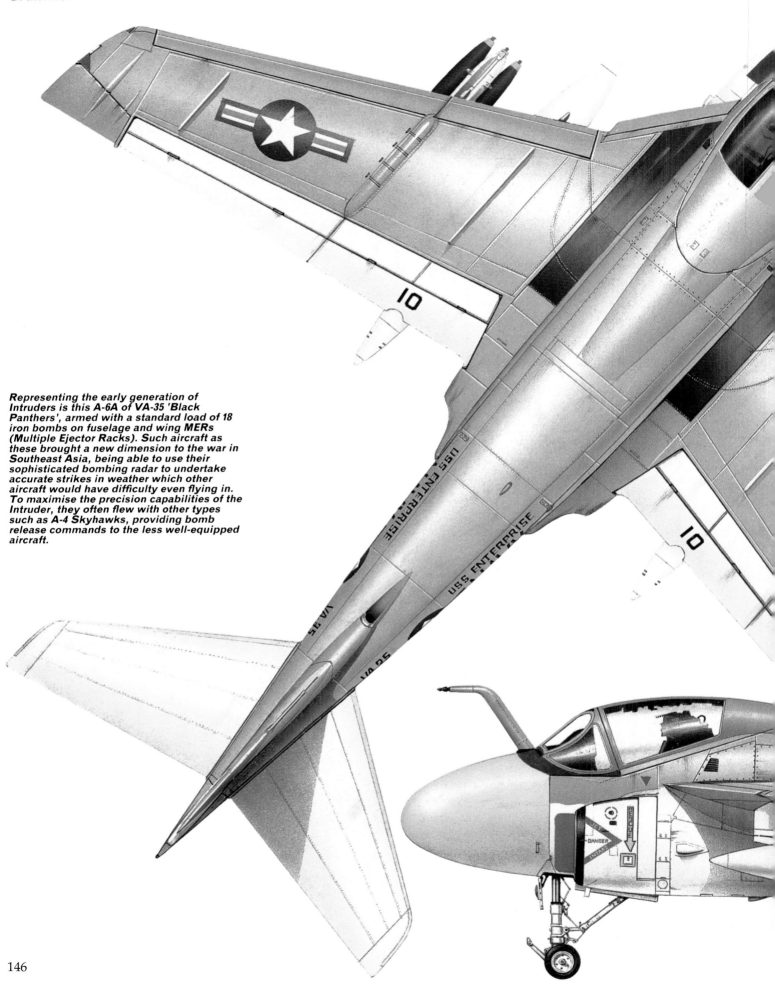

Representing the early generation of Intruders is this A-6A of VA-35 'Black Panthers', armed with a standard load of 18 iron bombs on fuselage and wing MERs (Multiple Ejector Racks). Such aircraft as these brought a new dimension to the war in Southeast Asia, being able to use their sophisticated bombing radar to undertake accurate strikes in weather which other aircraft would have difficulty even flying in. To maximise the precision capabilities of the Intruder, they often flew with other types such as A-4 Skyhawks, providing bomb release commands to the less well-equipped aircraft.

Specification
Grumman A-6A Intruder

Type: two-seat carrier- or shore-based all-weather attack aircraft

Powerplant: two 4218-kg (9,300-lb) thrust Pratt & Whitney J52-P-8B turbojets

Performance: maximum speed 1036 km/h (644 mph) at sea·level; cruising speed 763 km/h (474 mph); service ceiling 12,925 m (42,400 ft); range with maximum military load 1627 km (1,011 miles)

Weights: empty 12093 kg (26,660 lb); maximum take-off, catapult 26581 kg (58,600 lb), field 27397 kg (60,400 lb)

Dimensions: span 16.15 m (53 ft 0 in); length 16.69 m (54 ft 9 in); height 4.93 m (16 ft 2 in); wing area 49.13 m² (528.9 sq ft)

Armament: one underfuselage and four underwing attachment points for maximum external load of 8165 kg (18,000 lb)

General Dynamics F-111 'Aardvark'

Specification
General Dynamics F111 'Aardvark'

Type: two-seat multi-purpose attack aircraft

Powerplant: two 11385-kg (25,100-lb) thrust Pratt & Whitney TF-30-P-100 augmented turbofans

Performance: maximum speed at optimum altitude 2655 km/h (1,650 mph) or Mach 2.5; maximum speed at sea level 1473 km/h (915 mph) or Mach 1.2; service ceiling more than 17985 m (59,000 ft); range with maximum internal fuel 4707 km (2,925 miles)

Weights: empty 21398 kg (47,175 lb); maximum take-off 45359 kg (100,000 lb)

Dimensions: span unswept 19.20 m (63 ft 0 in); swept 9.74 m (31 ft 11½ in); length 22.40 m (73 ft 6 in); height 5.22 m (17 ft 1½ in)

Armament: one 20-mm multi-barrelled M61A-1 cannon and one 340-kg (750-lb) B43 bomb, or two B43 bombs in internal weapons bay; three underwing hardpoints on each outer wing panel, the inner four pivoting to keep stores aligned as wings sweep

After its disastrous first combat deployment to South East Asia, the F-111 returned in 1972 and fared considerably better, constantly demonstrating its ability to lay down ordnance with extreme accuracy in all weathers. This aircraft wears the 'NA' tailcode of the 474th Tactical Fighter Wing from Nellis AFB, Nevada, the first recipient of the type in service. It is shown loaded with fin-retarded Mk 82 'Snakeye' bombs and has its weapon bay doors open.

Northrop F-5E

Despite being the first recipient of the second-generation F-5E (illustrated) and F-5F two-seat derivative, the US Air Force only received a few. The initial deliveries were to the 425th TFTS, 58th TTW at Luke AFB, Arizona, where the type was principally involved in training foreign pilots. However, the type's similarity in size and performance to the MiG-21 made it an ideal choice for a dissimilar air combat aircraft to equip the newly-formed Aggressor Squadrons. Most of the USAF's F-5Es therefore wore Soviet-style camouflage and two-digit nose codes. The lion's share of the aggressor force served with the 64th and 65th Aggressor Squadrons of the 57th Fighter Weapons Wing at Nellis AFB, Nevada, although the 527th Aggressor Squadron at RAF Alconbury, England, and the 26th Aggressor Squadron at Clark AB, Philippines, were established to serve the European and Pacific forces, respectively. The F-5 was phased out of this role with the introduction of the F-16, although the Aggressor Squadrons were disbanded as a cost-cutting measure in 1990. Both the US Navy and Marine Corps continue to use the type in their own adversary programmes.

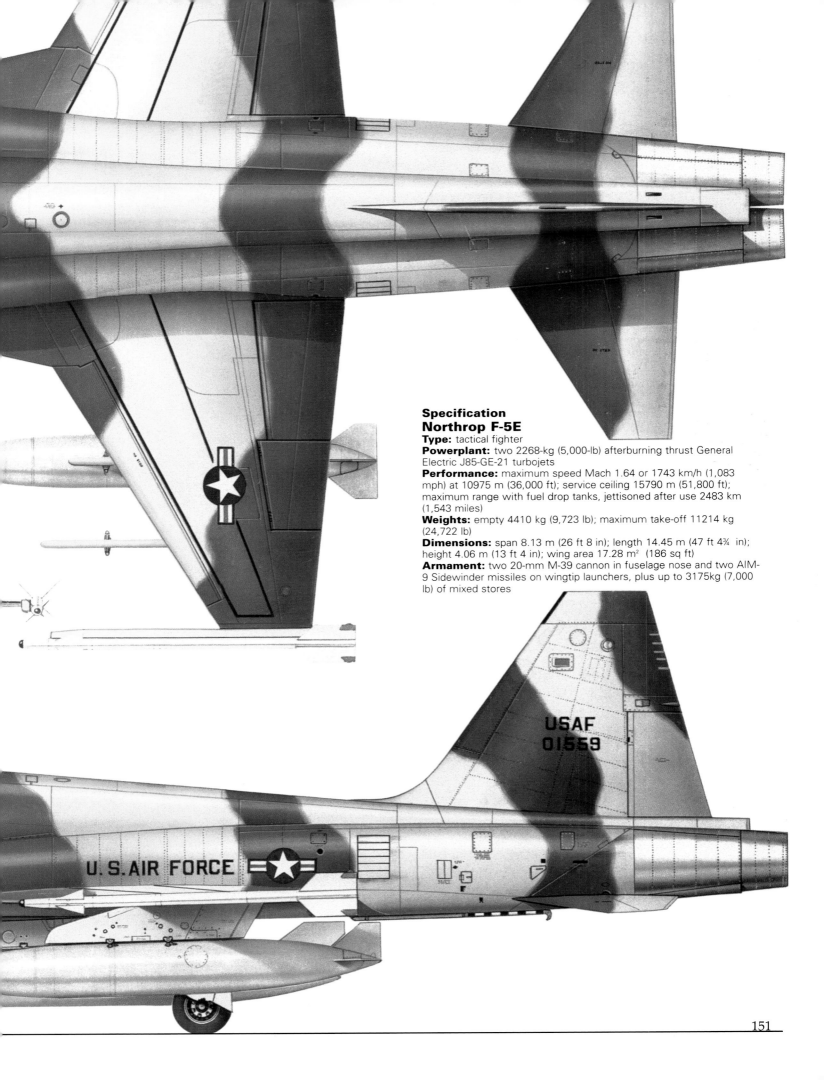

Specification
Northrop F-5E

Type: tactical fighter
Powerplant: two 2268-kg (5,000-lb) afterburning thrust General Electric J85-GE-21 turbojets
Performance: maximum speed Mach 1.64 or 1743 km/h (1,083 mph) at 10975 m (36,000 ft); service ceiling 15790 m (51,800 ft); maximum range with fuel drop tanks, jettisoned after use 2483 km (1,543 miles)
Weights: empty 4410 kg (9,723 lb); maximum take-off 11214 kg (24,722 lb)
Dimensions: span 8.13 m (26 ft 8 in); length 14.45 m (47 ft 4¾ in); height 4.06 m (13 ft 4 in); wing area 17.28 m² (186 sq ft)
Armament: two 20-mm M-39 cannon in fuselage nose and two AIM-9 Sidewinder missiles on wingtip launchers, plus up to 3175kg (7,000 lb) of mixed stores

Specification
Mikoyan-Gurevich MiG-25
Type: single-seat interceptor
Powerplant: two Tumanskii R-31 turbojets each with an afterburning thrust of 12250 kg (27,006 lb)
Performance: (estimated) maximum combat speed 2975 km/h (1,849 mph) or Mach 2.8; service ceiling 24395 m (80,000 ft); maximum combat radius 1450 km (901 miles)
Weights: (estimated) empty 20000 kg (44,092 lb); maximum take-off 36200 kg (79,807 lb)
Dimensions: span 13.95 m (45 ft 9¼ in); length 23.82 m (78 ft 1¾ in); height 6.10 m (20 ft 1¼ in); wing area 56.83 m² (611.73 sq ft)
Armament: underwing pylons for the carriage of up to four air-to-air missiles

The subject of this illustration is a MiG-25 interceptor which in early 1975 was serving with an unknown PVO unit in the Soviet Union (not the aircraft in which Lieutenant Belyenko defected in September 1976). It carries the main armament option: four of the giant AAMs known to NATO as AA-6 'Acrid' carried on wing pylons, those on the inboard pylons being fitted with IR homing heads and those on the outer pylons being guided by semi-active radar. A later radar homing head has a receiver aerial of greater diameter inside a bulged white radome, again with a pointed nose.

153

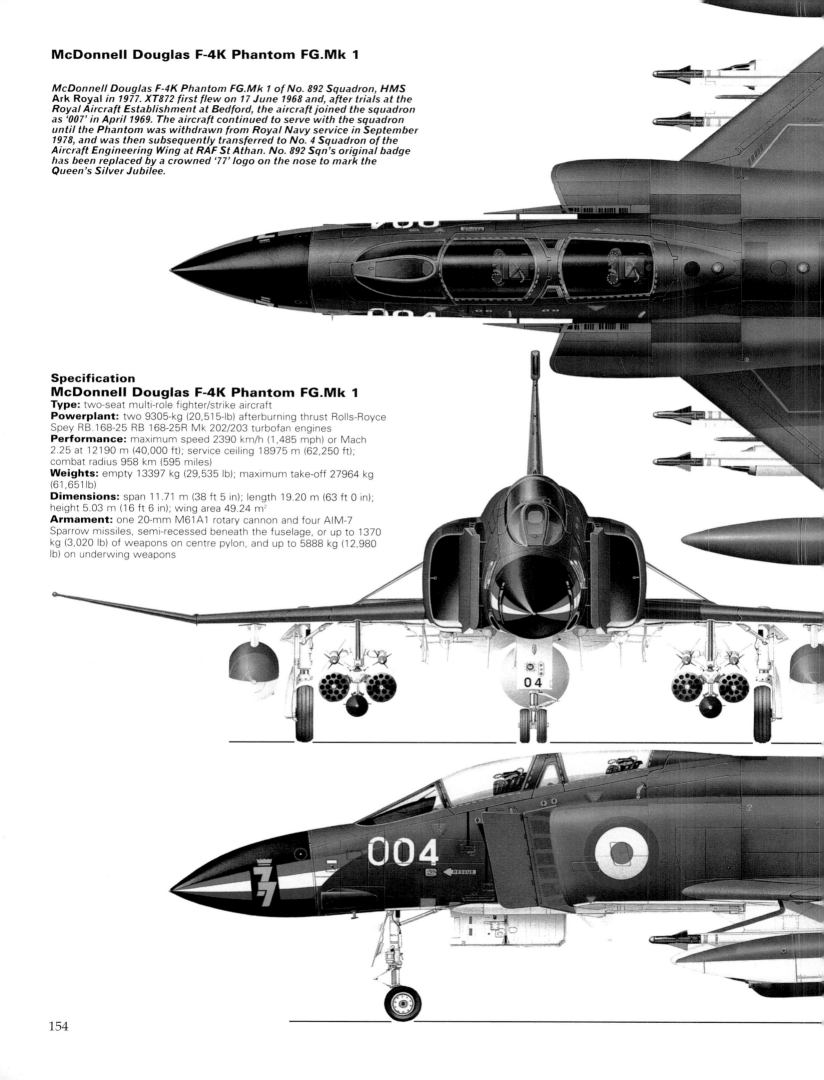

McDonnell Douglas F-4K Phantom FG.Mk 1

McDonnell Douglas F-4K Phantom FG.Mk 1 of No. 892 Squadron, HMS Ark Royal in 1977. XT872 first flew on 17 June 1968 and, after trials at the Royal Aircraft Establishment at Bedford, the aircraft joined the squadron as '007' in April 1969. The aircraft continued to serve with the squadron until the Phantom was withdrawn from Royal Navy service in September 1978, and was then subsequently transferred to No. 4 Squadron of the Aircraft Engineering Wing at RAF St Athan. No. 892 Sqn's original badge has been replaced by a crowned '77' logo on the nose to mark the Queen's Silver Jubilee.

Specification
McDonnell Douglas F-4K Phantom FG.Mk 1

Type: two-seat multi-role fighter/strike aircraft

Powerplant: two 9305-kg (20,515-lb) afterburning thrust Rolls-Royce Spey RB.168-25 RB 168-25R Mk 202/203 turbofan engines

Performance: maximum speed 2390 km/h (1,485 mph) or Mach 2.25 at 12190 m (40,000 ft); service ceiling 18975 m (62,250 ft); combat radius 958 km (595 miles)

Weights: empty 13397 kg (29,535 lb); maximum take-off 27964 kg (61,651lb)

Dimensions: span 11.71 m (38 ft 5 in); length 19.20 m (63 ft 0 in); height 5.03 m (16 ft 6 in); wing area 49.24 m²

Armament: one 20-mm M61A1 rotary cannon and four AIM-7 Sparrow missiles, semi-recessed beneath the fuselage, or up to 1370 kg (3,020 lb) of weapons on centre pylon, and up to 5888 kg (12,980 lb) on underwing weapons

Keith Fretwell.

Vought A-7D Corsair II

Specification
Vought A-7D Corsair II

Type: single-seat attack aircraft

Powerplant: one 64.5-kN (14,500-lb) Allison TF41-A-1 (licensed Rolls-Royce Spey) non-after-burning turbojet

Performance: maximum speed, clean 1065 km/h (662 mph) at 610 m (2000 ft) and with 2722 kg (6000 lb) of stores 1041 km/h (647 mph) at 1525 m (5,000 ft); radius of action 885 km (550 miles) with eight 500-lb (227-kg) bombs allowing 30 minutes at low-level in target area, or 1762 km (1,095 miles) with 12 500-lb (227-kg) bombs in hi-lo-hi mission; ferry range 4619 km (2,870 miles) with four 1137-litre (250-lmp gal) tanks

Weights: empty 8973 kg (19,781 lb); maximum take-off 19051 kg (42,000 lb)

Dimensions: span 11.81 m (38 ft 9 in); length 14.06 m (46 ft 1½ in); height 4.90 m (16 ft ¾ in); wing area 34.84 m² (375 sq ft)

Armament: one internal 20-mm M61 Vulcan cannon with 1,000 rounds, plus up to 15,000 lb (6804 kg) of ordnance on six wing and two fuselage pylons

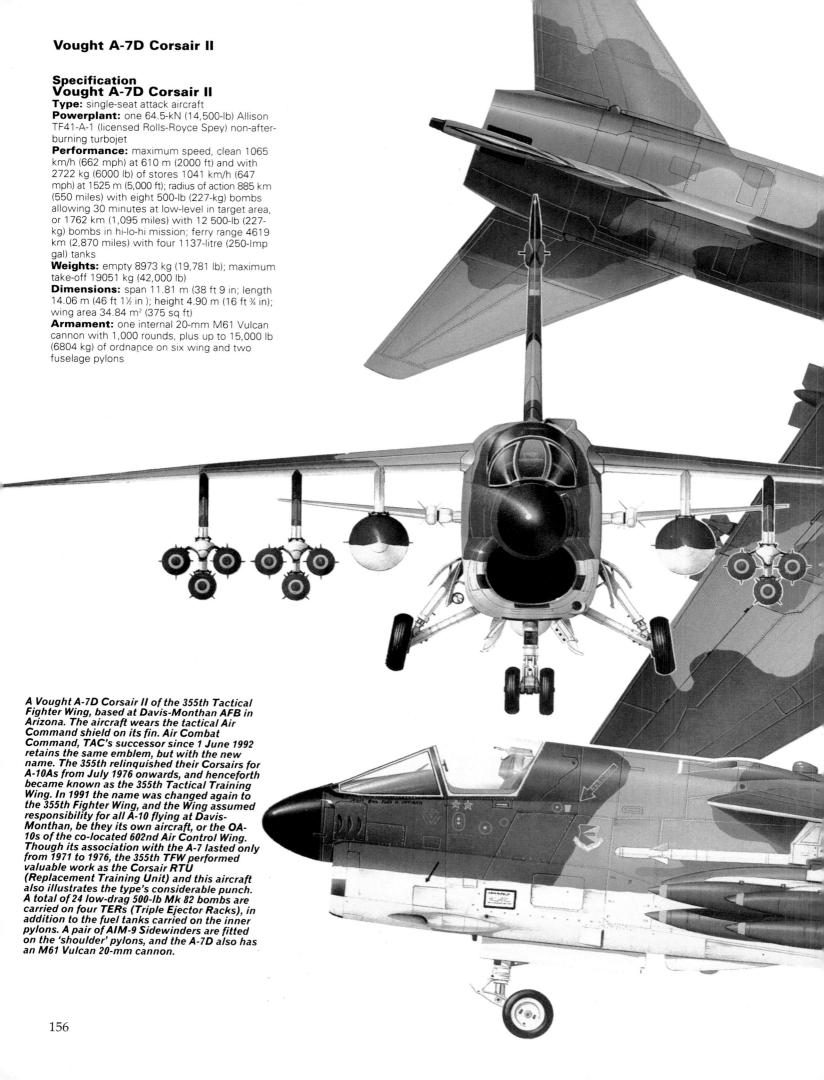

A Vought A-7D Corsair II of the 355th Tactical Fighter Wing, based at Davis-Monthan AFB in Arizona. The aircraft wears the tactical Air Command shield on its fin. Air Combat Command, TAC's successor since 1 June 1992 retains the same emblem, but with the new name. The 355th relinquished their Corsairs for A-10As from July 1976 onwards, and henceforth became known as the 355th Tactical Training Wing. In 1991 the name was changed again to the 355th Fighter Wing, and the Wing assumed responsibility for all A-10 flying at Davis-Monthan, be they its own aircraft, or the OA-10s of the co-located 602nd Air Control Wing. Though its association with the A-7 lasted only from 1971 to 1976, the 355th TFW performed valuable work as the Corsair RTU (Replacement Training Unit) and this aircraft also illustrates the type's considerable punch. A total of 24 low-drag 500-lb Mk 82 bombs are carried on four TERs (Triple Ejector Racks), in addition to the fuel tanks carried on the inner pylons. A pair of AIM-9 Sidewinders are fitted on the 'shoulder' pylons, and the A-7D also has an M61 Vulcan 20-mm cannon.

For much of their career, the SR-71s wore high visibility national markings over the top of the black paint that reduced radar reflectivity. During the last few years of their service all these markings were removed, leaving only a small serial in red on the fin, and the bare essentials in terms of warning stencils. Essentially a simple delta, the SR-71's remarkable shape owed much to the fuselage chines (which were attached to a standard cylindrical fuselage) and the considerable wing/fuselage/nacelle blending. Not only did this have an aerodynamic function, it also helped to reduce radar reflectivity. The sensors, including radars, electronic listening gear and cameras, were housed in four compartments in the chines, or in the detachable nose cone.

Specification
Lockheed SR-71 Blackbird
Type: two-seat reconaissance aircraft
Powerplant: two 14742-kg (32,500-lb) thrust Pratt & Whitney J58 afterburning bleed turbojets
Performance: maximum speed Mach 3 to 3.5 at 24385 m (80,000 ft); maximum sustained cruising speed Mach 3; unrefuelled range 4168 km (2,590 miles)
Weights: estimated maximum take-off 77111 kg (170,000 lb)
Dimensions: span 16.94 m (55 ft 7 in); length 32.74 m (107 ft 5 in); height 5.64 m (18 ft 6 in)

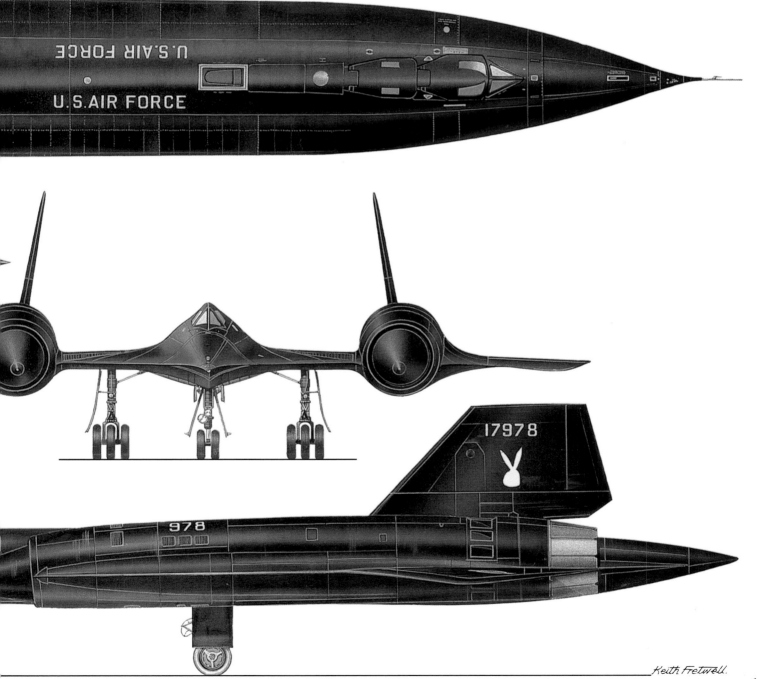

Keith Fretwell.

Keith Fretwell

Mikoyan-Gurevich MiG 23 Flogger-E

Specification
Mikoyan-Gurevich MiG-23 Flogger-E

Type: single-seat air-combat fighter
Powerplant: one Tumanskii R-29 turbojet engine with afterburning thrust of 12250 kg (27,560 lb)
Performance: (estimated) maximum combat speed 2975 km/h (1,849 mph) or Mach 2.8; service ceiling 24395 m (80,000 ft); maximum combat radius 1450 km (901 miles)
Weights: (estimated) empty 20000 kg (44,092 lb); maximum take-off 36200 kg (79,807 lb)
Dimensions: span 13.95 m (45 ft 9¼ in); length 23.82 m (78 ft 1¾ in); wing area 56.83 m² (611.73 sq ft)
Armament: underwing pylons for the carriage of up to four air-to-air missiles

Selected nations outside the Warsaw Pact were supplied with MiG-23 fighters by the Soviet Union, Libya being a major recipients. This is the downgraded 'Flogger-E' export version, featuring the 'Jay Bird' radar of the MiG-21 in a smaller nose radome, allied to basic AA-2 'Atoll'

missiles. Following the January 1989 shooting down of two Libyan MiG-23s by US Navy F-14 Tomcats, the US Department of Defense asserted that Libya had AA-7 'Apex' medium-range missile capability for its MiGs. However, no such missiles were observed by Israeli pilots during the 1982 'turkey shoot' against Syrian MiG-21s and MiG-23s, when over 80 Arab aircraft fell to F-15s and F-16s.

SEPECAT Jaguar

Until replaced by Tornado GR.Mk 1s, the Jaguar formed the main attack component of RAF Germany, flying from the bases at Laarbruch and Brüggen. This aircraft was based at the former, with No. 20 Squadron. It carries a typical battlefield air interdiction load, with four Hunting BL755 cluster bombs under the fuselage and iron bombs under the outer wing pylons. Two 30-mm ADEN cannon provides strafing capability. During the war with Iraq, Jaguars from the RAF's surviving squadrons (Nos 6, 41 and 54 Squadrons at RAF Coltishall) flew many strikes against targets in Kuwait and Iraq, using conventional and cluster bombs, and CRV7 rockets, the latter particularly effective against coastal targets. For Gulf service the Jaguars were hastily modified with overwing pylons for self-defence Sidewinder missiles.

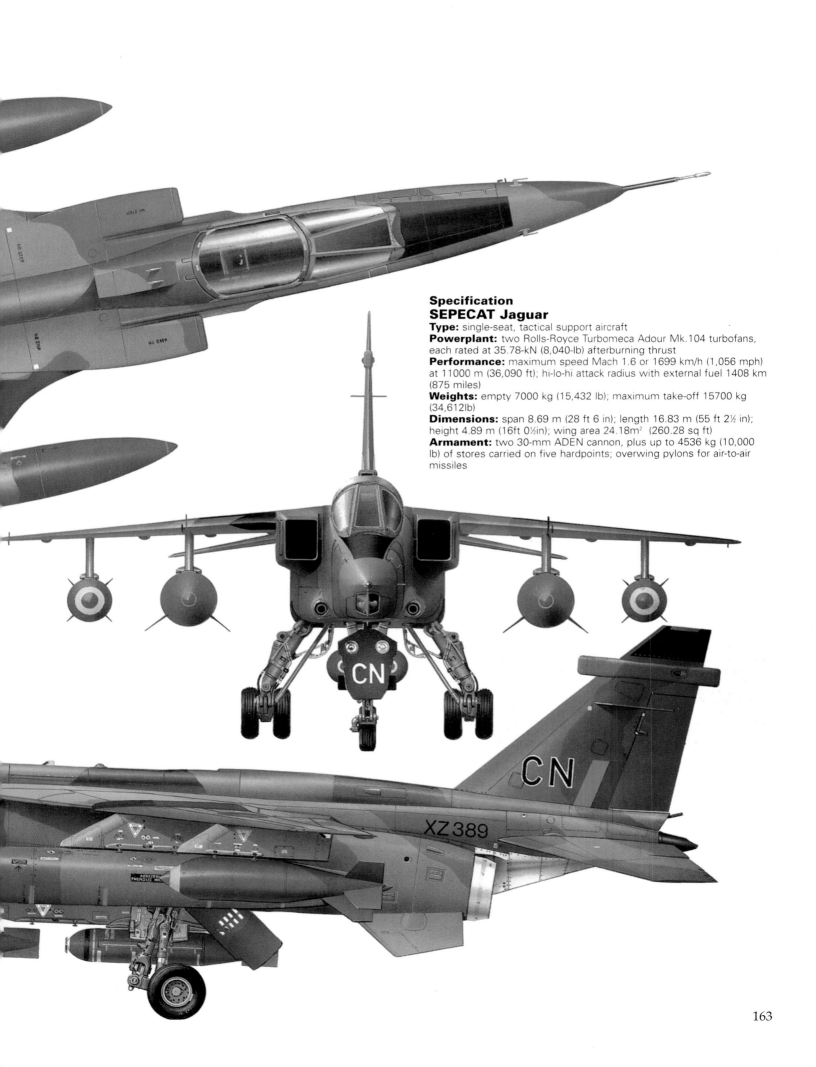

Specification
SEPECAT Jaguar

Type: single-seat, tactical support aircraft
Powerplant: two Rolls-Royce Turbomeca Adour Mk.104 turbofans, each rated at 35.78-kN (8,040-lb) afterburning thrust
Performance: maximum speed Mach 1.6 or 1699 km/h (1,056 mph) at 11000 m (36,090 ft); hi-lo-hi attack radius with external fuel 1408 km (875 miles)
Weights: empty 7000 kg (15,432 lb); maximum take-off 15700 kg (34,612lb)
Dimensions: span 8.69 m (28 ft 6 in); length 16.83 m (55 ft 2½ in); height 4.89 m (16ft 0½in); wing area 24.18m² (260.28 sq ft)
Armament: two 30-mm ADEN cannon, plus up to 4536 kg (10,000 lb) of stores carried on five hardpoints; overwing pylons for air-to-air missiles

Grumman F-14A Tomcat

This Grumman F-14A Tomcat, shown in the insignia of VF-143 'Pukin' Dogs', formed part of Carrier Air Wing CVW-7 aboard USS Dwight D. Eisenhower (CVN 69). The aircraft is carrying the standard maximum weapons load of four AIM-54A Phoenix, two AIM-7F Sparrow and two AIM-9L Sidewinder air-to-air missiles. The F-14A was also equipped with an integral Vulcan M6120-mm cannon for close-in air combat. The Tomcat was the US Navy's primary fleet defence fighter from 1974 until 2006.

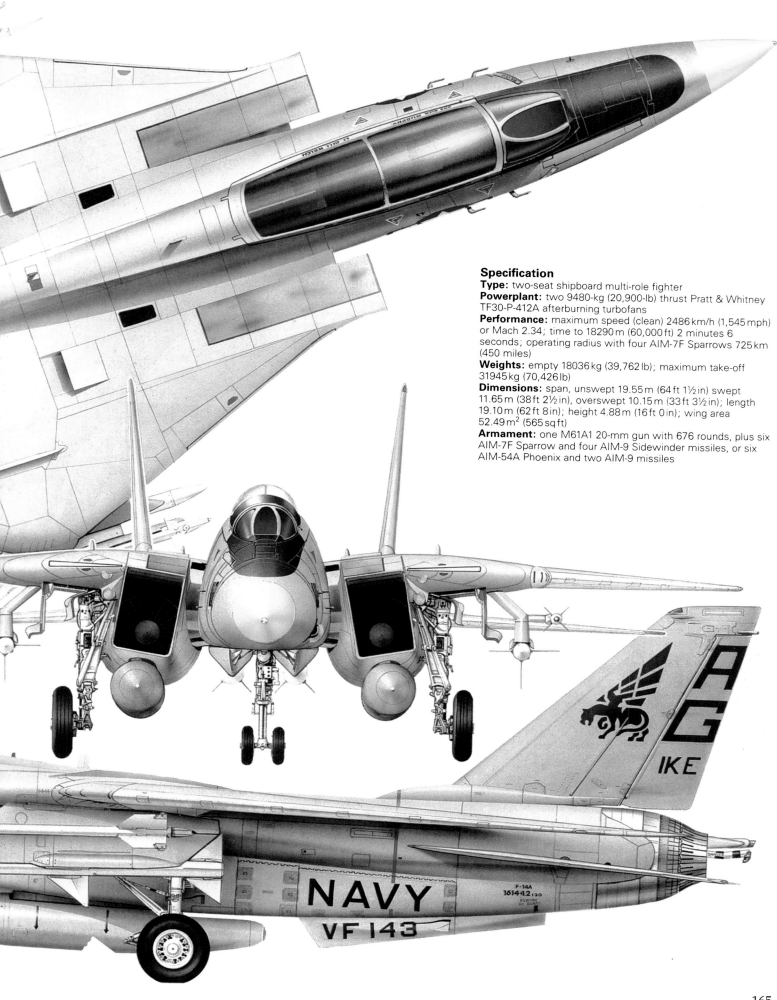

Specification

Type: two-seat shipboard multi-role fighter

Powerplant: two 9480-kg (20,900-lb) thrust Pratt & Whitney TF30-P-412A afterburning turbofans

Performance: maximum speed (clean) 2486 km/h (1,545 mph) or Mach 2.34; time to 18290 m (60,000 ft) 2 minutes 6 seconds; operating radius with four AIM-7F Sparrows 725 km (450 miles)

Weights: empty 18036 kg (39,762 lb); maximum take-off 31945 kg (70,426 lb)

Dimensions: span, unswept 19.55 m (64 ft 1½ in) swept 11.65 m (38 ft 2½ in), overswept 10.15 m (33 ft 3½ in); length 19.10 m (62 ft 8 in); height 4.88 m (16 ft 0 in); wing area 52.49 m² (565 sq ft)

Armament: one M61A1 20-mm gun with 676 rounds, plus six AIM-7F Sparrow and four AIM-9 Sidewinder missiles, or six AIM-54A Phoenix and two AIM-9 missiles

Saab Viggen AJ37

One of the most potent combat aircraft of the 1970s, the Saab 37 Viggen (Thunderbolt) was designed to carry out the four roles of attack, interception, reconnaissance and training. This AJ-37 served with wing F7 at Satenas, as denoted by the yellow number on the nose. It is seen equipped for precision attack with missiles, carrying a pair of RB75 Maverick missiles on the fuselage pylons and two of the huge RB04E anti-ship missiles under the wings. The centreline fuel tank was usually carried to extend range. The Viggen has been phased out in favour of the JAS-39 Gripen.

Specification
SAAB Viggen AJ37

Type: single-seat fighter

Powerplant: (AJ) RM8A afterburning turbofan, 11800 kg (26,015 lb) of thrust; (JA) RM8B afterburning turbofan, 12770 kg (28,153 lb) of thrust; fuel 9750 lb

Performance: maximum speed Mach 2 or 2112 km/h (1320 mph) at 12192 m (40,000 ft); Mach 1.1 or 1335 k/ph (835 mph) at sea level; initial climb 12200 m (40,000 ft) per min.; service ceiling: 18300 m (60,000 ft); combat radius hi-lo-hi 1000 km (620 miles)/ lo-lo-lo 500 km (310 miles)

Weights: empty 11800 kg (26,015 lb); maximum take-off 20450 kg (45,085 lb)

Dimensions: span 10.6 m (34 ft 9 in); length 15.45 m (50 ft 5 in)

Armament: one fixed belly-mounted 30-mm Oerlikon KCA cannon, and can carry either four Skyflash semi-active radar homing (SARH) or four Sidewinder air-to-air missiles

Sukhoi Su-17/20/22 'Fitters'

Late model 'Fitters' were known as Su-17s by the Soviet Air Force's Frontal Aviation and as Su-22s to their export customers. All shared the bulged spine that gave the type its distinctive 'humped-back' appearance, and taller squared-off tail fin. The 'Fitter-H' entered production in the early 1980s and served with Soviet and Hungarian Air Forces. This aircraft, unlike the subsequent 'Fitter-K', retained the Tumanskii R-29 engine of previous models, which was fitted with both an afterburner and water injection. While capable of carrying a full range of weapons, including the TN-1000 and -1200 series of free-fall nuclear bombs, the 'Fitter' shown here is armed simply with a pair of 'Advanced Atoll' AAMs, a load which does not accurately reflect its dedicated ground attack role.

Specification
Sukhoi Su-17/20/22 'Fitters'

Type: attack fighter
Powerplant: one 109.8-kN (24,692-lb) afterburning thrust Lyulka AL-21F-3 turbojet
Performance: maximum speed at optimum altitude Mach 2.17; service ceiling 18000 m (59,055 ft); combat radius (hi-lo-hi) 630 km (391 miles)
Weights: empty 10000 kg (22,046 lb), maximum take-off 14000 kg (30,865 lb)

Dimensions: span, unswept, 14 m (45 ft 11¾ in); swept 10.60 m (34 ft 9¾ in); length 18.75 m (61 ft 6¾ in); height 4.75 m (15 ft 7 in); wing area, unswept, 40.10 m (431.65 sq ft)
Armament: two 30-mm cannon in wing roots, plus eight external pylons for up to 4000 kg (8,818 lb) of mixed stores that can include air-to-surface missiles such as AS-7 (NATO 'Kerry'), bombs, nuclear weapons and rockets

Specification
Sukhoi Su-35 (Su-27m)
Type: long-range, twin-engine air-superiority fighter
Powerplant: 2 Lyulka AL-31F afterburning turbofans, 12,500 kg (27,500 lb) of thrust each
Performance: maximum speed Mach 2.35, 2550 k/ph (1,527 mph) at 11000 m (36,000 ft); Mach 1.1, 1520 k/ph (1,527 mph) at sea level; initial climb 15243 m per min. (50,000 ft per min.); service ceiling 18293 m (60,000 ft); combat radius 1553 km (930 miles); maximum range 4000 km (2,580 miles)
Weights: normal loaded 22000 kg (48,400 lb); maximum take-off 30000 kg (66,000 lb)
Dimensions: span 14.7 m (48 ft 2 in); length 21.92 m (71 ft 11 in)
Armament: six wing pylons (including two at the tips) and two fuselage pylons under the engine in-takes, all for air-to-air missiles; standard load is six AA-10, Alamo medium-range radar-guided missiles on the fuselage and underwing pylons, and two AA-8 Aphid or AA-11 Archer short-range infrared-homing missiles on each wingtip; maximum capacity of 6000 kg (13,225 lb) of bombs or air-to-surface missiles

The Sukhoi Su-35, derived from the Flanker-B and originally designated Su-27M, is a second-generation version with improved agility and enhanced operational capability. Its maiden flight was in 1988 and the aircraft seen here is one of eleven prototypes that were put through their paces up to 1994. Although it appears similar to the Su-27 it is in many ways a new type, with new systems and some new structure. The Su-35 is powered by a pair of Lyulka AL-35F turbofans, and is equipped with an improved multi-mode radar. This aircraft is carrying a pair of R-37s outboard, four R-77s and a trio of the new long-range AAM-L anti-AWACS weapon. The Su-35 utilises a completely new quadruplex fly-by-wire system, and the cockpit is fitted with three CRT displays.

171

McDonnell Douglas F-15C Eagle

Project Peace Sun saw the delivery of Saudi Arabia's first F-15s. Sixty-two aircraft – 46 F-15Cs and 16 F-15Ds – were delivered to replace long-serving English Electric Lightning F.Mk. 55s. The first aircraft began to arrive in January 1981 and were operational by August of that year. Prior to the Iraqi invasion of Kuwait in 1990, the US authorities had imposed a ceiling of 60 aircraft on the RSAF's F-15 fleet, but in the light of events this limit was rapidly disregarded. Twenty-four F-15C/Ds were taken from the 32nd Tactical Fighter Squadron and 36th Tactical Fighter Wing in Holland and Germany, and were used to form the newly created No. 42 Squadron at Dhahran. Saudi military aircraft use their squadron number to form the first half of their serials, and the rough stencilling of RSAF titles on the nose of this Eagle also marks it out as one of the hastily transferred aircraft.

Specification
McDonnell Douglas F-15C Eagle

Type: single-seat air-superiority fighter
Powerplant: two 106-kN (23,930-lb) afterburning thrust Pratt & Whitney F100-PW-100 turbofans
Performance: maximum speed (high, clean) Mach 2.5; zoom ceiling 30480 m (100,000 ft); unrefuelled flight endurance 5 hours 15 minutes
Weight: maximum take-off 30844 kg (68,000 lb)
Dimensions: span 13.05 m (42 ft 9¾ in); length 19.43 m (63 ft 9 in); height 5.63 m (18 ft 5½ in); wing area 56.48 m² (608 sq ft)
Armament: one M61A1 20-mm six-barrelled cannon and four AIM-9 Sidewinder, four AIM-7 Sparrow or eight AMRAAM air-to-air missiles; in the secondary attack role up to 7300 kg (16,000 lb) of weapons can be carried externally

ROYAL SAUDI AIR FORCE

General Dynamics F-16C Fighting Falcon

The F-16, designed and built by General
Dynamics, had its origin in a USAF requirement
of 1972 for a lightweight fighter and first flew on
2 February 1974. The F-16B and -D are two-seat
versions, while the F-16C, delivered from 1988,
featured numerous improvements in avionics and
was available with a choice of engine. F-16s have
seen action in the Lebanon (with the Israeli Air
Force), in the Gulf Wars and the Balkans. The F-16
Fighting Falcon, now produced by Lockheed
Martin, is the world's most prolific combat
aircraft, with over 2,000 in service with the United
States Air Force and a further 2,000 in service
with 19 other air forces around the world. The
aircraft seen here is from the 50th TFW at Hahn
AB in Germany.

Specification
General Dynamics F-16C Fighting Falcon

Type: single-seat air combat and ground-attack fighter

Powerplant: either one 10800-kg (23,700-lb) Pratt & Whitney F100-PW-220 or one 13150-kg (28,984-lb) General Electric F110-GE-100 afterburning turbofan

Performance: maximum level speed more than 2142 km/h (1,320 mph) or Mach 2.0 at 12190 m (40,000 ft); service ceiling above 15240 m (50,000 ft); operational radius 925 km (575 miles)

Weights: empty 7070 kg (15,586 lb); maximum take-off 16057 kg (35,400 lb)

Dimensions: span 9.45 m (31 ft 0 in); length 15.09 m (49 ft 6 in); height 5.09 m (16 ft 8 in); wing area 27.87m² (300 sq ft)

Armament: one General Electric M61A1 20-mm multi-barrelled cannon, a wingtip missile station on each wing plus one underfuselage and six underwing hardpoints enabling the carriage of a 9276-kg (20,450-lb) warload of air-to-air or air-to-surface missiles, ECM, reconaissance or rocket pods, iron or 'smart' bombs or fuel tanks

Keith Fretwell.

Dassault Super Etendard

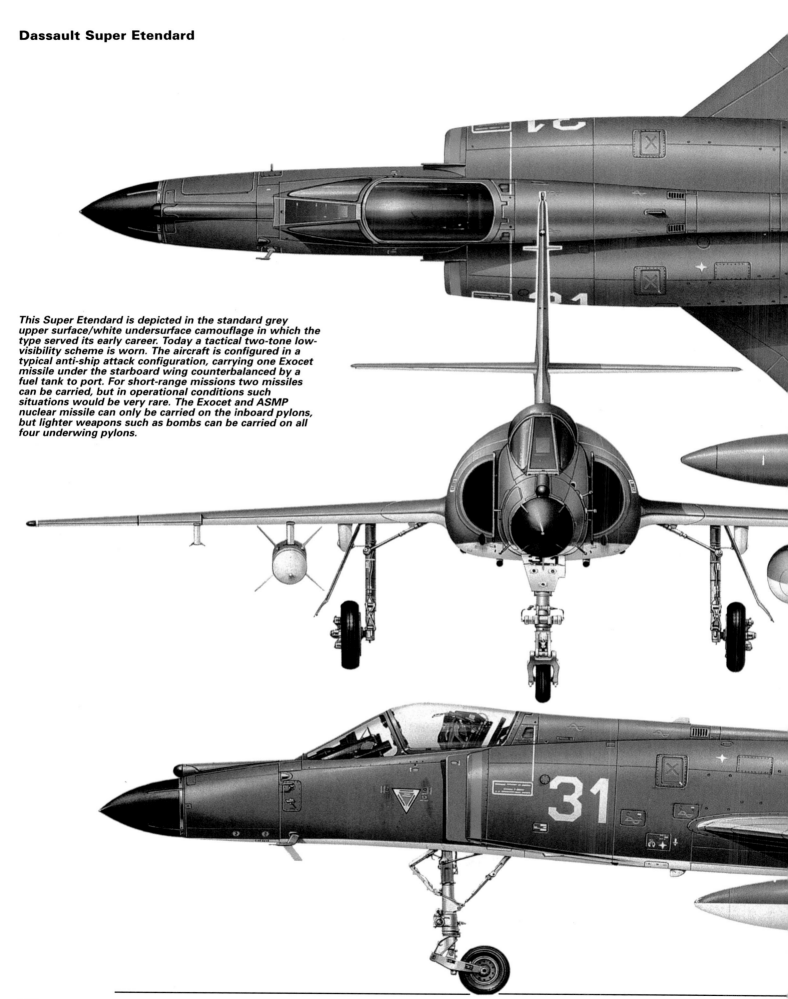

This Super Etendard is depicted in the standard grey upper surface/white undersurface camouflage in which the type served its early career. Today a tactical two-tone low-visibility scheme is worn. The aircraft is configured in a typical anti-ship attack configuration, carrying one Exocet missile under the starboard wing counterbalanced by a fuel tank to port. For short-range missions two missiles can be carried, but in operational conditions such situations would be very rare. The Exocet and ASMP nuclear missile can only be carried on the inboard pylons, but lighter weapons such as bombs can be carried on all four underwing pylons.

Specification
Dassault Super Etendard
Type: carrier-based attack and reconaissance aircraft
Powerplant: one SNECMA Atar 8K-50 5110-kg (11,265-lb) thrust turbojet
Performance: maximum speed at sea level or 1200 k/ph (745 mph); Mach 1 or 1085 k/ph (650 mph) at 10975 m (36,000 ft); initial climb 7500 m (24,600 ft) per min.; service ceiling 13175 m (45,000 ft)
Weights: empty 6500 kg (14,300 lb); maximum take-off 12000 kg (26,455 lb)
Dimensions: span 9.5 m (31 ft 6 in); length 14.31 m (46 ft 11 in)
Armament: typical payloads include one Exocet AM.39 and one drop tank, or one AN.52 free-fall nuclear bomb and one drop tank, or two drop tanks and two Matra R.550 Magic air-to-air missiles, or up to 2100 kg (4630 lb) of free-fall bombs, cluster bombs, laser-guided bombs, Napalm and rocket pods; they are also equipped to launch the ASMP nuclear stand-off missile

Fairchild A-10A Thunderbolt II

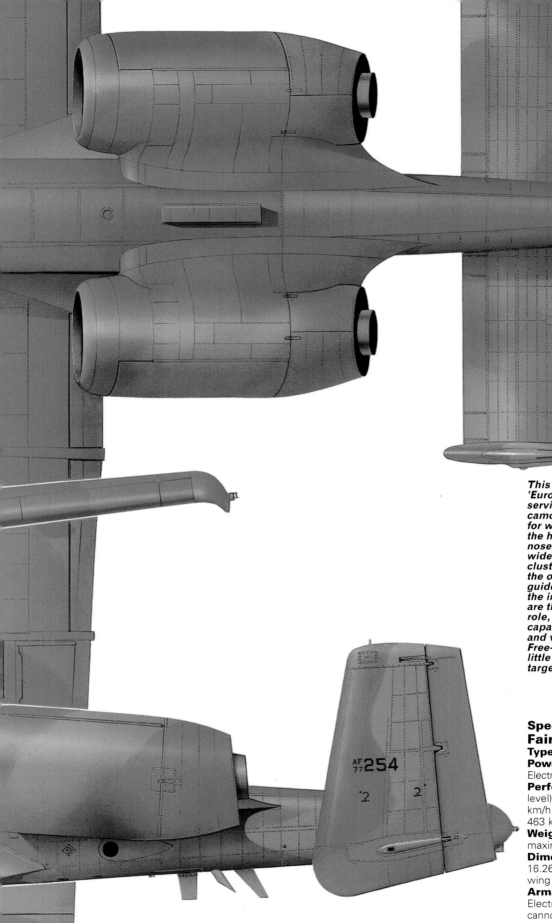

*This **A-10A** is depicted in the standard 'European One' or 'lizard' scheme adopted for service machines, this affording excellent camouflage for the very low level operations for which the A-10 is renowned. In addition to the huge 30-mm cannon firing through the nose, the A-10 can be equipped to launch a wide variety of ordnance. Depicted here are clusters of Maverick anti-armour missiles on the outboard pylons, with **HOBOS TV-**guided, and Paveway laser-guided bombs on the inner pylons. Mavericks and the cannon are the primary weapons in the anti-armour role, both affording a fair degree of stand-off capability, necessary given the slow speed and vulnerability to gunfire of the aircraft. Free-fall weapons are used only in areas with little defence, as the aircraft has to overfly the target in order to release them.*

Specification
Fairchild A-10A Thunderbolt II
Type: single-seat close-support aircraft
Powerplant: two 4112-kg (9,065-lb) thrust General Electric TF34-GE-100
Performance: maximum speed (clean, at sea level) 706 km/h (439 mph); cruising speed 555 km/h (345 mph) at sea level; loiter endurance at 463 km (288 miles) from base 1 hour 40 minutes
Weights: empty operating 11321 kg (24,959 lb); maximum take-off 22680 kg (50,000 lb)
Dimensions: span 17.53 m (57 ft 6 in); length 16.26 m (53 ft 4 in); height 4.47 m (14 ft 8 in); wing area 47.01 m² (506 sq ft)
Armament: primary weapon is the General Electric GAU-8/A Avenger 30-mm seven-barrel cannon, with a maximum firing rate of 4,200 rounds per minute. Its magazine contains 1,174 armour-piercing rounds, each weighing 0.73 kg (1.6 lb).In addition, three underfuselage and eight underwing stores pylons have a combined external load capacity of 7257 kg (16,000 lb)

VFA-113 were the first US Navy recipients of the F/A-18 Hornet, shore-based at NAS Lemoore in California. This example is shown in the standard air-to-air configuration carrying two AIM-9UM Sidewinders on the wingtip rails and two AIM-7FIM Sparrow missiles along the intake sides. For close-range work the Hornet has a M61A1 20-mm six-barrel cannon mounted in the nose. For greater combat persistence the Hornet can carry four additional Sidewinders on twin racks on the outboard pylon when fitted, although this has a corresponding adverse effect on performance and manoeuvrability. The F/A-18E/F Super Hornet is a more advanced development, which entered service with the US Navy in 1999.

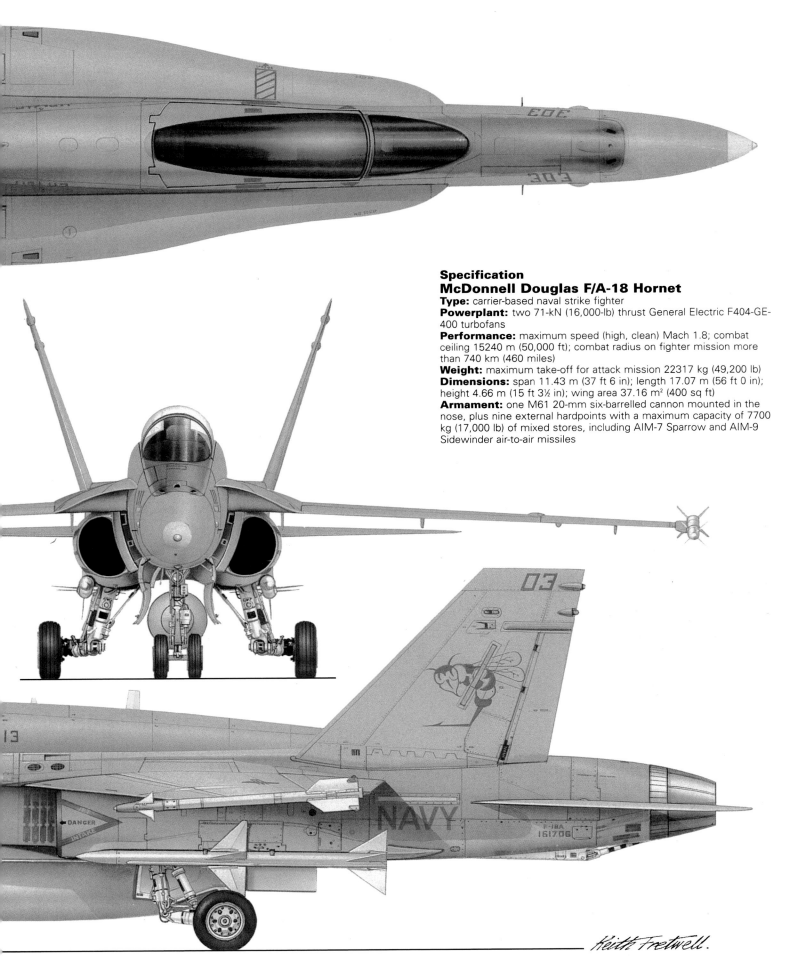

Specification
McDonnell Douglas F/A-18 Hornet
Type: carrier-based naval strike fighter
Powerplant: two 71-kN (16,000-lb) thrust General Electric F404-GE-400 turbofans
Performance: maximum speed (high, clean) Mach 1.8; combat ceiling 15240 m (50,000 ft); combat radius on fighter mission more than 740 km (460 miles)
Weight: maximum take-off for attack mission 22317 kg (49,200 lb)
Dimensions: span 11.43 m (37 ft 6 in); length 17.07 m (56 ft 0 in); height 4.66 m (15 ft 3½ in); wing area 37.16 m² (400 sq ft)
Armament: one M61 20-mm six-barrelled cannon mounted in the nose, plus nine external hardpoints with a maximum capacity of 7700 kg (17,000 lb) of mixed stores, including AIM-7 Sparrow and AIM-9 Sidewinder air-to-air missiles

British Aerospace/MBB/Aeritalia Tornado ADV (F2)

Specification
British Aerospace/MBB/Aeritalia Tornado ADV (F2)

Type: two-seat long-range interdiction aircraft (with an interceptor variant)

Powerplant: two 7273-kg (16,000-lb) thrust Turbo-Union RB.199 Mk104 afterburning turbofans; fuel 6982 kg (15,360 lb)

Performance: maximum speed Mach 2.27 or 2505 k/ph (1,500 mph) at 11000 m (36,000 ft); Mach 1.2, or 1536 k/ph (920 mph) at sea level; initial climb 15243 m per min. (50, 000 ft per min.); service ceiling 15243 m (50,000 ft); combat radius, 2.33-hr loiter, 626 km (275 miles)

Weights: normal loaded 21590 kg (47,600 lb); maximum take-off 27986 kg (61,700 lb)

Dimensions: span 13.9 m (45 ft 6 in); length 18.06 m (59 ft 3 in)

Armament: inboard pylons with side-mounted launch rails fortwo AIM-9 Sidewinder air-to-air missiles to be carried at all times; submunitions dispenser for airfield attack: 454-kg (1,000-lb) free-fall and retarded bombs; 454-kg (1,000-lb) Paveway laser-guided bombs; Napalm cannisters; BL.755 cluster bombs; rocket pods, Alarm anti-radiation missiles; Sea Eagle anti-ship missiles; and two tandem pairs of medium-range air-to-air missiles in semi-recessed belly wells

No. 29 Squadron at RAF Coningsby was the first front-line user of the Tornado ADV, becoming operational on 1 November 1987. In the NATO structure it was declared to SACLANT (Supreme Allied Commander Atlantic) and had a maritime air defence commitment. It also had out-of-area taskings, and was consequently one of the units deployed in Operation Granby to Saudi Arabia in 1991. After flying a heavy commitment of combat air patrol missions in support of the Allied effort against Iraq six aircraft returned to Coningsby in March. The squadron disbanded in 1998, later re-forming as the second squadron to receive the Eurofighter Typhoon.

Iain Wyllie

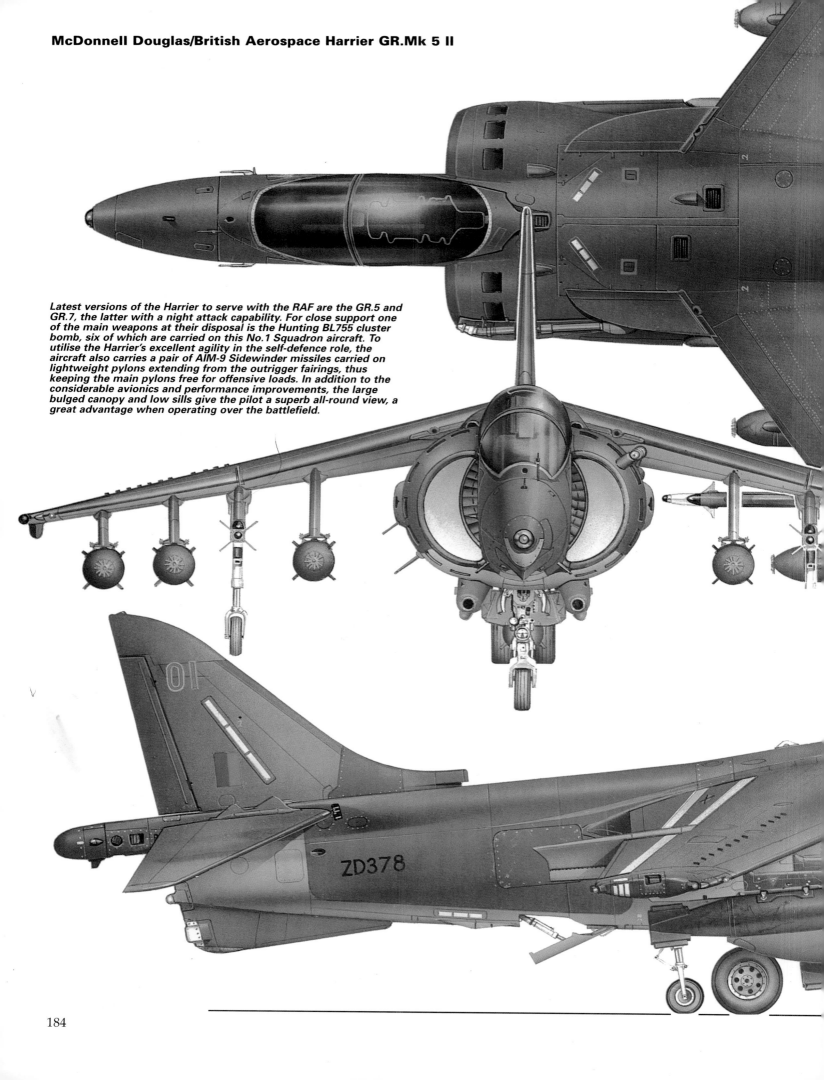

Latest versions of the Harrier to serve with the RAF are the GR.5 and GR.7, the latter with a night attack capability. For close support one of the main weapons at their disposal is the Hunting BL755 cluster bomb, six of which are carried on this No.1 Squadron aircraft. To utilise the Harrier's excellent agility in the self-defence role, the aircraft also carries a pair of AIM-9 Sidewinder missiles carried on lightweight pylons extending from the outrigger fairings, thus keeping the main pylons free for offensive loads. In addition to the considerable avionics and performance improvements, the large bulged canopy and low sills give the pilot a superb all-round view, a great advantage when operating over the battlefield.

Specification
McDonnell Douglas/British Aerospace
Harrier GR.Mk 5 II

Type: short take-off and vertical landing jet fighter/attack aircraft

Powerplant: Pegasus 105 engine of 95-kN (21,500-lb) thrust

Performance: maximum speed at sea level 1065 km/h (661 mph); maximum speed at altitude Mach 0.92; combat radius with two Harpoons, two Sidewinders and two 1136-litre (250-Imp gal) drop tanks 1128 km (701 miles)

Weights: empty 6344 kg (13, 968 lb); maximum external warload 6003 kg (13,235 lb); maximum take-off 14061 kg (31,000 lb); maximum VTO 9342 kg (20,595 lb)

Dimensions: span 9.25 m (30 ft 4 in); length 14.5 m (47 ft 9 in); height 3.5 m (11 ft 8 in); wing area 21.3 m² (230 sq ft)

Armament: two 25-mm ADEN cannon and nine weapon stations mounted under the fuselage and wings, the extra two wing points for self defence Sidewinder air-to-air missiles, or four Maverick laser-guided air-to-surface missiles, six Mk 83 or 15 Mk 82 bombs, or 12 rocket pods, or four 1136-litre (250-Imp gal) drop tanks

Keith Fretwell

Lockheed F-117 Stealth Fighter

The angular shape of the F-117 is now well-known the world over, yet few have seen the aircraft outside air displays. Certainly Iraqi gunners during the 1991 Gulf War had little knowledge of its whereabouts until its bombs exploded, pilots only returning triple-A fire after the weapons had hit their targets. For the first missions against Iraq, F-117s were escorted by jamming aircraft, but these actually increased the amount of fire before the weapons release, as the jamming gave the Iraqis prior warning of an attack. Afterwards the jammers supporting the F-117s only turned on their equipment after the strike to cover the egress, or used their jammers to deceive defenders. For the most part the F-117s used the GBU-27 bomb, a steel-cased 900 kg (2,000 lb) penetration bomb with the Paveway 3 laser-guidance package. Special treatment makes the GBU-27 'stealthy' so as to preserve the low-observable features of the F-117 during the weapon release.

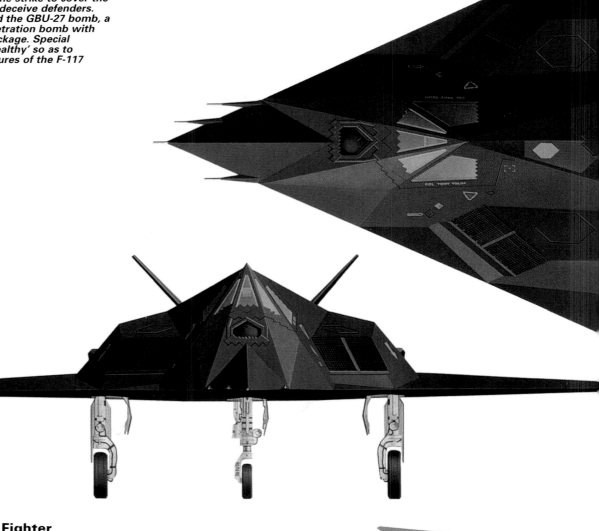

Specification
Lockheed F-117 Stealth Fighter
Type: single-seat stealth strike fighter
Powerplant: two 4900-kg (10,800-lb) thrust General Electric F404-GE-F102 turbofans
Performance: maximum speed Mach 1; normal operating speed Mach 0.9
Weights: empty operating 13609 kg (30,000 lb); maximum take-off 23814 kg (52,500 lb)
Dimensions: span 13.20 m (43 ft 4 in); length 20.08 m (65 ft 11 in); height 3.78 m (12 ft 5 in); wing area 105.9 m² (1,140 sq ft)
Armament: underfuselage internal weapons can accommodate the full range of USAF tactical fighter ordnance but principally two 907-kg (2,000-lb) bombs of GBU-10/GBU-27 laser-guided type, or AGM-65 Maverick or AGM-89 HARM air-to-surface missiles

Eurofighter Typhoon

The Eurofighter Typhoon programme dates back more than three decades. The joint development programme between the UK, Germany, Italy and Spain has always focused on producing a versatile and affordable swing-role combat aircraft to meet the future needs of air forces in the partner nations and around the globe, and the end result is an aircraft with a high thrust-to-weight ratio and remarkable performance. As well as the Eurofighter Typhoon's air combat role, the UK is already looking to introduce an 'austere' ground-attack capability, with a targeting pod and GPS/laser-guided bombs.

Weapons intregration initially focused on air-to-air missiles, but now trials are well advanced to introduce precision ground strike. A wide range of weapons will give Eurofighter a true swing-role capability to tackle all kinds of missions in a single flight. Despite amazing agility and ferocious performance, the Typhoon is extremely docile to fly. Pilots enjoy carefree handling thanks to the advanced flight-control system. It is this range of capabilities, coupled with its affordability, that is making the Typhoon extremely attractive to potential export customers.

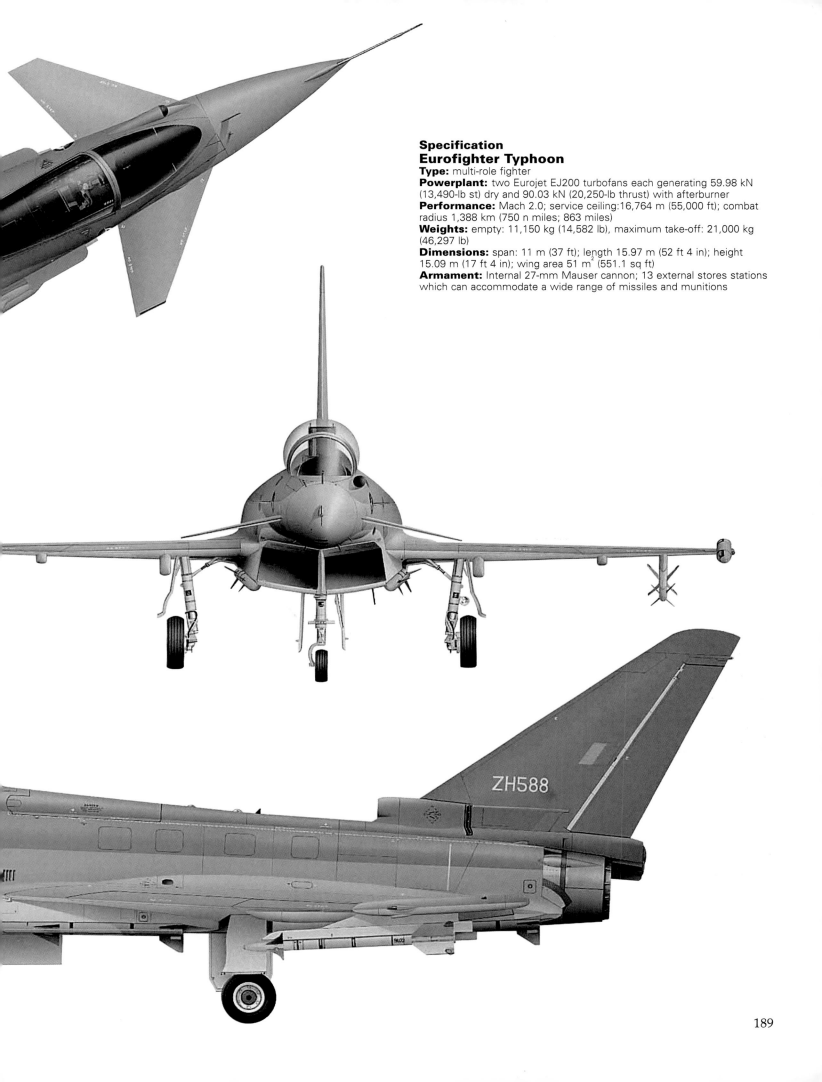

Specification
Eurofighter Typhoon

Type: multi-role fighter

Powerplant: two Eurojet EJ200 turbofans each generating 59.98 kN (13,490-lb st) dry and 90.03 kN (20,250-lb thrust) with afterburner

Performance: Mach 2.0; service ceiling:16,764 m (55,000 ft); combat radius 1,388 km (750 n miles; 863 miles)

Weights: empty: 11,150 kg (14,582 lb), maximum take-off: 21,000 kg (46,297 lb)

Dimensions: span: 11 m (37 ft); length 15.97 m (52 ft 4 in); height 15.09 m (17 ft 4 in); wing area 51 m² (551.1 sq ft)

Armament: Internal 27-mm Mauser cannon; 13 external stores stations which can accommodate a wide range of missiles and munitions

Lockheed Martin F-22A Raptor

Specification
Lockheed Martin F-22A Raptor

Type: multi-role fighter

Powerplant: two 155.61 kN (35,000-lb) thrust Pratt & Whitney F119-PW-100 turbofans, each with two-dimensional thrurst vectoring

Performance: maximum speed Mach 1.7 at 9144 m (30,000 ft); service ceiling 15,240 m (50,000 ft); combat radius n/a

Weights: empty 14,365 kg (31,670 lb); maximum take-off almost 27,216 kg (60,000 lb)

Dimensions: span 13.05 m (44 ft 6 in); length 18.09 m (62 ft 1 in); height 5.12 m (16 ft 8 in); wing area 78m^2 (840 sq ft)

Armament: cheek weapons bays for AIM-9 Sidewinders, main weapon bay for Joint Direct Attack Munitions and AIM-120 AMRAAM. Internal General Dynamics M61 20-mm cannon.

The Lockheed Martin F-22A Raptor is the ultimate air dominance superfighter, designed to penetrate enemy airspace and achieve a first-look, first-kill capability against multiple targets. Stealthy and very agile, it strikes lethal blows to fighters in the air or hits targets on the ground using precision weapons – yet remaining invisible to radar. This impressive beast was born out of the USAF's Advanced Tactical Fighter (ATF) competition to replace the F-15C Eagle. One of the Raptor's key attributes is Supercruise, which means that it can fly faster than the speed of sound for extended periods of time without using afterburner. To keep it super-stealthy, the Raptor is designed to operate as a 'clean' aircraft, with its weapons carried in internal bays, though it can be configured with four underwing hardpoints. The Raptor's development modernization process will ensure that the aircraft receives emerging weapons and sensors as they become available, such as the new Small Diameter Bomb (SDB).

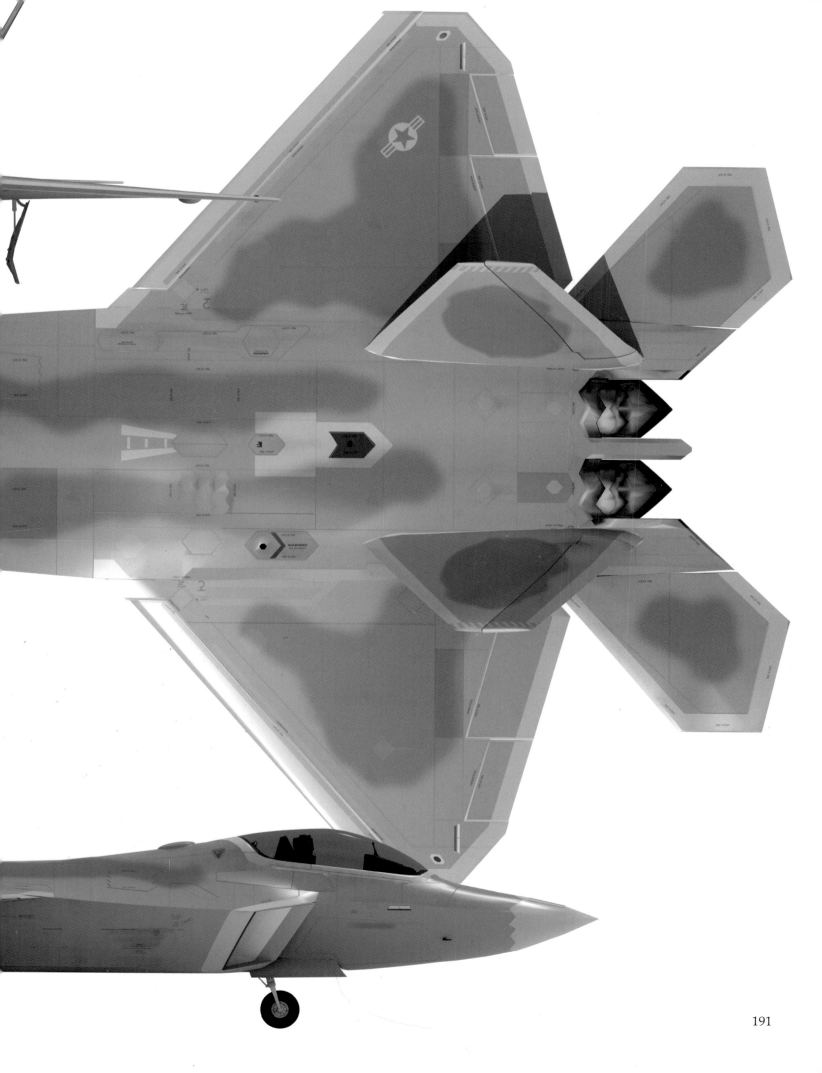

Index